PREVENTING CRIME
What Works for Children, Offenders, Victims and Places

PREVENTING CRIME

What Works for Children, Offenders, Victims and Places

Edited by

Brandon C. Welsh

Department of Criminal JusticeandCriminology
University of Massachusetts Lowell
Lowell, MA, USA

David P. Farrington

Institute of Criminology
UniversityofCambridge, UK

 Springer

Brandon C. Welsh
Department of Criminal Justice
 and Criminology
University of Massachusetts Lowell
870 Broadway Street, Suite 2
Lowell, MA 01854-3044
USA

David P. Farrington
Institute of Criminology
University of Cambridge
Sidgwick Avenue
Cambridge CB3 9DT
UK

ISBN 978-0-387-69168-8   e-ISBN 978-0-387-69169-5

Library of Congress Control Number: 2007932292

Printed on acid-free paper.

9 8 7 6 5 4 3 2 1

springer.com

TABLE OF CONTENTS

FOREWORD

Preventing Crime: What Works for Children, Offenders, Victims, and Places is the first book that details the role of the Campbell Collaboration in assessing outcomes in crime and justice. I first heard about the Campbell Collaboration in the summer of 1999 and immediately decided to be part of this valiant effort to change the way crime and justice, education, and social welfare were implemented around the world. As a longtime champion of research I was impressed by the way the Campbell Collaboration looked at programs and policies. This book represents the first step in setting the framework for how to go about reinventing crime and justice and gives a good example for both education and social welfare. Of course, this does not come without challenges. The first challenge is to find out what works through high quality scientific research. The second challenge is to get public officials to embrace the findings and take action.

Crime and justice, as well as education, have been sidetracked by fads, political expediency, and private agendas. In the United States, welfare to work has become the exception. Numerous randomized controlled studies have been conducted that led to major changes in welfare to work, which have proven to be quite effective. And, more importantly, the United States government has acted on these studies to make changes for the betterment of the underclass of society.

There is an undercurrent in both the United Kingdom and here in the United States for using high quality scientific research to find out what works and what doesn't work in implementing social policy. And it is picking up steam.

The Jerry Lee Foundation is dedicated to solving the problems of the inner cities. The problems of crime, lack of education, and social welfare (jobs) are the mission of the Jerry Lee Foundation. I believe that governments around the world have enough money and resources to solve most of society's problems, if only we would invest in scientific research to find out what works. This would allow us to better target our resources on what works and quit spending money on what doesn't work.

I for one am very optimistic that within 20 years time, high quality scientific research will be the rule rather than the exception in determining public policy. This book, which brings together the leading researchers in evidence-based criminology and public policy, represents an important step forward towards this aim.

Jerry Lee
President
Jerry Lee Foundation
Board Member
Campbell Collaboration

Brandon C. Welsh and David P. Farrington, eds.
Preventing Crime: What Works for Children, Offenders, Victims, and Places, vii
© 2007 *Springer.*

PREFACE

As the title indicates, the main aim of this book is to advance knowledge on what works to prevent crime. It brings together leading evidence-based research on the effects on crime of a wide range of interventions that have been organized around four key domains in criminology and criminal justice: at-risk children, offenders, victims, and places. Importantly, policy implications of the effects of these different interventions are also explored. Another key aim of this book is to make the field of evidence-based crime prevention, along with the method of systematic review, known to a much wider audience. This includes students, policymakers at the local, state, and federal levels, and scholars and researchers. They all share an interest in the study of crime prevention and come from a wide range of disciplines, including criminology and criminal justice, sociology, psychology, psychiatry, public health, mental health, social work, economics, and education.

We view these aims as indispensable to get more of what works best in preventing crime into policy and practice at the local level. Indeed, it was with these aims in mind that an exciting partnership was born and this project was launched. In 2000, the newly formed Campbell Collaboration, named after the influential experimental psychologist Donald T. Campbell, established its Crime and Justice Steering Committee (CJSC) to oversee the preparation, maintenance, and dissemination of systematic reviews of the highest quality research on the effects of criminological interventions. Work began right away and within a couple of years the first wave of reviews was nearing completion. The 13 topics reported here represent only a start; reviews of many other topics are underway and planned for the future.

During this time the CJSC was fortunate to have in attendance at some of its meetings a representative of Springer Publishing. This was the beginning of a partnership between a group who wished to inform a wide audience about the importance of using scientific evidence and results about what works to inform crime policy (the CJSC) and a leading international publishing company who is also interested in contributing to more effective crime policy and has the means to reach this wider audience (Springer Publishing). The product of this happy collaboration is this book, *Preventing Crime: What Works for Children, Offenders, Victims, and Places*.

This book is organized into five sections. Preceding these sections is an introductory chapter that sets the stage for this volume, by describing evaluation research designs and summarizing different review methods for assessing the accumulated evidence of the effects of types of crime prevention programs. The first section comprises two chapters that look at what works in intervening in the

Brandon C. Welsh and David P. Farrington, eds.
Preventing Crime: What Works for Children, Offenders, Victims, and Places, ix–x
© 2007 *Springer*.

lives of children who are at-risk for delinquency and later criminal offending. The second section comprises five chapters that examine what works in preventing offenders from committing further offenses in the community. In the third section there are three chapters that address what works for victims of crime. Section four includes three chapters that describe what works in preventing crime at high-crime places or areas at high risk for criminal activity. The final section includes one chapter that summarizes the main conclusions about what works for at-risk children, offenders, victims, and places, and identifies future directions for research and policy development to advance evidence-based crime prevention and contribute to a safer society.

ACKNOWLEDGMENTS

This book was surely a team effort. We wish to thank the members of the Campbell Crime and Justice Group, who supported this project from its inception and remained enthusiastic throughout. We are particularly grateful to Lawrence Sherman and Jerry Lee for their far-sighted support of the Campbell venture. The contributors to this volume are especially deserving of our thanks for producing high quality reviews of research and writing in a clear and intelligible way for a broad readership. Finally, we are grateful to our brilliant editor Welmoed Spahr and the Springer Publishing team who made this project a reality as well as an enjoyable experience along the way.

Brandon C. Welsh
David P. Farrington

CHAPTER 1

EVIDENCE-BASED CRIME PREVENTION*

Brandon C. Welsh

University of Massachusetts Lowell

David P. Farrington

Cambridge University

INTRODUCTION

Crime prevention should be rational and based on the best possible evidence. One would expect that decision-makers would take careful account of any available evidence on what works. How can a program that has produced no discernable evidence of effectiveness, as shown through numerous evaluations, be considered for implementation? Unfortunately, this happens all the time. Consider the short-lived revival of the prison deterrence program known as Scared Straight despite past evaluations that showed that it had failed to deter juvenile delinquents from future criminal activity (Finckenauer and Gavin, 1999; Petrosino et al., 2000). Consider also the long-standing school-based substance abuse prevention program known as DARE (Drug Abuse and Resistance Education) for which the accumulated evidence shows that it has a trivial effect on substance use and crime (Gottfredson et al., 2002; U.S. General Accounting Office, 2003). Many other examples exist in this country and elsewhere.

There are many considerations involved in selecting and implementing new crime prevention programs (as well as in expanding effective programs or putting an end to ineffective or harmful ones). For example, there may be different government priorities, such as military defense spending, environmental protection, or prescription drug benefits for seniors, which are competing for scarce public resources. National polls may show that the public is more concerned with public policy issues other than crime prevention. Other political considerations include the worry by politicians that they may be perceived as soft on crime by supporting non-criminal justice crime prevention efforts (see Gest, 2001), as well as the short time horizons of politicians (Tonry and Farrington, 1995b), which makes programs that show results only in the longer term less appealing to those who are trying to get elected every few years. Regrettably, it seems that evidence

---

* We thank Jerry Lee and Jon Baron for helpful comments on an earlier draft of this chapter.

Brandon C. Welsh and David P. Farrington, eds.
Preventing Crime: What Works for Children, Offenders, Victims, and Places, 1–17
© 2007 *Springer.*

of what works best is rarely a factor in implementing new crime prevention programs. Political and policy considerations often dominate.

Evidence-based crime prevention attempts to avoid these mistakes by ensuring that the best available evidence is considered in any decision to implement a program designed to prevent crime. As noted by Petrosino (2000:635), "An evidence-based approach requires that the results of rigorous evaluation be rationally integrated into decisions about interventions by policymakers and practitioners alike."

This is an approach that has garnered much support in medicine (Halladay and Bero, 2000; Millenson, 1997). But even in medicine, a discipline noted for its adherence to scientific principles and high educational requirements, most practice is "shaped by local custom, opinions, theories, and subjective impressions" (Sherman, 1998:6). Of course, making available scientific evidence on what works best to policymakers and practitioners (regardless of the discipline) and having them put it into practice are two entirely different things.

Support for evidence-based crime prevention is growing (see Welsh and Farrington, 2001). This growth has been fostered by a number of recent developments, including a movement toward an evidence-based approach in other disciplines, such as medicine (Millenson, 1997) and education (Mosteller and Boruch, 2002); large-scale, government- and foundation-sponsored reviews of "what works" in crime prevention (Goldblatt and Lewis, 1998; Sherman et al., 1997; 2002; Tonry and Farrington, 1995a); and, most recently, the establishment of the Campbell Collaboration and its Crime and Justice Group (Farrington and Petrosino, 2000; 2001; Farrington et al., 2001). This book marks a further installment in an international movement to advance evidence-based crime prevention research, policy, and practice.

This chapter describes evaluation research designs for assessing effects of crime prevention programs, summarizes different review methods for assessing accumulated evidence of the effects of types of crime prevention programs, reports on the development and activities of the Campbell Collaboration and its Crime and Justice Group, and presents the aims and organization of this book.

EVALUATION RESEARCH

When can we have confidence that the reported conclusions of an evaluation of a crime prevention program – whether they suggest that it is effective, ineffective, or, worse yet, harmful – are valid? This is a central question for an evidence-based approach to preventing crime.

High Quality Evaluations

It is surely stating the obvious to say that not all evaluations of crime prevention programs are equally valid. The methodological quality of evaluations can indeed vary greatly. According to Cook and Campbell (1979) and Shadish et al. (2002), methodological quality depends on four criteria: statistical conclusion validity, internal validity, construct validity, and external validity. Descriptive validity, which refers to the adequacy of reporting of information, could be added as a fifth criterion of the methodological quality of evaluation research (Farrington, 2003; see also Lösel and Koferl, 1989). "Validity refers to the correctness of inferences about cause and effect" (Shadish et al., 2002:34).

Statistical conclusion validity is concerned with whether the presumed cause (the intervention) and the presumed effect (the outcome) are related. The main threats to this form of validity are insufficient statistical power – the probability of correctly rejecting the null hypothesis when it is false – to detect the effect (e.g., because of small sample size) and the use of inappropriate statistical techniques.

Internal validity refers to how well the study unambiguously demonstrates that an intervention (e.g., parent training) had an effect on an outcome (e.g., delinquency). Here, some kind of control condition is necessary to estimate what would have happened to the experimental units (e.g., people or areas) if the intervention had not been applied to them – termed the "counterfactual inference." The main threats to internal validity are:

- Selection: the effect reflects preexisting differences between experimental and control conditions.
- History: the effect is caused by some event occurring at the same time as the intervention.
- Maturation: the effect reflects a continuation of preexisting trends, for example, in normal human development.
- Instrumentation: the effect is caused by a change in the method of measuring the outcome.
- Testing: the pretest measurement causes a change in the posttest measure.
- Regression to the mean: where an intervention is implemented on units with unusually high scores (e.g., areas with high crime rates), natural fluctuation will cause a decrease in these scores on the posttest, which may be mistakenly interpreted as an effect of the intervention. The opposite (an increase) happens when the interventions are applied to low-crime areas or low-scoring people.
- Differential attrition: the effect is caused by differential loss of units (e.g., people) from experimental compared to control conditions.
- Causal order: it is unclear whether the intervention preceded the outcome (Shadish et al., 2002:55).

Construct validity refers to the adequacy of the operational definition and measurement of the theoretical constructs that underlie the intervention and the outcome. For example, if a program aims to investigate the effect of interpersonal skills training on offending, did the training program really target and change interpersonal skills, and were arrests a valid measure of offending? The main threats to this form of validity rest on the extent to which the intervention succeeded in changing what it was intended to change (e.g., how far there was treatment fidelity or implementation failure) and on the validity and reliability of outcome measures (e.g., how adequately police-recorded crime rates reflect true crime rates).

External validity refers to how well the effect of an intervention on an outcome is generalizable or replicable in different conditions: different operational definitions of the intervention and various outcomes, different persons, different environments, and so on. It is difficult to investigate this within one evaluation study. External validity can be established more convincingly in systematic reviews and meta-analyses of a number of evaluation studies (see below). As noted by Shadish et al. (2002:87), the main threats to this form of validity consist of interactions of causal relationships (effect sizes) with types of persons, settings, interventions, and outcomes. For example, an intervention designed to reduce offending may be effective with some types of people and in some types of places but not in others. A key issue is whether the effect size varies according to the degree to which those who carried out the research had some kind of stake in the results.

An evaluation of a crime prevention program is considered to be high quality if it possesses a high degree of internal, construct, and statistical conclusion validity. Put another way, one can have a great deal of confidence in the observed effects of an intervention if it has been evaluated with a design that controls for the major threats to these three forms of validity. Experimental (randomized and non-randomized) and quasi-experimental research designs are the types of evaluation designs that can best achieve this.

The randomized controlled experiment is considered the "gold standard" in evaluation research designs. It is the most convincing method of evaluating crime prevention programs (Farrington, 1983; Farrington and Welsh, 2005). The key feature of randomized experiments is that the random assignment equates the experimental and control groups before the experimental intervention on all possible extraneous variables. Hence, any subsequent differences between the groups must be attributable to the intervention. Randomization is the only method of assignment that controls for unknown and unmeasured confounders as well as those that are known and measured. However, the randomized experiment is only the most convincing method of evaluation if it is implemented with full integrity. To the extent that there are implementation problems (e.g., problems of maintaining random assignment, differential attrition, cross-over between control and experimental conditions), internal validity could be reduced in it.

Another important feature of the randomized experiment is that a sufficiently large number of units (e.g., people or areas) need to be randomly assigned to ensure that the treatment group is equivalent to the comparison group on all extraneous variables (within the limits of statistical fluctuation). As a rule of thumb, at least 50 units in each category are needed (Farrington, 1997). This number is relatively easy to achieve with individuals, but very difficult to achieve with larger units such as communities, schools, or classrooms (see below).

An evaluation design in which experimental and control units are matched or statistically equated (e.g., using a prediction score) prior to intervention – what is called a non-randomized experiment – has less internal validity than a randomized experiment. It is important to note that statistical conclusion validity and construct validity may be just as high for a non-randomized experiment as for a randomized experiment.

In area-based studies, the best and most feasible design usually involves before and after measures in experimental and comparable control conditions, together with statistical control of extraneous variables. This is an example of a quasi-experimental evaluation design. Even better, the effect of an intervention on crime can be investigated after controlling (e.g., in a regression equation) not only for prior crime but also for other factors that influence crime. Another possibility is to match two areas and then to choose one at random to be the experimental area. Of course, several pairs of areas would be better than only one pair. These are the best ways of dealing with threats to internal validity when random assignment of units to experimental and control conditions cannot be achieved. Here again, statistical conclusion validity and construct validity may not be any different from a randomized experiment.

ASSESSING RESEARCH EVIDENCE

Just as it is crucial to use the highest quality evaluation designs to investigate the effects of crime prevention programs, it is also important that the most rigorous methods be used to assess the available research evidence. Efforts to assess if a particular crime prevention strategy (e.g., developmental, situational), intervention modality (e.g., parent training, improved street lighting), or some other feature of crime prevention programs works can take many different forms. The main types of review methodology include the single study, narrative, vote-count, systematic, and meta-analytic.

Single Study Review Method

Not only is the single study method self-explanatory, its limitations – in comparison with the other methods – are blatantly evident. In this method, a single evaluation study, usually of high quality methodologically (e.g., a randomized controlled experiment), is used to represent a body of research on a particular type of intervention. The well known Perry Preschool program (Schweinhart et al., 1993) has long been used by advocates of early childhood intervention to show the beneficial results that this type of intervention can have on delinquency and later offending. Despite Perry's beneficial results, as well as findings from cost-benefit analyses that showed that it returned to society savings far in excess of the costs to run the program (see Barnett, 1996; Greenwood et al., 2001), it is by no means representative of other early childhood interventions that have measured effects on criminal activity (see Farrington and Welsh, 2002, 2003).

Narrative Review Method

Narrative reviews of the literature quite often include many studies and may be very comprehensive. Their main drawback, however, is researcher bias. This bias, whether intentional or not, typically starts right from the beginning with a less than rigorous methodology for searching for studies. More often than not, the researcher will limit his or her search to published sources or even self-select studies to be included, based on the researcher's familiarity with them, quite possibly leaving many studies out of the review. This can sometimes lead to an incorrect interpretation of the particular intervention's effect on crime; for example, what should have been presented as a desirable effect is instead reported as an uncertain effect (i.e., unclear evidence of an effect). The one conceivable advantage to the narrative review is that the reader can usually glean a great deal more information about individual studies than would otherwise be possible in the more rigorous methods of vote count, systematic review, or meta-analysis.

Vote-Count Review Method

The vote-count method adds a quantitative element to the narrative review, by considering statistical significance (the probability of obtaining the observed effect if the null hypothesis of no relationship were true). In essence, this method tallies-up the "number of studies with statistically significant findings in favor of the hypothesis and the number contrary to the hypothesis" (Wilson, 2001:73). The main problem with using statistical significance is that it depends partly on sample size and partly on effect size. For example, a significant result may reflect a small effect in a large sample or a large effect in a small sample.

A more comprehensive vote-count method was developed by Sherman and his colleagues (1997) to help them draw conclusions about what works, what does not work, what is promising, and what is unknown in preventing crime in seven major institutional settings: families, communities, schools, labor markets, places (e.g., urban centers, homes), police agencies, and courts and corrections. In addition to statistical significance, their vote-count method integrated a "scientific methods scale" (SMS) that was largely based on the work of Cook and Campbell (1979). In constructing the SMS, the main aim was to devise a simple scale measuring internal validity that could easily be communicated to scholars, policymakers, and practitioners. Thus, a simple five-point scale was used rather than a summation of scores (e.g., from 0–100) on a number of specific criteria. It was intended that each point on the scale should be understandable, and the scale is as follows (see Welsh et al., 2002:18–19):

> Level 1: Correlation between a prevention program and a measure of crime at one point in time (e.g., areas with CCTV have lower crime rates than areas without CCTV).

This design fails to rule out many threats to internal validity and also fails to establish causal order.

> Level 2: Measures of crime before and after the program, with no comparable control condition (e.g., crime decreased after CCTV was installed in an area).

This design establishes causal order but fails to rule out many threats to internal validity. Level 1 and level 2 designs were considered inadequate and uninterpretable by Cook and Campbell (1979).

> Level 3: Measures of crime before and after the program in experimental and comparable control conditions (e.g., crime decreased after CCTV was installed in an experimental area, but there was no decrease in crime in a comparable control area).

This was considered to be the minimum interpretable design by Cook and Campbell (1979), and it is also regarded as the minimum design that is adequate for drawing conclusions about what works in the book *Evidence-Based Crime Prevention* (Sherman et al., 2002). It rules out many threats to internal validity, including history, maturation/trends, instrumentation, testing effects, and differential attrition. The main problems with it center on selection effects and regression to the mean (because of the non-equivalence of the experimental and control conditions).

> Level 4: Measures of crime before and after the program in multiple experimental and control units, controlling for other variables that influence crime (e.g., victimization of premises under CCTV surveillance decreased compared to victimization of control premises, after controlling for features of premises that influenced their victimization).

This design has better statistical control of extraneous influences on the outcome and hence deals with selection and regression threats more adequately.

> Level 5: Random assignment of program and control conditions to units (e.g., victimization of premises randomly assigned to have CCTV surveillance decreased compared to victimization of control premises).

As noted above, providing that a sufficiently large number of units are randomly assigned, those in the experimental condition will be equivalent (within the limits of statistical fluctuation) to those in the control condition on all possible extraneous variables that influence the outcome. Hence, this design deals with selection and regression problems and has the highest possible internal validity.

In light of the fact that the SMS as defined above focuses only on internal validity, all evaluation projects were also rated on statistical conclusion validity and on construct validity. Specifically, the following four aspects of each study were rated:

For statistical conclusion validity:

1. Was the statistical analysis appropriate?
2. Did the study have low statistical power to detect effects because of small samples?
3. Was there a low response rate or differential attrition?

For construct validity:

4. What was the reliability and validity of measurement of the outcome?

External validity was addressed to some extent in the rules for accumulating evidence from different evaluation studies. The overriding aim was again simplicity of communication of findings. The aim was to classify all program types into one of four categories: what works, what does not work, what is promising, and what is unknown.

What works. These are programs that prevent crime in the kinds of social contexts in which they have been evaluated. Programs coded as working must have at least two level-3 to level-5 evaluations showing statistically significant and desirable results and the preponderance of all available evidence showing effectiveness.

What does not work. These are programs that fail to prevent crime. Programs coded as not working must have at least two level-3 to level-5 evaluations with statistical significance tests showing ineffectiveness and the preponderance of all available evidence supporting the same conclusion.

What is promising. These are programs wherein the level of certainty from available evidence is too low to support generalizable conclusions, but wherein there is some empirical basis for predicting that further research could support such conclusions. Programs are coded as promising if they were found to be effective in significance tests in one level-3 to level-5 evaluation and in the preponderance of the remaining evidence.

What is unknown. Any program not classified in one of the three above categories is defined as having unknown effects.

This vote-count method has great utility as part of meta-analytic and systematic reviews. However, one of the limitations of the vote-count method is that equal weight is given to all studies irrespective of methodological quality. (For other limitations of the vote-count method, see Wilson, 2001:73–74.)

Systematic Review Method

The systematic review and the meta-analytic review (described below) are the most rigorous methods for assessing the effectiveness of criminological interventions. Systematic reviews, according to Johnson et al. (2000:35), "essentially take an epidemiological look at the methodology and results sections of a specific population of studies to reach a research-based consensus on a given study topic." They use rigorous methods for locating, appraising, and synthesizing evidence from prior evaluation studies, and they are reported with the same level of detail that characterizes high quality reports of original research. The key features of systematic reviews include the following:

– *Explicit objectives.* The rationale for conducting the review is made clear.
– *Explicit eligibility criteria.* The reviewers specify in detail why they included certain studies and rejected others. What was the minimum level of methodological quality? (Here is where the SMS is sometimes employed.) Did they consider only a particular type of evaluation design, such as randomized

experiments?[1] Did the studies have to include a certain type of participant, such as children or adults? What types of interventions were included? What kinds of outcome data had to be reported in the studies? All criteria or rules used in selecting eligible studies should be explicitly stated in the final report.

- *The search for studies is designed to reduce potential bias.* Because there are many potential ways in which bias can compromise the results of a review, the reviewers must explicitly state how they conducted their search of potential studies to reduce such bias. How did they try to locate studies reported outside scientific journals? How did they try to locate studies in foreign languages? All bibliographic databases that were searched should be made explicit so that potential gaps in coverage can be identified.

- *Each study is screened according to eligibility criteria, with exclusions justified.* The searches will undoubtedly locate many citations and abstracts to potentially relevant studies. Each of the reports of these potentially relevant studies must be screened to determine if it meets the eligibility criteria for the review. A full listing of all excluded studies and the justifications for exclusion should be made available to readers.

- *Assembly of the most complete data possible.* The systematic reviewer will generally try to obtain all relevant evaluations meeting the eligibility criteria. In addition, all data relevant to the objectives of the review should be carefully extracted from each eligible report and coded and computerized. Sometimes, original study documents lack important information. When possible, the systematic reviewer will attempt to obtain these data from the authors of the original report.

- *Quantitative techniques are used, when appropriate and possible, in analyzing results.* A systematic review may or may not include a meta-analysis (described below). The use of meta-analysis may not be appropriate due to a small number of studies, heterogeneity across studies, or different units of analysis of the studies (i.e., a mix of area- and individual-based studies). But when suitable, meta-analyses should be conducted as part of systematic reviews.

- *Structured and detailed report.* The final report of a systematic review is structured and detailed so that the reader can understand each phase of the research, the decisions that were made, and the conclusions that were reached (Farrington et al., 2001:340–341).

As noted by Petrosino et al. (2001:20), "The foremost advantage of systematic reviews is that when done well and with full integrity, they provide the most reliable and comprehensive statement about what works." Systematic reviews are not, however, without their limitations; although these limitations or challenges

---

1   The criterion of methodological quality that is used for including (or excluding) studies is perhaps the "most important and controversial" in conducting systematic reviews (Farrington and Petrosino, 2001:42). How high to set the "bar" of methodological rigor as part of a review of the literature, systematic or other, is a question that all researchers face. (For a brief discussion of this issue in the context of the vote-count review method, see MacKenzie, 2000.)

appear to be more closely linked with administrative and dissemination issues, such as getting them in the hands of decision-makers (see Petrosino et al., 2001). Some of the challenges that face the "substance" of systematic reviews include the transparency of the process (e.g., the need to state the reasons why studies were included or excluded) and the need to reconcile differences in coding of study characteristics and outcomes by multiple researchers (i.e., inter-rater reliability).

Meta-Analytic Review Method

A meta-analysis involves the statistical or quantitative analysis of the results of prior research studies (Lipsey and Wilson, 2001). Since it involves the statistical summary of data (in particular, effect sizes), it requires a reasonable number of intervention studies that are sufficiently similar to be grouped together; there may be little point in reporting an average effect size based on a very small number of studies. Nevertheless, quantitative methods can be very important in helping the reviewer determine the average effect of a particular intervention.

One major product of a meta-analysis is a weighted average effect size, although there is usually also an attempt to investigate factors that predict larger or smaller effect sizes in different studies. Each effect size is weighted according to the sample size on which it is based, with larger studies having greater weights in calculating the average.

Strengths of the meta-analytic review method include its transparent nature – the explication of its methods and the studies involved – which makes it easily replicated by other researchers, its ability to handle a very large number of studies that may be overwhelming for other review methods, and the "statistical methods of meta-analysis help guard against interpreting the dispersion in results as meaningful when it can just as easily be explained as sampling error" (Wilson, 2001:84). Limitations of meta-analysis include, on a practical side, its time consuming nature and its inability to synthesize "[c]omplex patterns of effects found in individual studies" (Wilson, 2001:84). A major problem is how to select effect sizes for analysis in studies that measure many different outcomes.

Systematic reviews – incorporating meta-analytic techniques – of high quality research evidence have received increased attention in recent years in the social sciences generally and in criminology and criminal justice specifically. This is part of a broader interest in evidence-based policy and practice in public services (Davies et al., 2000) and in crime prevention (Sherman, et al., 2002). At the forefront of the development of systematic reviews in criminology and criminal justice is the newly formed Campbell Crime and Justice Group.

THE CAMPBELL CRIME AND JUSTICE GROUP

Named after the influential experimental psychologist Donald T. Campbell (Campbell, 1969), the Campbell Collaboration was set up for the purpose of preparing, maintaining, and disseminating evidence-based research on the effects of interventions in the social sciences, including education, social work and social welfare, and crime and justice. Its Crime and Justice Group aims to prepare and maintain systematic reviews of criminological interventions and to make them accessible electronically to practitioners, policymakers, scholars, the mass media, and the general public.

From Cochrane to Campbell

In 1993, the Cochrane Collaboration was established to prepare, maintain, and make accessible systematic reviews of research on the effects of health care and medical interventions. The Cochrane Collaboration established collaborative review groups (CRGs) to oversee the preparation and maintenance of systematic reviews in specific areas, such as heart disease, infectious diseases, and breast cancer. For example, the Cochrane Injuries Group prepares systematic reviews relevant to the prevention, treatment, and rehabilitation of traumatic injury. All reviews produced by Cochrane CRGs follow a uniform structure. The same level of detail and consistency of reporting is found in each, and each review is made accessible through the *Cochrane Library*, a quarterly electronic publication.

The success of the Cochrane Collaboration in reviewing health care interventions stimulated international interest in establishing a similar infrastructure for conducting systematic reviews of research on the effects of social welfare, educational, and criminological interventions. Following several exploratory meetings, the Campbell Collaboration was officially founded at a meeting in Philadelphia in February 2000.

Following the example of the Cochrane Collaboration, the Campbell Collaboration aims to prepare rigorous and systematic reviews of high-quality research evidence about what works. Recognizing that evidence is changing all the time, the Campbell Collaboration is committed to updating reviews on a periodic basis. Through international networking, it ensures that relevant evaluation studies conducted across the world are taken into account in its systematic reviews and that evidence from these reviews is made accessible globally through language translation and worldwide dissemination.

The Crime and Justice Group

At the Philadelphia meeting, the Campbell Collaboration appointed a Crime and Justice Steering Committee (CJSC) to coordinate the work of the Crime and Justice Group. The CJSC currently consists of 16 members from 13 countries.[2]

---

2 The members are: Catherine Blaya (European Observatory of Violence in Schools, France), Ulla Bondeson (University of Copenhagen, Denmark), David Farrington (University of Cambridge, U.K., co-chair), Vicente Garrido (University of Valencia, Spain), Peter Grabosky (Australian National University, Australia), Martin Killias (University of Lausanne, Switzerland), Jerry Lee (Jerry Lee Foundation, U.S.), Friedrich Lösel (University of Erlangen-Nuremberg, Germany), Jacqueline Mallender (Matrix Research and Consulting, U.K.), Jonathan Shepherd (University of Wales College of Medicine, U.K.), Lawrence Sherman (University of Pennsylvania), Chuen-Jim Sheu (National Central Police University, Taiwan), Richard Tremblay (University of Montreal, Canada), Hiroshi Tsutomi (University of Shizuoka, Japan), Peter Van Der Laan (Netherlands

The broad mission of the CJSC is to oversee the preparation, maintenance, and dissemination of systematic reviews of the highest quality research on the effects of criminological interventions. Reviews are focused on interventions designed to prevent delinquency or crime (presently the main focus of the CJSC), as well as those attempting to improve the management or operations of the criminal justice system.

Preparation of Systematic Reviews. The CJSC oversees the preparation of systematic reviews by working closely with authors. Figure 1 shows the steps involved in conducting a systematic review. Once the title of a systematic review has been accepted by the Area Coordinator, or in the case of the Crime and Justice Group, the CJSC, a Principal Advisor is recruited to marshal the review through the remaining steps. Principal Advisors are highly qualified researchers in the field of criminology and criminal justice and are very often experts on the review topic. The next step is the development of a protocol or comprehensive plan for a systematic review by the author, which details, among other things, the background to the review, objectives, strategies for searching the literature, selection criteria for studies, and strategies for data extraction and analysis. The protocol is then sent out to two external reviewers and a methods specialist for substantive comments. The Principal Advisor is tasked with collecting the comments and forwarding them, along with any the Principal Advisor may have, to the author. Once the Principal Advisor is satisfied with the draft protocol, it is submitted to the CJSC for approval. This results in the publication of the protocol in the Campbell Collaboration Reviews of Interventions and Policy Effects Database or C2-RIPE. As illustrated in Figure 1, this editorial process is then repeated for the systematic review itself.

The CJSC currently oversees systematic reviews on a wide range of topics, including child skills training, juvenile curfews, boot camps, policing crime "hot spots", electronic monitoring, and community based alternatives versus custody. At the time of writing, 36 titles of systematic reviews had been registered with the Crime and Justice Group, and six protocols had been approved for publication in C2-RIPE. The 13 systematic reviews presented in this book (chapters 2 through 14), although not officially approved Campbell Collaboration reviews, are presently in various stages of development and are expected to be approved and disseminated as Campbell reviews in due course.

Maintenance of Systematic Reviews. One of the problems that currently hinders the role of systematic reviews as an evidence-based resource in criminology and criminal justice is that they tend to be "one-off" exercises conducted as time, funding, and interest permit. Traditional print journals often lack the capacity for or interest in updating reviews once they have been published. As existing reviews become outdated, funding agencies usually pay for another set of researchers to start anew trying to locate, retrieve, code, and analyze many of the same studies.

Institute for the Study of Crime and Law Enforcement), David Weisburd (Hebrew University, Israel, co-chair), and David Wilson (George Mason University). Michael Schlossman serves as the coordinator of the CJSC.

FIGURE 1. *Steps in Conducting a Systematic Review*

Systematic review authors or Steering Committee define the research question or topic
↓
Authors submit the proposed title and expected completion date to the relevant Coordinator
↓
Steering Committee Chair and/or Coordinator assign project to Principal Advisor[1]
↓
Authors complete and submit a draft protocol with assistance from Principal Advisor
↓
Principal Advisor and Editorial Team reviews the draft protocol[2]
↓
Principal Advisor approves the protocol and submits it to C2-RIPE
↓
Authors complete a draft review and submit it to Principal Advisor
↓
Principal Advisor obtains external comments and critiques of draft from the Editorial Team[3]
↓
Authors receive and incorporate feedback from the Editorial Team
(this step may involve multiple iterations)
↓
Authors submit final review
↓
Review is published in Campbell Collaboration Reviews of Intervention and Policy Effectiveness[4]
↓
Versions of the review are developed for use by multiple audiences

Notes:
[1] A list of Principal Advisors is approved by the Steering Committee.
[2] At this step, the Principal Advisor is strongly encouraged to establish an Editorial Team that will comment on and critique the draft protocol. The Editorial Team may consist of members of the Steering Committee, methodologists, and other experts in the field. The Principal Advisor contacts the Methods Group Coordinator or Chair to select a methods group member to serve on the Editorial Team.
[3] If an Editorial Team was established for the protocol, they also would serve for the draft review.
[4] The Campbell Collaboration Secretariat is responsible for maintaining and monitoring the contents of the C2-RIPE.

Source: Campbell Collaboration (2003).

Typically, previous researchers do not share their raw or coded data with new researchers, which militates against the development of cumulative knowledge. Although the results of new reviews may not be duplicative, the resources and effort that go into them most certainly are.

The CJSC plans to overcome this state of affairs by having systematic reviews updated every two or three years. These updates will take account of new studies, cogent criticisms, and methodological advances. One of the ways that the CJSC helps to ensure that systematic reviews are maintained over time is that researchers, upon submitting a title to do a review, are asked to make a commitment to periodically update their review. Another way that the CJSC plans to maintain systematic reviews is by establishing links between funding agencies and researchers; lack of funding is a major deterrent to updating reviews.

Accessability of Systematic Reviews. Like Cochrane's CRGs, Campbell's Crime and Justice Steering Committee acts as a vehicle for bringing to the attention of practitioners, policymakers, and others the most rigorous and up-to-date evidence on what works to prevent crime. At present, systematic reviews are disseminated or published in a wide range of outlets, such as government reports, academic journals, World Wide Web documents, and online publications. Each of these publication outlets has its own set of rules, structure, jargon and technical language, quality assurance methods, and capacity for detail and thoroughness.

Through the electronic publication of C2-RIPE, this archive will standardize the way systematic reviews are reported. Most importantly, systematic reviews will be more up-to-date and more easily accessible to those who need the evidence for their decision-making.

AIMS AND ORGANIZATION OF THE BOOK

The main aim of this book is to advance knowledge on what works to prevent crime. It brings together leading evidence-based research on the effects on crime for a wide range of interventions that have been organized around four important domains in criminology and criminal justice: at-risk children, offenders, victims, and places. Policy implications of the effects of these different interventions are also explored.

Another important aim of this book is to make the field of evidence-based crime prevention, along with the method of systematic review, known to a much wider audience. This includes students, policymakers at the local, state, and federal levels, and scholars and researchers, all of whom share an interest in the study of crime prevention and come from a wide range of disciplines, including criminology and criminal justice, sociology, psychology, psychiatry, public health, mental health, social work, economics, and education.

This book has 15 chapters. The next 14 chapters are organized into four main parts. Part I comprises two chapters that look at what works in intervening in the lives of children who are at-risk for delinquency and later criminal offending. In chapter 2, Odette Bernazzani and Richard Tremblay examine early parent training (a family-based intervention that most often also involves the children), and in chapter 3, Friedrich Lösel and Andreas Beelmann examine child social skills training.

Part II comprises five chapters that examine what works in preventing offenders from committing further offenses in the community. In chapter 4, Mark Lipsey and Nana Landenberger examine cognitive-behavioral interventions. In chapter 5, David Wilson and Doris MacKenzie report on the effects of military-style boot camp interventions. In chapter 6, Anthony Petrosino, Carolyn Turpin-Petrosino, and John Buehler assess the effects of the popular prison deterrence program known as Scared Straight and other juvenile awareness programs. In chapter 7, Ojmarrh Mitchell, Doris MacKenzie, and David Wilson examine incarceration-based drug treatment, and in the final chapter in this part (chapter 8), Cynthia McDougall, Mark Cohen, Amanda Perry, and Raymond Swaray assess the monetary costs and benefits of different types of criminal sentences.

Part III includes three chapters that address what works for victims of crime. In chapter 9, Lynette Feder and David Wilson report on the effects of mandated batterer intervention programs to reduce domestic violence. In chapter 10, Heather Strang and Lawrence Sherman report on the effects of restorative justice to reduce victimization, and in chapter 11, Graham Farrell and Ken Pease review evaluations of the prevention of repeat residential burglary victimization.

Part IV includes three chapters that address what works for places. In chapter 12, Anthony Braga reports on the effects of policing crime "hot spots." In chapters 13 and 14, we review the effects of closed-circuit television (CCTV) surveillance and improved street lighting on crime, respectively.

Part V includes one chapter, written by us, that summarizes the main conclusions of this book about what works for at-risk children, offenders, victims, and places, and identifies some directions for research and policy development to advance evidence-based crime prevention and contribute to a safer society.

REFERENCES

Barnett, W. Steven. 1996. *Lives in the Balance: Age-27 Benefit-Cost Analysis of the High/Scope Perry Preschool Program.* Ypsilanti, MI: High/Scope Press.

Campbell Collaboration. 2003. A Flow Chart of the Steps in Conducting a Campbell Review. Retrieved July 3, 2003, from http://www.campbellcollaboration.org/Fraguidelines.html.

Campbell, Donald T. 1969. Reforms as Experiments. *American Psychologist* 24: 409–429.

Cook, Thomas D., and Donald T. Campbell. 1979. *Quasi-Experimentation: Design and Analysis Issues for Field Settings.* Chicago: Rand McNally.

Davies, Huw T.O., Sandra M. Nutley, and Peter C. Smith, eds. 2000. *What Works? Evidence-Based Policy and Practice in Public Services.* Bristol, England: The Policy Press.

Farrington, David P. 1983. "Randomized Experiments on Crime and Justice." In *Crime and Justice: An Annual Review of Research,* Vol. 4, edited by Michael Tonry and Norval Morris, 257–308. Chicago: University of Chicago Press.

——. 1997. Evaluating a Community Crime Prevention Program. *Evaluation* 3: 157–173.

——. 2003. Methodological Quality Standards for Evaluation Research. *Annals of the American Academy of Political and Social Science* 587: 49–68.

——, and Anthony Petrosino. 2000. Systematic Reviews of Criminological Interventions: The Campbell Collaboration Crime and Justice Group. *International Annals of Criminology* 38: 49–66.

——, and Anthony Petrosino. 2001. The Campbell Collaboration Crime and Justice Group. *Annals of the American Academy of Political and Social Science* 578: 35–49.

——, and Brandon C. Welsh. 2001. Systematic Reviews and Cost-Benefit Analyses of Correctional Interventions. *Prison Journal* 81: 339–359.

Farrington, David P., and Brandon C. Welsh. 2002. "Family-Based Crime Prevention." In *Evidence-Based Crime Prevention,* edited by Lawrence W. Sherman, David P. Farrington, Brandon C. Welsh, and Doris Layton MacKenzie, 22–55. New York: Routledge.

——. 2003. Family-Based Prevention of Offending: A Meta-Analysis. *Australian and New Zealand Journal of Criminology* 36: 127–151.

——. 2005. Randomized Experiments in Criminology: What Have We Learned in the Last Two Decades? *Journal of Experimental Criminology* 1: 9–38.

Finckenauer, James O., and Patricia W. Gavin. 1999. *Scared Straight: The Panacea Phenomenon Revisited.* Prospect Heights, IL: Waveland Press.

Gest, Ted. 2001. *Crime and Politics: Big Government's Erratic Campaign for Law and Order.* New York: Oxford University Press.

Goldblatt, Peter, and Chris Lewis, eds. 1998. *Reducing Offending: An Assessment of Research Evidence on Ways of Dealing with Offending Behaviour.* Home Office Research Study, No. 187. London: Research and Statistics Directorate, Home Office.

Gottfredson, Denise C., David B. Wilson, and Stacy Skroban Najaka. 2002. "School-Based Crime Prevention." In *Evidence-Based Crime Prevention,* edited by Lawrence W. Sherman, David P. Farrington, Brandon C. Welsh, and Doris Layton MacKenzie, 56–164. New York: Routledge.

Greenwood, Peter W., Lynn A. Karoly, Susan S. Everingham, Jill Houbé, M. Rebecca Kilburn, C. Peter Rydell, Matthew Sanders, and James Chiesa. 2001. "Estimating the Costs and Benefits of Early Childhood Interventions: Nurse Home Visits and the Perry Preschool." In *Costs and Benefits of Preventing Crime,* edited by Brandon C. Welsh, David P. Farrington, and Lawrence W. Sherman, 123–148. Boulder, CO: Westview Press.

Halladay, Mark, and Lisa Bero. 2000. Implementing Evidence-Based Practice in Health Care. *Public Money and Management* 20: 43–50.

Johnson, Byron R., Spencer De Li, David B. Larson, and Michael McCullough. 2000. A Systematic Review of the Religiosity and Delinquency Literature: A Research Note. *Journal of Contemporary Criminal Justice* 16: 32–52.

Lipsey, Mark W., and David B. Wilson. 2001. *Practical Meta-Analysis.* Thousand Oaks, CA: Sage.

Lösel, Friedrich, and Peter Koferl. 1989. "Evaluation Research on Correctional Treatment in West Germany: A Meta-Analysis." In *Criminal Behavior and the Justice System: Psychological Perspectives,* edited by Hermann Wegener, Friedrich Lösel, and Jochen Haisch, 334–355. New York: Springer-Verlag.

MacKenzie, Doris Layton. 2000. Evidence-Based Corrections: Identifying What Works. *Crime & Delinquency* 46: 457–471.

Millenson, Michael L. 1997. *Demanding Medical Excellence: Doctors and Accountability in the Information Age.* Chicago: University of Chicago Press.

Mosteller, Frederick, and Robert F. Boruch, eds. 2002. *Evidence Matters: Randomized Trials in Education Research.* Washington, DC: Brookings Institution Press.

Petrosino, Anthony. 2000. How Can We Respond Effectively to Juvenile Crime? *Pediatrics* 105: 635–637.

——, Robert F. Boruch, Haluk Soydan, Lorna Duggan, and Julio Sanchez-Meca. 2001. Meeting the Challenges of Evidence-Based Policy: The Campbell Collaboration. *Annals of the American Academy of Political and Social Science* 578: 14–34.

——, Carolyn Turpin-Petrosino, and James O. Finckenauer. 2000. Well Meaning Programs Can Have Harmful Effects! Lessons From Experiments of Programs Such as Scared Straight. *Crime & Delinquency* 46: 354–379.

Schweinhart, Lawrence J., Helen V. Barnes, and David P. Weikart. 1993. *Significant Benefits: The High/Scope Perry Preschool Study Through Age 27.* Ypsilanti, MI: High/Scope Press.

Shadish, William R., Thomas D. Cook, and Donald T. Campbell. 2002. *Experimental and Quasi-Experimental Designs for Generalized Causal Inference.* Boston: Houghton Mifflin.

Sherman, Lawrence W. 1998. *Evidence-Based Policing.* Washington, DC: Police Foundation.

——, David P. Farrington, Brandon C. Welsh, and Doris Layton MacKenzie, eds. 2002. *Evidence-Based Crime Prevention.* New York: Routledge.

Sherman, Lawrence W., Denise C. Gottfredson, Doris Layton MacKenzie, John E. Eck, Peter Reuter, and Shawn D. Bushway. 1997. *Preventing Crime: What Works, What Doesn't, What's Promising.* Washington, DC: National Institute of Justice, U.S. Department of Justice.

Tonry, Michael, and David P. Farrington, eds. 1995a. *Building a Safer Society: Strategic Approaches to Crime Prevention. Crime and Justice: A Review of Research,* Vol. 19. Chicago: University of Chicago Press.

——. 1995b. "Strategic Approaches to Crime Prevention." In *Building a Safer Society: Strategic Approaches to Crime Prevention. Crime and Justice: A Review of Research*, Vol. 19, edited by Michael Tonry and David P. Farrington, 1–20. Chicago: University of Chicago Press.

U.S. General Accounting Office. 2003. *Youth Illicit Drug Use Prevention: DARE Long-Term Evaluations and Federal Efforts to Identify Effective Programs*. Report GAO-03–172R. Washington, DC: Author.

Welsh, Brandon C., and David P. Farrington. 2001. Toward an Evidence-Based Approach to Preventing Crime. *Annals of the American Academy of Political and Social Science* 578: 158–173.

——, Lawrence W. Sherman, and Doris Layton MacKenzie. 2002. What Do We Know About Crime Prevention? *International Annals of Criminology* 40: 11–31.

Wilson, David B. 2001. Meta-Analytic Methods for Criminology. *Annals of the American Academy of Political and Social Science* 578: 71–89.

PART I: WHAT WORKS FOR CHILDREN

CHAPTER 2

EARLY PARENT TRAINING*

Odette Bernazzani and Richard E. Tremblay

University of Montreal

INTRODUCTION

Disruptive behavior in children can be defined as an array of behavior problems that include opposition to adults, hyperactivity, stealing, lying, truancy, extreme non-compliance, aggression, physical cruelty to people and animals, and destructive and sexually coercive behaviors (American Psychiatric Association, 1994; Quay and Hogan, 1999a). Oppositional-Defiant Disorder, Conduct Disorder, and Attention-Deficit/Hyperactivity Disorder are the diagnostic categories most often used in the psychiatric field to refer to children presenting severe disruptive behavior patterns. Although epidemiological studies in this area face important measurement problems and are limited by sample size (Lahey et al., 1999:23), it has been suggested that the three forms of disruptive behaviors account for up to two-thirds of all childhood and adolescent psychiatric disorders (Quay and Hogan, 1999b). Most children manifest disruptive behaviors during early child-hood, and show a gradual decline in frequency with age (Broidy et al., 1999; Lahey et al., 1999:23; Nagin and Tremblay, 1999; Tremblay, 2000; McCord et al., 2001). The term delinquent behavior refers to disruptive behaviors sanctioned by the law. Age of the child that performs a disruptive behavior is generally a key factor in deciding whether the behavior is, or is not, sanctioned by the law (McCord et al., 2001).

BACKGROUND

Longitudinal studies have shown that there are long-term consequences of disruptive behavior disorders for the individual, family, friends, community, and even the following generation (White et al., 1990; Farrington, 1995; Fergusson and Horwood, 1998; Serbin et al., 1998; Frick and Loney, 1999:507; Loeber, 2001; Côté et al., 2001). Prevention appears a worthy goal as treatment programs have shown a modest impact (Chamberlain, 1999:495; Kavale et al., 1999:441). The developmental trajectories of disruptive behaviors are a major reason to argue

* We thank the following agencies for financial support: Canadian Institute for Advanced Research, FCAR, Fonds de la Recherche en Santé du Québec, Molson Foundation, Social Sciences and Humanities Research Council of Canada, and St-Justine Hospital Research Centre.

Brandon C. Welsh and David P. Farrington, eds.
Preventing Crime: What Works for Children, Offenders, Victims, and Places, 21–32
© 2007 *Springer.*

for very early prevention. There is good evidence that chronic disruptive behavior leading to serious delinquency appears during early childhood (Moffit et al., 1996; Broidy et al., 1999; Nagin and Tremblay, 1999). There is also evidence to suggest that children with disruptive behavior problems become increasingly resistant to change with age despite treatment efforts (Kazdin, 1985; Frick and Loney, 1999:507; Tremblay, 2000). All these considerations underscore the need for early preventive programs targeting high risk families.

During the past 40 years, parenting programs have been offered in a variety of settings and to a variety of families. Many of these programs have targeted families with school age disruptive children (Patterson, 1982; Webster-Stratton et al., 1988; Kazdin et al., 1992; Tremblay et al., 1995; Hawkins et al., 1999). Parenting interventions as early as pregnancy have recently been stimulated by the evidence of reduced delinquent behavior in adolescents of poorly educated mothers who received a home visitation program during pregnancy and the first two years following birth (Olds et al., 1998). These home visitation programs are aimed at a wide range of outcomes, including maternal physical and psychosocial health, parenting skills, and children's psychosocial development and physical health. The long-term impact on delinquency of intensive home visitation during a period of more than two years supports the hypothesis that quality of family environment during the early years is a key to delinquency prevention (Patterson et al., 1992; Yoshikawa, 1994; McCord et al., 2001; Nagin and Tremblay, 2001). Early parenting interventions generally postulate that quality of parent-child relations will facilitate learning of control over impulsive, oppositional, and aggressive behavior, thus reducing disruptive behavior and its long-term negative impact on social integration.

The current review aims to address whether early parenting and home visitation programs are effective in preventing behavior problems and delinquency in children.

SUMMARY OF RESEARCH METHODS

Search Criteria and Strategy

The review was limited to families with a child under age three at the start of the intervention to ensure that the interventions were provided early in the child's life. However, no limits were set concerning the child's age at the end of the intervention. In addition, selected interventions could target either the general population (universal intervention) or a high risk group (selective intervention). Studies were eligible for this review when parent training or support was a major component of the intervention, although not necessarily the only one.

The original aim of the review was to assess the impact of the interventions on the children's delinquent behavior. However, since we found only one study assessing delinquency, we used a broader scope in our review and selected studies with outcome measures of disruptive behaviors. These assessments included self-reported delinquency, self-, parent-, or teacher-rated measures of disruptive behavior, and observer-rated assessments of disruptive behavior in the classroom.

Only studies employing random assignment or quasi-experimental (pre- and post-intervention assessments and adequate control groups) designs were included.

Our starting point for searching through the literature was two previous reviews. The first (Mrazek and Brown, 1999) reviewed psychosocial interventions during the pre-school years designed to enhance child development according to a wide variety of outcomes. The second review (Tremblay et al., 1999) focused on programs targeting families of pre-adolescents for the prevention of disruptive behavior. In addition, several other major sources of information were searched: Two major electronic databases, PsyINFO and MEDLINE (1967 to 2001); the *Cochrane Library*; the *Future of Children* publications, as well as all the potentially relevant review articles identified during the search (Gomby et al., 1993; 1999; Yoshikawa, 1995; Vitaro et al., 1996; Culross, 1999; Barlow and Coren, 2001). A wide search strategy was used to ensure that relevant studies were not missed. Hence, the search terms excluded study design and reflected a wide age group and a wide range of behavior problems. The following search terms were used: "parent training," "childhood," "pre-school," "delinquency," "conduct disorder," "antisocial behavior," "aggression," "physical aggression," and "behavior problems."

Identification of Studies

Titles and abstracts of studies identified through our searches were reviewed to determine whether they met the inclusion criteria. Studies were selected for methodological quality using the criteria suggested by Mrazek and Brown (1999). These authors have extensively reviewed outcomes in psychosocial prevention and early intervention in young children. They have developed an instrument called the Threats to Trial Integrity Score (TTIS) that allows for the measurement of the quality of the design of a controlled trial, whether it is randomized or not. This scale assesses the potential threat regarding ten dimensions of quality design on a four-point scale, from Null or Minimal risk (0), Low Risk (1), Moderate Risk (2), and High Risk (3). Scores for each of the ten dimensions are combined in a weighted fashion to obtain a global score (for additional information, see Mrazek and Brown, 1999). The authors then categorized this ordinal scale into a five level Trial Quality Grade. Each trial was classified as a one- to five-star design. The five-star designs were the highest scoring trials based on TTIS score (about 5%). The four-star designs were among the top quarter of trials; the three-star designs were in the second quartile, and so forth. Mrazek and Brown suggested concentrating on trials with five- and four-star designs as they are clearly well-designed studies. Mrazek and Brown identified 165 prevention studies with preschool children, but only thirty-four met the four- or five-star classification. Of the 34 studies, a total of six trials met our inclusion criteria. Three additional trials were identified in Tremblay et al. (1999), but they were not kept in our review, as they did not meet the four-star criteria design of Mrazek and Brown (1999).

TABLE 1.   Sample Characteristics of Studies Included in the Review

Study	Target Population	Country	Final N[c]
Cullen (1976)	[Universal][a]	Australia	246
Johnson and Breckenridge (1982) Johnson and Walker (1987)	Low-Income Mexican-American families [Selective][b]	U.S	139
Kitzman et al. (1997)	Pregnant women with at least 2 of the following: unmarried, less than 12 years of education, unemployed Most subjects were African-American [Selective]	U.S.	743
McCarton et al. (1997)	Low-birth-weight premature infants [Selective]	U.S.	874
Olds et al. (1986, 1998)	Women who were young (<19 years), unmarried or of low SES [Selective]	U.S.	323
Scarr and McCartney (1988)	All families with a 2-year-old child in a Bermudian parish [Universal]	Bermuda	117
St-Pierre and Layzer (1999)	Families with incomes below the poverty level [Selective]	U.S.	<2000 (exact number not available)

[a] Universal preventive intervention: Intervention that targets the general population.
[b] Selective preventive intervention: Intervention that targets high risk groups.
[c] Sample number related to outcomes examined in this review.

The PsyINFO search yielded 151 new abstracts, none of which were included in the review. Most of them were excluded because they targeted older children. Others were excluded for methodological reasons, mostly because of the absence of a control group. Searching the *Cochrane Library* and the *Future of Children* publications generated a further four reviews that provided information about one trial that had not already been identified and met our criteria.

Thus, seven studies met our criteria. The data have been summarized using effect sizes, but have not been combined in a meta-analysis due to the small number of studies and the presence of substantial heterogeneity among them.

RESULTS

Sample Characteristics

All seven studies were randomized controlled experiments (see Table 1). All but two were conducted in the U.S. Two interventions targeted the general population (universal preventive interventions), while the remaining five were selective preventive interventions (i.e., they targeted high risk groups, mostly socially disadvantaged families or, in one study, premature babies). Boys and girls were included in all studies. Two studies targeted minority groups: African Americans and Mexican Americans. The latter study was the only one that did not attempt to obtain a representative population sample due to major recruitment challenges. While it can be argued that nearly all studies tried to involve families, in practice, most studies intervened mainly with mothers.

In total, 7,917 families were randomly assigned to receive parent training or to a control group. One study had over 4,000 participants involving 21 sites, two had over 1,000 participants, three had over 300, and one had 125. Attrition rates varied greatly from one study to another, ranging from 20% to 67%. Sample numbers relevant to our review varied from 117 to more than 2,000 (see right-hand column of Table 1).

Intervention Characteristics

Four interventions began when the child was 12 months old or younger (see Table 2). All four continued beyond age two, up to either age three, five, or six. Two trials began during the prenatal period and both continued up to two years. Finally, one trial began when children were 24 months old and ended when they were about four years. Overall duration of interventions ranged from more than two to six years. Length of follow-up ranged from immediate end of intervention

TABLE 2. *Intervention Characteristics of Studies Included in the Review*

Study	Average Age at Start of Intervention	Intervention Period (Child's Age)	Type of Intervention
Cullen (1976)	3 months	Up to 6 years	Clinic-based interview with general practitioner
Johnson and Breckenridge (1982) Johnson and Walker (1987)	12 months	1 to 3 years	Home visits, family workshops and child development center
Kitzman et al. (1997)	16.5 weeks (gestational age)	Prenatal to 2 years	Home visits
McCarton et al. (1997)	7 weeks	Up to 3 years	Home visits, parent groups, child development center
Olds et al. (1986, 1998)	25 weeks (gestational age)	Prenatal to 2 years	Home visits
Scarr and McCartney (1988)	24 months	2 to 4 years	Home visits
St-Pierre and Layzer (1999)	Not available	Younger than 1 year and up to 5 years	Home visits, child development center

to 13 years following the end. The longest follow-up was for the Elmira (New York) project (Olds et al., 1998). Nearly all studies (six) involved intensive home visitation. Half of these had additional intervention components, either the participation in a child development center or parent groups. One study involved a clinic-based interview conducted with mothers by a general practitioner. In all but one study (Scarr and McCartney, 1988), control groups were offered a non-intensive follow-up that included screening procedures, pediatric surveillance, free-transportation, or annual contact by the secretary of the study.

Effectiveness of Early Parent Training

Overall, results concerning the effectiveness of parent training in the prevention of behavior problems in children were mixed (see Table 3). Four studies reported no evidence of effectiveness, two reported beneficial effects, and one study reported mainly beneficial effects with some harmful effects. Of the studies with significant results, which provided sufficient data to calculate an effect-size, the treatment effect ranged from 0.25 to 1.05 (calculations from Mrazek and Brown, 1999). All but one study (Scarr and McCartney, 1988) included mother reports of disruptive behavior. Two studies also included teacher or school reports (Johnson and Walker, 1987; Olds et al., 1998), and one study used self-reported delinquency (Olds et al., 1998). Only two of the seven studies were designed to target specifically behavior problems: the Houston Parent-Child Development Center Program (Johnson and Breckenridge, 1982; Johnson and Walker, 1987) and the Brusselton study (Cullen, 1976). Most studies looked at behavior problems among a wide range of other outcomes; for example, cognitive development and physical health. The child's age at evaluation varied greatly from one study to another, ranging from two to 15 years. Only two studies reported differential effects according to gender, but both girls and boys had benefited from the interventions.

Only one study (Olds et al., 1998) evaluated the effectiveness of home visitation and parent training on delinquent behaviors. Although not initially designed with the aim of preventing delinquency, the Elmira project reported beneficial effects on the child's delinquent behavior 13 years after the end of the intervention (age 15). However, the beneficial effect of the intervention concerned a subgroup of children of poor, young, and unmarried women only (n = 68). The intervention was an intensive nurse home visiting program that started early during the pregnancy of high risk women and continued during the first two years after birth. The nurses promoted several aspects of maternal functioning and well-being, including competent care of the children. The nurses completed an average of nine home visits during pregnancy and 23 home visits from birth to the child's second year (Olds et al., 1997).

CONCLUSIONS AND POLICY IMPLICATIONS

A very limited number of well-designed studies including both early interventions and outcomes related to disruptive behaviors were available for this review. In

TABLE 3. Effectiveness of Early Parent Training (Outcome Findings)

Study	Outcome	Effect size[a]	P value	Direction of Outcome[b]
Cullen (1976)	AT AGE 6			
	Mother reports			*Beneficial*
	Talked loudly	< -0.25	<0.05	T
	Hit or struck others	< -0.25	<0.05	T
		< -0.35	<0.05	G
	Exaggerated/ told untruths	< -0.35	<0.05	G
				Harmful
	Late for school	>0.42	<0.001	T
		>0.48	<0.01	B
Johnson and	AT AGE 5.3			
Breckenridge	*Mother reports*			
(1982)	Behavior Assessment			*Beneficial*
Johnson and	– Destructive	-1.05	<0.01	B
Walker (1987)	– High Activity	-0.55	<0.05	B
	AT AGE 5.5			
	Teacher reports			
	Classroom Behavior Inventory			*Beneficial*
	– Hostility Scale	-0.46	0.01	T
		-0.66	0.01	B
	Behavior Problems			
	– Disrupts	$-0.42; -0.53$	0.019; 0.038	T; B
	– Obstinate	$-0.48; -0.61$	0.007; 0.018	T; B
	– Restless	$-0.47; -0.70$	0.008; 0.007	T; B
	– Fights	$-0.46; -0.68$	0.01; 0.008	T; B
	– Impulsive	$-0.58; -0.54$	0.025; 0.03	B; G
Kitzman et al.	AT AGE 2			
(1997)	*Mother reports*			
	Child Behavior Checklist			NS
McCarton	AT AGE 8			
et al.	*Mother reports*			
(1997)	Child Behavior Checklist			NS
	Behavior Profile			NS

Continued

addition, overall results were mixed: four studies reported no evidence of effectiveness, two reported beneficial effects, and one study reported mainly beneficial effects with some harmful effects. The latter effects, however, concerned one specific item only, "late for school." Studies varied greatly from one another on various aspects, including outcome measures, child's age at evaluation, the nature and duration of the intervention, and sample size. Studies reporting beneficial effects showed no specific patterns, allowing one to be able to distinguish them

TABLE 3. Continued

Study	Outcome	Effect size[a]	P value	Direction of Outcome[b]
Olds et al. (1986, 1998)	AT AGE 15			
	Child reports			
	– Running away	NA[c]	0.003	*Beneficial*[d]
	– Arrests	NA	0.03	"
	– Convictions; probation violations	NA	<0.001	"
	– Number of sex partners	NA	0.003	"
	– Days having consumed alcohol	NA	0.03	"
	– Minor antisocial acts			"
	– Major delinquent acts			NS
	– Externalizing problems			NS
	– Acting-out problems			NS
	– Incidence of times stopped by police			NS
	– Alcohol impairment			NS
	– Days using drugs			NS
	Parent reports			
	– Similar scales			NS
	School reports			
	– Incidence of short- or long-term school suspensions			NS
Scarr and McCartney (1988)	AT 45 MONTHS			
	Blind examiner			
	Childhood Personality Scale			NS
	Infant Behavior Record			NS
St-Pierre and Layzer (1999)	AT AGE 3, 4 AND 5			
	Mother reports			
	Child Behavior Checklist			NS
	– Total score			
	– Externalizing Score			
	– Internalizing Score			

[a] Effect-size calculations are taken from Mrazek and Brown (1999). They can be either negative or positive and their interpretation depends on the way the outcome measure is coded.
[b] T = total sample; B = boys; G = girls.
[c] Insufficient data provided to calculate an effect-size.
[d] The beneficial outcomes concerned only the subgroup of children of poor, young, and unmarried women.

from the other studies. In this context, it is impossible to make a definitive statement as to whether early parent training and support is effective in preventing disruptive behaviors in children and delinquency during adolescence. Thus, caution is suggested in the interpretation of the existing studies, especially in the context of policy recommendations.

Similar caution has already been expressed with respect to home visiting programs that provide an important amount of parent training. Some authors have argued that home visits are a necessary but insufficient component of programs seeking to help families and young children (Weiss, 1993). More recently, a major review of six home visiting models that were being, or had been, implemented nationally in the U.S. concluded that results regarding the effectiveness of home visiting for a wide range of outcomes were quite modest, at the most (Gomby et al., 1999).

Several factors can contribute to these overall disappointing results (for excellent reviews of these factors, see Gomby et al., 1999; St-Pierre and Layzer, 1999). The heterogeneity in the definition of parent training and the absence of evidence regarding which components of parent training are most effective appear most relevant to our own review. The three studies reporting beneficial results varied greatly with regards to the nature of the intervention. The Elmira project (Olds et al. 1998), an intensive nurse home visitation program that emphasized parental development and was provided during the first two years of the child's life, had a significant effect on children of poor, young, and unmarried women. Several aspects of maternal functioning were promoted in addition to the competent care of the child, including maternal personal development and positive health behaviors. In addition, an important focus was put on the involvement of other family members and people in the social network.

On the other hand, the Brusselton project in Australia (Cullen, 1976) was significantly different in nature and intensity. Counselling sessions (only 20– to 30-minutues long) were provided by the same general practitioner to all mothers living in a rural community. Four sessions were provided during the first two years of life followed by two sessions per year for the next four years. Although significantly less intensive, the duration of the Brusselton intervention was three times longer than the Elmira intervention. The progress of the child formed the basis of each interview in the Brusselton study. Mothers were encouraged to accept themselves as they were and to reflect on, and eventually modify, their child-rearing practices. Finally, the third study showing beneficial effects on disruptive behaviors, the Houston project (Johnson and Breckenridge, 1982), targeted low-income Mexican-American families and combined several intervention components that all emphasized parenting skills: Home visits, family workshops, and participation in a child development center. Fathers were strongly encouraged to participate. This heterogeneity in the small number of studies showing beneficial effects underscores the fact that little information is available to guide intervention programs when they choose to target parent education. As St-Pierre and Layzer (1999) pointed out, the field of parent education targeting young families seems to suffer from a lack of evidence about what intervention components are most important, which parents are more likely to benefit from the intervention, how long it should last, and whether parent training should be combined with other intervention types.

It is of interest to note that the Brusselton and Houston studies were the only two initially designed to prevent behavior disorders, and both reported beneficial effects. This, perhaps, highlights the relevancy of developing specific models for the prevention of behavior problems rather than using general models to improve a wide range of maternal and child outcomes. In their review of major U.S. home visiting programs targeting broad outcomes, Gomby et al. (1999) advocated a more modest view of the potential of home visiting programs. In addition, they strongly recommended the use of new models to improve the overall effectiveness of home visiting programs. We believe this recommendation is especially relevant for interventions targeting the prevention of children's disruptive behavior problems, as well as delinquency. Without any doubt, many additional studies are required in order to identify the characteristics of early parent training and support programs that can prevent the development of disruptive behavior disorders and delinquency.

Overall, caution is suggested in the interpretation of findings of research on the effectiveness of early parent training for the prevention of disruptive behavior problems in children and juvenile delinquency, due to three important considerations: (1) the limited number of adequately designed studies; (2) results of the well-designed studies available are mixed and, where positive, often modest in magnitude; and (3) very few studies (two out of seven) were specifically designed to prevent disruptive behaviors in children. Since there is good evidence from longitudinal studies that disruptive behavior starts during the pre-school years and often leads to juvenile delinquency, there is clearly a need for numerous studies to test different types of early interventions specifically designed for the prevention of disruptive behavior problems and juvenile delinquency. We believe that useful policy recommendations will be possible to establish only once additional crucial information becomes available.

REFERENCES

American Psychiatric Association. 1994. *Diagnostic and Statistical Manual of Mental Disorders*. Fourth ed. Washington DC: Author.

Barlow, Jane, and Esther Coren. 2001. Parent-Training for Improving Maternal Psychosocial Health. *The Cochrane Library*, Issue 2. Oxford, UK: Update Software.

Broidy, Lisa, Daniel Nagin, and Richard E. Tremblay. 1999. The Linkage of Trajectories of Childhood Externalizing Behaviors to Later Violent and Nonviolent Delinquency. Paper presented at the Biennial Meeting of the Society for Research in Child Development, Albuquerque, NM, April.

Chamberlain, Patricia. 1999. "Residential Care for Children and Adolescents with Oppositional Defiant Disorder and Conduct Disorder." In *Handbook of Disruptive Behavior Disorders*, edited by Herbert C. Quay and Anne. E. Hogan, 495–506. New York: Kluwer Academic/Plenum.

Côté, Sylvana, Mark Zoccolillo, Richard E. Tremblay, Daniel Nagin, and Frank Vitaro. 2001. Predicting Girls' Conduct Disorder in Adolescence from Childhood Trajectories of Disruptive Behaviors. *Journal of the American Academy of Child and Adolescent Psychiatry* 40: 678–684.

Cullen, Kevin J. 1976. A Six-Year Controlled Trial of Prevention of Children's Behavior Disorders. *Journal of Paediatrics* 88: 662–666.

Culross, Patti L. 1999. Summary of Home Visiting Program Evaluation Outcomes. *Future of Children* 9: 195–223.

Farrington, David. P. 1995. The Development of Offending and Antisocial Behavior from Childhood: Key Findings from The Cambridge Study in Delinquent Development. *Journal of Child Psychology and Psychiatry* 36: 929–964.

Fergusson, David M., and L. John Horwood. 1998. Early Conduct Problems and Later Life Opportunities. *Journal of Child Psychology and Psychiatry* 39:1097–1108.

Frick, Paul J., and Bryan R. Loney. 1999. "Outcomes of Children and Adolescents with Oppositional Defiant Disorder and Conduct Disorder." In *Handbook of Disruptive Behavior Disorders*, edited by Herbert C. Quay and Anne. E. Hogan, 507–524. New York: Kluwer Academic/Plenum.

Gomby, Deanna S., Patti L. Culross, and Richard E. Behrman. 1999. Home Visiting: Recent Program Evaluations-Analysis and Recommendations. *Future of Children* 9: 4–26.

Gomby, Deanna S., Carol S. Larson, Eugene M. Lewit, and Richard E. Behrman. 1993. Home Visiting: Analysis and Recommendations. *Future of Children* 3: 6–22.

Hawkins, J. David, Richard F. Catalano, Richard Kosterman, Robert Abbott, and Karl G. Hill. 1999. Preventing Adolescent Health-Risk Behaviors by Strengthening Protection During Childhood. *Archives of Pediatrics and Adolescent Medicine* 153: 226–234.

Johnson, Dale L., and James N. Breckenridge. 1982. The Houston Parent-Child Development Center and the Primary Prevention of Behavior Problems in Young Children. *American Journal of Community Psychology* 10: 305–316.

Johnson, Dale L., and Todd T. Walker. 1987. Primary Prevention of Behavior Problems in Mexican-American Children. *American Journal of Community Psychology* 15: 375–395.

Kavale, Kenneth A., Steven R. Forness, and Hill M.Walker. 1999. "Interventions for Oppositional Defiant Disorder and Conduct Disorder in the Schools." In *Handbook of Disruptive Behavior Disorders*, edited by Herbert C. Quay and Anne E. Hogan, 441–454. New York: Kluwer Academic/Plenum.

Kazdin, Alan E. 1985. *Treatment of Antisocial Behavior in Children and Adolescents*. Homewood, Il: Dorsey Press.

Kazdin, Alan E., Todd C. Siegel, and Debra Bass. 1992. Cognitive Problem-Solving Skills Training and Parent Management Training in the Treatment of Antisocial Behavior in Children. *Journal of Consulting and Clinical Psychology* 60: 733–747.

Kitzman, Harriet, David L. Olds, Charles R. Henderson, Carole Hanks, Robert Cole, Robert Tatelbaum, Kenneth M. McConnochie, Kimberly Sidora, Dennis W. Luckey, David Shaver, Kay Engelhardt, David James, and Kathryn Barnard. 1997. Effect of Prenatal and Infancy Home Visitation by Nurses on Pregnancy Outcomes, Childhood Injuries and Repeated Childbearing. *Journal of the American Medical Association* 278: 644–652.

Lahey, Benjamin B., Terri L. Miller, Rachel A. Gordon, and Anne W. Riley. 1999. "Developmental Epidemiology of the Disruptive Behavior Disorders." In *Handbook of Disruptive Behavior Disorders*, edited by Herbert. C. Quay and Anne E. Hogan, 23–48. New York: Kluwer Academic/Plenum.

Loeber, Rolf. 2001. Developmental Aspects of Juvenile Homicide. Paper presented at the Biennial Meeting of the Society for Research in Child Development, Minneapolis, MN, April 19–22.

McCarton, Cecilia M., Jeanne Brooks-Gunn, Ina F. Wallace, Charles R. Bauer, Forrest C. Bennet, Judy C. Bernbaum, Sue Broyles, Patrick H. Casey, Marie C. McCormick, David T. Scott, Jon Tyson, James Tonascia, and Curtis L. Meinert. 1997. Results at Age 8 Years of Early Intervention for Low-Birth-Weight Premature Infants: The Infant Health and Development Program. *Journal of the American Medical Association* 277: 126–132.

McCord, Joan, Cathy S. Widom, and Nancy E. Crowell, eds. 2001. *Juvenile Crime, Juvenile Justice*. Washington, DC: National Academy Press.

Moffitt, Terrie. E., Avshalom Caspi, Nigel Dickson, Phil S. Silva, and Warren Stanton. 1996. Childhood-Onset Versus Adolescent-Onset Antisocial Conduct Problems in Males: Natural History from Ages 3 to 18 Years. *Development & Psychopathology* 8: 399–424.

Mrazek, Patricia. J., and C. Henricks Brown. 1999. *An Evidenced-Based Literature Review Regarding Outcomes in Psychosocial Prevention and Early Intervention in Young Children*. Toronto, Canada: Invest in Kids Foundation.

Nagin, Daniel, and Richard E. Tremblay. 1999. Trajectories of Boys' Physical Aggression, Opposition, and Hyperactivity on the Path to Physically Violent and Non-Violent Juvenile Delinquency. *Child Development* 70: 1181–1196.

——. 2001. Parental and Early Childhood Predictors of Persistent Physical Aggression in Boys from Kindergarten to High School. *Archives of General Psychiatry* 58: 389–394.

Olds, David L., Charles R. Henderson, Robert Chamberlin, and Robert Tatelbaum. 1986. Preventing Child Abuse and Neglect: A Randomized Trial of Nurse Home Visitation. *Pediatrics* 78: 65–78.

Olds, David L., Harriet Kitzman, Robert Cole, and JoAnn Robinson. 1997. Theoretical and Empirical Foundations of a Program of Home Visitation for Pregnant Women and Parents of Young Children. *Journal of Community Psychology* 25: 9–25.

Olds, David L., Charles R. Henderson, Robert Cole, John Eckenrode, Harriet Kitzman, Dennis Luckey, Lisa Pettitt, Kimberly Sidora, Pamela Morris, and Jane Powers. 1998. Long-Term Effects of Nurse Home Visitation on Children's Criminal and Antisocial Behavior: 15-Year Follow-Up of a Randomized Controlled Trial. *Journal of the American Medical Association* 280: 1238–1244.

Patterson, Gerald R. 1982. *Coercive Family Process*. Eugene, OR: Castalia.

——, John B. Reid, and Thomas J. Dishion. 1992. *Antisocial Boys*. Eugene, OR: Castalia.

Quay, Herbert C., and Anne E. Hogan, eds. 1999a. *Handbook of Disruptive Behavior Disorders*. New York: Kluwer Academic/Plenum.

——. 1999b. "Preface." In *Handbook of Disruptive Behavior Disorders*, edited by Herbert. C. Quay and Anne. E. Hogan, ix-x. New York: Kluwer Academic/ Plenum.

St-Pierre, Robert G., and Jean I. Layzer. 1999. Using Home Visits for Multiple Purposes: The Comprehensive Child Development Program. *Future of Children* 9: 134–151.

Scarr, Sandra, and Kathleen McCartney. 1988. Far from Home: An Experimental Evaluation of the Mother-Child Home Program in Bermuda. *Child Development* 59: 531–543.

Serbin, Lisa A., Jessica M. Cooperman, Patrica L. Peters, Pascale M. Lehoux, Dale M. Stack, and Alex E. Schwartzman. 1998. Intergenerational Transfer of Psychosocial Risk in Women with Childhood Histories of Aggression, Withdrawal, or Aggression and Withdrawal. *Developmental Psychology* 34: 1246–1262.

Tremblay, Richard E. 2000. The Development of Aggressive Behaviour During Childhood: What Have We Learned in The Past Century? *International Journal of Behavioral Development* 24: 129–141.

——, Linda Kurtz, Louise C. Mâsse, Frank Vitaro, and Robert O. Pihl. 1995. A Bimodal Preventive Intervention for Disruptive Kindergarten Boys: Its Impact Through Mid-Adolescence. *Journal of Consulting and Clinical Psychology* 63: 560–568.

Tremblay, Richard. E., David LeMarquand, and Frank Vitaro. 1999. "The Prevention of Oppositional Defiant Disorder and Conduct Disorder." In *Handbook of Disruptive Behavior Disorders*, edited by Herbert C. Quay and Anne E. Hogan, 525–555. New York: Kluwer Academic/Plenum.

Vitaro, Frank, Mirella De Civita, and Linda Pagani. 1996. The Impact of Research-Based Prevention Programs on Children's Disruptive Behavior. *Exceptionality Education Canada* 5: 105–135.

Webster-Stratton, Carolyn, Mary Kolpacoff, and Terri Hollinsworth. 1988. Self-Administered Videotape Therapy for Families with Conduct-Problem Children: Comparison with Two Cost-Effective Treatments and a Control Group. *Journal of Consulting and Clinical Psychology* 56: 558–566.

Weiss, Heather B. 1993. Home Visits: Necessary but Not Sufficient. *The Future of Children* 3: 113–128.

White, Jennifer L., Terrie E. Moffitt, Felton Earls, Lee Robins, and Phil A. Silva. 1990. How Early Can We Tell? Predictors of Childhood Conduct Disorder and Adolescent Delinquency. *Criminology* 28: 507–533.

Yoshikawa, Hirokazu. 1994. Prevention as Cumulative Protection: Effects of Early Family Support and Education on Chronic Delinquency and its Risks. *Psychological Bulletin* 115: 28–54.

——. 1995. Long-Term Effects of Early Childhood Programs on Social Outcomes and Delinquency. *The Future of Children* 5: 51–75.

CHAPTER 3

CHILD SOCIAL SKILLS TRAINING*

Friedrich Lösel and Andreas Beelmann

University of Erlangen-Nuremberg

INTRODUCTION

Early developmental prevention of aggressive, delinquent, and other forms of antisocial behavior has become a very important field of research and policymaking in many countries (Farrington and Coid, 2003; Loeber and Farrington, 1998, 2001; McCord and Tremblay, 1992; Peters and McMahon, 1996). There are a number of reasons for this. First, conduct disorders are among the most frequent behavioral and emotional problems in young people (Lahey et al., 1999). Extremely violent, single cases and alarming crime statistics have particularly sensitized societies for this issue (Lösel and Bliesener, 2003). Whereas most youngsters show only adolescence-limited and less serious forms of antisocial behavior, the problem behavior of "early starters" is often particularly stable (Moffitt, 1993). Approximately one-half of this group will embark upon a relatively persistent and serious path of antisocial behavior (Moffitt et al., 1996; Patterson et al., 1998). These early and stable deviants cause a lot of suffering for parents, teachers, peers, and, in the long run, also for themselves. They accumulate problems such as social competence deficits, deviant peer group affiliation, school failure, or low work qualification and unemployment (Lösel and Bender, 2003; Thornberry, 1998). Many of these youngsters develop into intensive offenders who are responsible for more than one-half of classic crime (Loeber et al., 1998). Their behavior is difficult to change. Although specific modes of offender treatment are more successful than the "nothing works" doctrine suggested, effect sizes in this field are only moderate (see Lösel, 1995, 2001a). Furthermore, antisocial behavior in childhood possesses a marker function for other psychiatric disorders in adulthood (Robins and Price, 1991).

BACKGROUND

These considerations have led to increased interest in programs of early developmental prevention, such as parent training, home visits, day care, family therapy,

---

* This research was supported by grants from the Smith Richardson Foundation and the German Federal Ministry for the Family, Seniors, Women, and Youth. We wish to thank Birgit Plankensteiner for her help in coding studies and Jonathan Harrow for English-language, native-speaker advice.

preschool- or school-based child training, teacher training, multisystemic therapy, or combined programs in more complex community-oriented approaches (e.g., Beelmann, 2000; Farrington and Coid, 2003; Farrington and Welsh, 2003; Gottfredson, 2001; Loeber and Farrington 2001; McCord and Tremblay, 1992; Sherman et al., 1997; Wasserman and Miller 1998). One strategy applied relatively frequently is social skills training for children and youths. Such trainings are mainly based on cognitive-behavioral concepts of social learning and problem solving (e.g., Bierman et al., 1996; Kazdin, 1996; Shure, 1992). They typically contain a structured program with a limited number of sessions teaching adequate modes of social perception, identification of emotions, causal attribution, perspective taking and empathy, alternative thinking, anticipation and evaluation of consequences, self-control, anger management, interpersonal problem-solving, and related skills. More comprehensive approaches, which are combined with parent- and/or teacher-oriented programs and may extend over years of school- or preschool education, should not be subsumed under this specific category.

Social skills training for children is based on numerous studies demonstrating aggression-prone schemata of social information processing and deficits in social problem-solving as reliable risk factors for antisocial behavior (e.g., Akhtar and Bradley 1991; Crick and Dodge 1994; Frick, 1998). Compared with other types of prevention, these programs also have practical advantages; for example, they can reach the whole target population (e.g., at school), may generate relatively low costs (e.g., group training delivered by regular teachers), are less difficult to implement in everyday practice than family-oriented or combined programs, and may raise no serious ethical and legal problems regarding selection and negative side effects (Kazdin and Wassell, 1999; LeBlanc, 1998; Lösel, 2002; Offord et al., 1998; Prinz and Miller, 1994). These advantages led not only to many small-scale studies but also, more recently, to some large-scale, well-designed programs of social skills training for children (e.g., Conduct Problems Prevention Research Group, 1999, 2002).

Various reviews of outcome evaluations suggest that social skills training is a promising approach to the prevention of antisocial behavior and crime (e.g., Ang and Hughes, 2001; Beelmann, 2000; Beelmann et al., 1994; Brestan and Eyberg, 1998; Denham and Almeida, 1987; Durlak and Wells, 1997; Erwin, 1994; Greenberg, 2001; Kazdin, 1996; Lösel and Beelmann, 2003; Magee Quinn et al., 1999; Schneider, 1992; Sherman et al., 1997; Tremblay and Craig, 1995; Tremblay et al., 1999; Wasserman and Miller, 1998; Wilson et al., 2001). However, a number of problems still need to be taken into account (see, e.g., Beelmann et al., 1994; Bullis et al., 2001; Gottfredson, 2001; Gresham, 1998; Lösel, 2002). For example, many studies in this field do not meet rigorous criteria of methodological quality. In addition, the most substantial effects are found in those criteria that are relatively close to the training contents (e.g., social-cognitive skills). More generalizable outcomes in everyday behavior, in contrast, are less well investigated, seem to be smaller, and not yet consistent. This is particularly the case when we look at outcomes that are measured after a longer followup.

Against this background, the Crime and Justice Group of the Campbell

Collaboration (Farrington & Petrosino, 2001) launched a systematic and up-to-date meta-analysis of methodologically sound studies on the preventive effects of child skills training. The first results of 84 randomized controlled studies containing 135 comparisons have recently been published (Lösel and Beelmann, 2003). Despite a wide range of positive and negative effects, the majority confirmed the benefits of treatment. The mean postintervention effect (0 to 2 months after the program) was $d = .38$. Only a minority of studies measured outcome after longer time intervals. The mean follow-up effect (3 or more months after training) was $d = .28$. There were no significant differences between various modes of treatment. However, other moderators, such as sample size and type of randomization, had an impact on effect size.

Our previous analysis examined not only outcomes in terms of antisocial behavior but also related measures of social skills and social-cognitive skills. Although the skills criteria revealed larger effects than the measures of antisocial behavior, most of our previous analyses integrated all three categories. We also did not differentiate between various forms and measures of antisocial behavior. Therefore, a more specific analysis of outcomes in antisocial behavior is necessary before we can draw conclusions for policymaking and practice. In accordance with this aim, the present chapter reports analyses of direct measures of antisocial behavior. As in our previous study, only randomized controlled studies are used.

SUMMARY OF RESEARCH METHODS

Criteria for Inclusion of Studies

In selecting evaluation studies for inclusion in this review, the following eligibility criteria were used:

1. The study had to contain an evaluation addressing only a social competence training program for the prevention of antisocial behavior in children and youth. We excluded all studies evaluating additional program components (e.g., programs with parent training, teacher training, or home visits). Likewise, we did not include programs focusing on other areas of problem behavior, such as internalizing problems.
2. The study had to have a treatment and control group that were compared in an experimental (randomized) design. Although quasi-experiments were excluded in principle, we did include stratified modes of randomization (e.g., randomized field trial, randomized block design, matching plus randomization). However, pre- and post-intervention data had to be available.
3. Treated youngsters had to be between the ages of 0 to 18 years.
4. The program had to be preventive in a narrow sense. We included studies on primary or universal prevention and on targeted prevention in at-risk groups (selective or indicated prevention). We also included programs for youngsters with conduct disorders or oppositional-defiant disorders, because these targeted specific at-risk groups. However, we excluded treatment programs for already adjudicated delinquents or other clinical groups.

5. The studies had to report outcomes in a measure of antisocial behavior (e.g., self-report, parent report, teacher report, peer report, observational data, or official records). Data had to be reported in sufficient detail to permit effect size computation.
6. We included all retrievable published or unpublished reports in the English or German languages that had appeared not later than the year 2000.

Search Strategies

First, we carried out an intensive check of electronic databases, such as PsychInfo, Medline, ERIC, and Dissertation Abstracts. Second, the references from reviews on child skills training and the prevention of antisocial behavior were checked systematically. Third, the references given in already identified primary studies were analyzed for further relevant publications.

A total of 851 articles were identified with these strategies. From these, 230 reports were excluded in a first round because they did not fulfill the selection criteria. The remaining 621 articles (80% published and 20% unpublished) were checked in more detail. By excluding studies step by step, we ended up with 55 research reports that met our eligibility criteria (see Appendix 1). Because a number of reports contained more than one treatment or control group or carried out separate analyses for children and adolescents or boys and girls, the final database for this meta-analysis was 89 treatment-control group comparisons. These contained 9,109 youngsters of whom 4,603 (50.1%) belonged to the treatment groups.

Coding and Computation of Effect Sizes

The second author and a trained student coded all comparisons according to a detailed scheme. This contained characteristics of publication (e.g., year, country), methods (e.g., design, followup), intervention programs (e.g., type, intensity, setting), and the trained children (e.g., age, gender, risk factors). A selection of these variables is presented in the Results section (see Table 1). Two coders analyzed a subsample of 24 comparisons independently. Interrater agreement varied between 81% and 100% depending on category ($M = 96.3\%$).

Because most outcomes were quantitative variables, we used Cohen's (1988) *d* coefficient to compute effect sizes (ES). When relevant data were available, we computed the ES as the difference between the pre-post difference scores in the treatment group and the control group divided by the pooled standard deviation in the pretest. If no means and standard deviations were reported, re-computation and ES-estimation techniques were used (see Lipsey and Wilson, 2001). If the reports mentioned nonsignificant results without details, we counted this as a zero effect. Although a nonsignificant result does not necessarily mean "no effect" (see Weisburd et al., 2003), the lack of statistical data did not permit a less conservative strategy.

Integration and Statistical Analysis

In several comparisons, the postintervention measures were not assessed immediately after the training but several months later. Other studies had shorter follow-up periods than these posttests. Therefore, we used a common time metric to avoid confusion. Due to the small number of studies with relatively long follow-up periods (see Table 1), we used only two categories: all ESs measured within two months after treatment (postintervention) and all ESs measured three months or more after treatment (followup). This strategy produced 183 posttest ESs (80.6%) and 46 follow-up ESs (19.4%). We computed a separate ES for each

TABLE 1.   Descriptive Characteristics of the Comparisons

Study Characteristics	Coding	Frequency	Percent
General Study Characteristics			
Publication year[a]	Up to 1980	11	20.1
	1981–1990	24	43.6
	1991–2000	20	36.4
Publication type[a]	Journal article	49	89.1
	Book, Chapter	2	3.6
	Unpublished	4	7.3
Country[a]	USA	48	87.3
	Canada	4	7.3
	Other	3	5.5
Methodological Characteristics			
Sample size	< 30	32	36.0
	30–49	31	34.8
	50–149	10	11.2
	150–500	12	13.5
	500	4	4.5
Type of outcome comparison[b]	Postintervention only	69	77.5
	Post and follow-up	13	14.6
	Follow-up only	7	7.9
Time at latest outcome measurement	Up to 1 month	50	60.7
	1–2 months	5	4.5
	3–6 months[c]	17	12.3
	12 months[c]	11	12.3
	> 12 months[c]	6	5.6
Treatment Characteristics			
Type of treatment	Behavioral	26	29.2
	Cognitive	17	19.1
	Cognitive-behavioral	26	29.2
	Counseling, psychotherapy, etc.	20	22.4

Continued

TABLE 1   Continued

Study Characteristics	Coding	Frequency	Percent
Number of sessions	Up to 10	33	37.1
	11–30	30	33.7
	31–60	17	19.1
	> 100	1	1.1
	Not specified	8	9.0
Treatment duration	Up to 1 month	12	13.5
	1–2 months	27	30.3
	2–4 months	29	32.6
	4–6 months	9	10.4
	6–12 months	11	12.4
	> 12 months	1	1.1
Format of treatment	Individual training	9	10.4
	Group training	69	77.8
	Individual + Group training	5	5.9
	Self-instruction	2	2.2
	Individual coaching	4	3.7
Setting	Preschool/Kindergarten	7	7.9
	School	64	71.9
	Clinic, Special education unit	9	10.1
	Community	6	6.7
	Other	3	3.4
Trainer	Teachers	21	23.6
	Psycho-social professionals	28	31.5
	Study authors, research staff	17	19.1
	Supervised students	12	13.5
	Others	3	3.4
	Not specified	8	9.0
Child Characteristics			
Age (years)	4–6	16	18.0
	7–9	35	39.3
	10–12	22	24.7
	13–15	14	15.7
	16–18	2	0.2
Gender (% male)	0	5	5.6
	40–59	29	32.6
	60–79	18	20.2
	80–99	12	13.5
	100	19	21.3
	Not specified	6	6.7
Type of prevention	Universal	14	15.7
	Selective	28	31.5
	Indicated	47	52.8

[a] Based on 55 research reports.

[b] Post = all effects measured within two months after treatment; follow-up = all effects measured three months or more after treatment.

[c] Due to a lack of control group data, not all of these longer-term measurements could be used for effect size computation.

of the outcomes assessing a specific construct. Then, the various effects were integrated within and also across the various outcome categories. Accordingly, there was only one ES for each category and each comparison at the different times of measurement.

When computing mean effects, we followed Hedges and Olkin's (1985) approaches for weighting sample size. At first, the fixed model was applied to integrate the single effects. Because most effect size distributions remained heterogeneous, we finally used the random (mixed) model to estimate ES (see Lipsey and Wilson, 2001). The latter model was also applied in all our moderator analyses.

RESULTS

Descriptive Characteristics

Table 1 contains descriptive characteristics of the 89 comparisons integrated in this meta-analysis. Most studies were conducted during the last two decades in the United States and were published in journals. The low rate of unpublished reports may have been due to the relatively high methodological standard for study selection (i.e., randomized trials). Nearly 70% of the comparisons had sample sizes lower than 50 and even more had no follow-up assessment. Most comparisons that assessed the stability of effects had relatively short time intervals. Although six comparisons contained an outcome measurement after more than one year, only one of these reported control group data that were adequate for ES computation.

Nearly four-fifths of the programs had a behavioral and/or cognitive orientation. Combined approaches addressing both problematic modes of thinking and concrete patterns of social behavior were most frequent. Other programs, such as counseling, psychotherapy, or intensive care, were investigated less frequently. Most programs were relatively short interventions. Over one third contained no more than ten sessions and nearly one-half of the programs lasted no longer than two months. The typical format was a group training carried out in the school setting. Approximately one-third of trainers were psychosocial professionals; the next-largest groups were teachers followed by research staff.

The mean age of the trained children varied from 4 to 18 years. More than 80% of the comparisons addressed children younger than 12. Most studies contained mixed samples of boys and girls. However, in line with the higher prevalence of antisocial behavior in males, boys were overrepresented. Programs targeting children who already exhibited some form of antisocial behavior (indicated prevention) or who had other risk factors (selective prevention) were more frequent than programs for unselected groups (universal prevention).

ESs could be calculated from a widespread assessment of antisocial behavior. Table 2 shows the distribution of the type, informant, and assessment methods for single outcome measures. At postintervention and follow-up, nearly one-half

TABLE 2.   *Distribution of Outcome Measurements of Antisocial Behavior by Type, Informant, and Method of Assessment*

Type, informant, and assessment method of outcome measures	Postintervention		Follow up	
	n (ES)	%	*n* (ES)	%
Type				
Aggressive behavior	86	47.0	23	50.0
Disruptive behavior (school)	33	18.0	2	4.3
Delinquent behavior	17	9.3	16	34.8
Oppositional behavior	13	7.1	0	0.0
Antisocial behavior (unspecified)	34	18.6	5	10.9
Informant				
Teachers	88	48.1	11	23.9
Experts	44	24.0	4	8.7
Self	18	9.8	23	50.0
Parents	14	7.7	4	8.7
Peers	11	6.0	4	8.7
Official records	9	4.9	0	0.0
Assessment method				
Questionnaires	108	59.0	36	78.3
Behavior observation	53	29.0	6	13.0
Record analysis	9	4.9	0	0.0
Interviews	8	4.4	4	8.7
Tests	5	2.7	0	0.0

Notes: ES = effect size; postintervention = all ESs measured within two months after treatment; followup = all ESs measured three months or more after treatment.

of all dependent variables related to aggressive behavior. Less than 10% of postintervention measures addressed delinquency. At follow up, nearly one-third of ESs belonged to this category. Nearly one-fifth of postintervention ESs were based on unspecified measures of antisocial behavior, such as global externalizing scores.

More than 70% of all postintervention measures contained teacher or expert ratings. A much smaller number were based on information from parents and peers or official data sources (i.e., school or police records). Self-report measures accounted for only 10% of the postintervention measures, but for one-half of the follow-up assessments. Most criteria were assessed via questionnaires (59% at postintervention, 78% at follow-up) and behavior observations (29% and 13%, respectively). All other strategies had only a low frequency.

Overall Effects

Figure 1 shows the distribution of the single ESs. According to Cohen's (1988) classification, nearly one-half of the outcomes revealed a small, medium, or large positive effect (48% at postintervention, 46% at follow-up). Approximately two-fifths (44% at postintervention and 39% at followup) of ESs were close to zero

FIGURE 1.   *Distribution of Single Effect Sizes (d)*

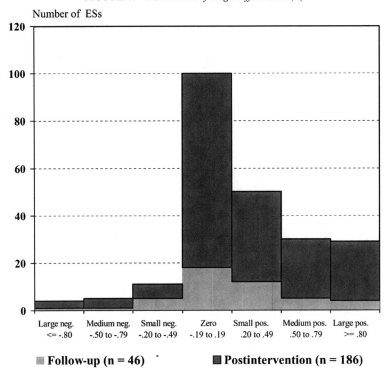

Follow-up (n = 46)　　　■ Postintervention (n = 186)

and nearly one out of ten (7% at postintervention, 15% at followup) were negative (i.e., the control group did better than the treatment group.

The mean of all unweighted postintervention ESs was $M = 0.30$ $(SD = 0.68)$ and the mean followup effect was slightly smaller at $M = 0.23$ $(SD = 0.60)$. When we computed only one effect size for each comparison and applied the random model of weighting for sample size (Lipsey & Wilson, 2001), the mean effect was $d = .29$ for postintervention outcome and $d = .21$ at follow-up (see Table 3).

Unspecific measures of antisocial behavior showed the highest postintervention effect; delinquent behavior revealed the smallest. However, delinquent behavior was the only category in which we also found a significant follow-up effect. There was a similar effect on aggressiveness, but this failed to attain significance due to heterogeneity. Overall, the small number of comparisons in most categories did not allow a reliable estimation of follow-up differences.

Comparisons between the sources of information showed mostly significant postintervention effects. However, official records and self-reports produced a nonsignificant effect. This may also be the reason for the small effects on delinquency mentioned above: Eleven of 17 single ESs in this category were assessed via self-report or official records. In the follow-up data, the source of information revealed heterogeneous results. Only the effect in teacher ratings was

TABLE 3.   Effect Sizes for Measures of Antisocial Behavior by Type, Informant, and Assessment Method

Type, informant, and assessment method of outcome measures	Postintervention		Follow-up	
	d	n	d	n
Type				
Aggressive behavior	0.24*	52	0.17	16
Oppositional/disruptive behavior	0.30*	28	1.03	2
Delinquent behavior	0.18*	11	0.19*	4
Antisocial behavior (unspecified)	0.36*	22	0.70	4
Informant				
Teachers	0.27*	59	0.41*	11
Experts	0.36*	24	0.05	1
Self	0.16	15	−0.01	7
Peers	0.24*	10	0.11	4
Parents	0.55*	8	0.66	4
Official records	0.23	8	–	–
Assessment method				
Questionnaires	0.23*	58	0.22*	15
Behavioral observation	0.48*	30	0.63	3
Other (tests, interview, file analysis)	0.23*	18	0.11	4
Total	0.29*	82	0.22*	20

Notes: ES = effect size; * ES differs significantly from zero; d = weighted mean effect size (random model); n = number of treatment-control group comparisons; postintervention = all ESs measured within two months after treatment; followup = all ESs measured three months of more after treatment.

significant. Regarding the type of assessment instrument, ESs from behavioral observations were higher than those from other instruments. The follow-up data revealed only a significant effect in questionnaires for which a relatively large number of studies was available.

Moderator Analysis

For reasons of space, we shall not present moderator analyses on all the variables listed in Table 1. We shall select only a few variables that are particularly relevant for practice and policymaking: mode of treatment, treatment dosage, age of children, type of prevention, and sample size (small- or large-scale programs). Due to the small number of studies available in some categories, we did not differentiate between the various types of antisocial behavior and used the overall outcome indicator only. Table 4 contains the respective mean ESs based on the random model of integration.

In the postintervention outcome, we found substantial and nearly significant differences between the four modes of treatment, χ^2 $(df = 3) = 7.60$, $p < .06$. Cognitive-behavioral programs were most successful. Furthermore, only this type

TABLE 4. *Relation Between Study Characteristics and Postintervention and Follow-up Effect-Size*

Moderator/Category	Postintervention		Follow-up	
	d	*n*	*d*	*n*
Type of treatment				
Behavioral	0.15	25	0.12	4
Cognitive	0.13	15	−0.06	3
Cognitive-behavioral	0.50*	26	0.50*	7
Counseling, Therapy, Other	0.38*	16	0.18	6
Treatment dosage[a]				
Low	0.22	24	0.12	3
Moderate	0.30*	49	0.17	11
Intensive	0.45*	9	0.32*	6
Age of children				
4–6	0.21	16	0.12	1
7–12	0.25*	50	0.18*	17
13 and older	0.59*	16	0.82*	2
Type of prevention				
Universal	0.08	13	−0.05	2
Selective	0.13	27	0.17	10
Indicated	0.52*	42	0.48*	8
Sample size				
<30	0.47*	32	0.15	6
30–49	0.22*	31	0.43	4
50–150	0.19	8	0.32	4
>150	0.23	11	0.10	6

[a] Coding: low = up to ten sessions or two months duration; moderate = 11 to 40 sessions or three to eight months duration; intensive = more than 40 sessions or eight months duration.

Note: d = weighted mean effect size (random model); n = number of comparisons; * effect size differs significantly from zero.

of program had significant effects in all areas of antisocial behavior (not shown in Table 4): $d = .39$ ($n = 20$ comparisons) for aggressive behavior, $d = .73$ (5) for oppositional-disruptive behavior, $d = .37$ (5) for delinquency, and $d = .54$ (17) for unspecified antisocial behavior. Counseling, care, and therapy programs also revealed a significant overall effect, as well as significant effects of $d = .53$ (8) on aggression and $d = .50$ (7) on unspecified antisocial behavior. Only cognitive-behavioral programs had a significant follow-up effect ($d = .50$, $n = 7$). Monomodal behavioral or cognitive programs had no significant effect at either postintervention or follow-up measurement.

There was no significant outcome difference between low, moderate, or intensive doses of programs ($p > .10$). However, the latter revealed the largest mean ES in postintervention and follow-up comparisons.

Looking at the age of participants, we found a tendency for programs with older children to have higher postintervention effects, χ^2 ($df = 2$) = 5.27, $p < .10$.

At follow-up, there was a similar trend ($p > .10$). The moderating effect of the children's age was probably related to the type of prevention: Twelve out of 16 postintervention comparisons with older children followed an indicated model of prevention that showed higher ESs than the other strategies, χ^2 (2) = 12.89, $p < .01$. With the exception of delinquency, this difference could be found for all types of antisocial behavior: χ^2 (2) = 10.68, $p < .01$ for aggressive behavior; χ^2 (2) = 0.89, $p < .05$ for oppositional-disruptive behavior; and χ^2 (2) = 11.73, $p < .01$ for unspecified antisocial behavior. In addition, there was a trend showing that indicated preventive treatments also resulted in a higher follow-up effect, χ^2 (2) = 4.57, $p < .10$.

No significant moderating effect could be found when we compared effects in the four categories of sample size. However, the smallest samples (up to 30) revealed a significantly stronger postintervention effect than the other three categories together, χ^2 (1) = 4.06, $p < .05$. At both postintervention and followup, comparisons with the largest samples had relatively low effects.

Although Table 4 focuses on only a few variables, it should be mentioned that most other study characteristics did not reveal stronger moderator effects. For example, the outcome differences between the various training formats, intervention settings, and types of trainer were not significant at either postintervention or followup (all $ps > .10$).

CONCLUSIONS AND POLICY IMPLICATIONS

The most important message from our meta-analysis is the overall positive and significant effect of social competence training on the antisocial behavior of children and youths. Although there are fewer randomized studies on this outcome indicator than in our previous synthesis of research (Lösel & Beelmann, 2003), results are based on a large data set of 55 research reports, 89 treatment-control group comparisons, and 9,109 youngsters of whom 50% were assigned to a program. However, the mean effects of $d = .29$ (postintervention) and $d = .21$ (follow-up) are smaller than in our previous meta-analysis (.38 and .29, respectively), which referred not only to direct measures of antisocial behavior but also to intermediate outcomes in social and social-cognitive competencies. This is plausible insofar as the latter measures are very similar to the content of child skills training. The smaller outcome in measures of concrete aggressive, delinquent, and other everyday behavior is in accordance with previous meta-analyses (e.g., Beelmann et al., 1994) and large-scale single studies of child skills training, such as Fast Track (e.g., Conduct Problems Prevention Research Group, 1999).

Regarding child skills training as an approach to crime prevention, it must also be emphasized that postintervention effects on aggressive and delinquent behavior are smaller than those on other forms or general assessments of antisocial behavior. In the follow-up, the number of ESs in the various outcome categories is too small to reveal a clear picture of differential results. However, the significant effect of $d = .19$ on delinquency is encouraging.

Although the followup intervals in studies on child skills training are much shorter than in most evaluations of offender treatment, the mean effect is in the same range (see Lösel, 1995, 2001a). It is also similar to that found in family-based programs of crime prevention (see Farrington and Welsh, 2003). A d coefficient of approximately .20 is equivalent to a correlation of $r = .10$, which indicates approximately a ten percentage point more positive outcome in treated groups than in control groups. Because many child skills programs are relatively short and delivered in group settings, such a small effect may well pay off with respect to cost-effectiveness (Welsh and Farrington, 2001). However, more long-term outcome studies are needed to demonstrate these potential benefits. This is also necessary because studies with relatively long-term followups of child skills trainings (e.g., Dishion and Andrews, 1995; Hundert et al., 1999; Kazdin et al., 1987; Lochman et al., 1983, Michelson et al., 1993) reveal a rather heterogeneous mix of large, small, zero, and negative outcomes. Some other long-term studies fail to present sufficient control group data for a comparative evaluation.

A further important message from our review is the broad range of outcomes, varying from highly positive to negative ESs. Although programs are planned and implemented in the best interest of youngsters and society, some interventions produced outcomes that are even worse than in the untreated control group. Therefore, we must take great care to ensure that we select and implement programs that are truly beneficial and do not harm the clientele (McCord, 1978, 2003). Our data suggest that some types of intervention are more successful than others. In particular, cognitive-behavioral programs consistently show not only the largest overall effect but also a significant impact on all types of antisocial behavior. These effects are relatively reliable insofar as they are based on the largest number of studies.

The positive outcome of cognitive-behavioral child skills programs is in accordance with the "what works" literature on offender treatment (e.g., Lipsey and Wilson, 1998; Lösel, 1995, 2001a; McGuire, 2002). The finding that purely behavioral or cognitive child skills programs have no significant effect points to the necessity of multi-modal prevention. Multi-modality may also be one reason why the more heterogeneous care, counseling, therapeutic, and other programs show positive effects on aggressive and generalized antisocial behavior. A further reason may be that these programs do not just contain unstructured casework but also intensive guidance that includes elements of a cognitive behavioral approach (e.g., Grossman and Tierney, 1998).

Our data further show that the source of information on the child's antisocial behavior is relevant for effect size. Parent's ratings of child behavior reveal the strongest postintervention effects. In the followup, the mean effect in this category is also relatively strong. However, it is based on only a small number of studies and thus not significant. In contrast, teacher ratings reveal a significant program effect in postintervention and follow-up measurements. The outcome data from parents and teachers may contain some reactivity effects, because both these informants normally know whether a youngster has been assigned to a program or not. However, the consistent postintervention effects in expert observations and peer ratings suggest that the more frequently used parent and teacher information does not create an artificially positive picture. Nonetheless, there is no significant effect in either self-reports or official records. In the latter category, we are even unable to find one single study investigating follow-up effects. The relatively rare use of both self-reports and official records may be due to the focus on developmental prevention and thus the younger age of the samples. On the other hand, we must emphasize the particular lack of significant and more long-term effects in those data sources that are most frequently used in research and policymaking on juvenile delinquency (see Loeber et al., 1998). More child skills program evaluations on these outcomes are needed to guide policymaking on the prevention of criminality.

Another finding from our research synthesis is also relevant for policymaking: Whereas common sense would lead us to expect the strongest program effects in young children (e.g., before behavioral problems can consolidate), we have found the highest ESs in studies on youth samples (13 years and older). In addition, programs addressing youngsters who have already developed some behavioral problems (indicated prevention) have the largest effect, whereas programs for general cohorts or unselected groups (universal prevention) have the lowest effect and are even nonsignificant. At first glance, this result seems to be counterintuitive. However, it cannot be interpreted as an artifact of regression to the mean, because we have analyzed only randomized studies (with equivalent treatment and control groups). Another explanation is more plausible: Although there may be positive learning processes in a large proportion of low-risk children in unselected groups, most of these youngsters will not develop serious behavioral problems even without the programs. As a consequence, there are no significant mean differences in outcome behavior compared with untreated control groups. In high-risk groups, however, the programs do have an impact that can be demonstrated in evaluations of indicated prevention. Again, these findings on prevention are in line with research on delinquency treatment in which high-risk samples showed larger effects (Lipsey and Wilson, 1998). As a consequence for policymaking, one can suggest a program focus on groups that are already on the track to antisocial behavior.

Although universal programs are easier to implement and avoid problems of stigmatization (e.g., LeBlanc, 1998; Lösel, 2002), risk-focused programs may also be more adequate to ensure sufficient treatment intensity. In addition, risk-focused programs may have lower costs and thus be more viable from an economic perspective. However, the finding of larger effects in indicated prevention should not be overgeneralized to extremely risky youngsters such as "fledgling psychopaths" (Lynam, 1996). We suggest a more differentiated interpretation based on an inverted U-shaped relationship between risk level and ES in program evaluations (Lösel, 2001b).

In addition to the moderator effects of child and program characteristics, we have also found that sample size may have an impact on outcome. Although this tendency was less clear than in our previous analysis, small samples revealed the strongest postintervention effects. One reason for this may be a publication bias:

Larger samples are more likely to reveal the significance of a true low effect (Weisburd et al., 2003). Due to author or editor decisions, this significant result may be published more frequently than the same, but nonsignificant, effect in a smaller sample. In contrast, studies with small samples may only be published when they have relatively large effects. Although such a publication bias cannot be ruled out completely, our previous analysis did not suggest that this is the main reason for a moderating effect of sample size (Lösel and Beelmann, 2003). Issues of program implementation also have to be taken into account. For example, in large studies, difficulties in maintaining program integrity and homogeneity of samples may reduce design sensitivity and thus lead to smaller effects (Lösel and Wittmann, 1989; Weisburd et al., 1993). In accordance with this interpretation, Farrington and Welsh (2003) found an inverse correlation between sample size and the effects of family-based crime prevention programs, and Lipsey and Wilson (1998) reported a similar relation in studies on young offender treatment. We need to have more follow-up data and more process evaluations on the implementation and integrity of child skills programs before we can draw sound conclusions from our data on sample size. However, as a preliminary recommendation, we would suggest that child skills training should not focus too strongly on large-scale implementations of low-dosage, universal prevention programs.

Due to the small number of studies in many subcategories, our more differentiated analyses address only single moderators that may be partially confounded with each other. Although such confounded variables cause problems for meta-analysis (e.g., Lipsey, 2003), they characterize concrete prevention programs in practice. Nevertheless, our conclusions for policymaking must be regarded with caution. However, our review does not just contain analyses of general and differential program effects, but also reveals deficits and blind spots in research. As Tables 1 and 2 show, more well controlled studies with longer follow-up periods and official records of delinquent behavior are needed. It also becomes clear that few randomized studies have been performed outside the United States. This is not just because we have restricted our meta-analysis to English- and German-language reports. Other English-speaking countries also reveal few randomized studies and the situation is even worse in German-speaking countries and other parts of the world. Facing this deficit, we must bear in mind that programs and findings from the United States cannot simply be transferred to other cultural contexts without local evaluation. We are currently preparing an additional analysis of nonrandomized but high-quality evaluations of child skills training as a measure of crime prevention. Perhaps, this will help to reduce the various blind spots and too rarely investigated areas disclosed in this chapter.

Overall, our systematic review reveals that there are a substantial number of randomized experiments addressing the efficacy of social skills training in preventing aggressive, delinquent, and other antisocial behavior in children and youths. These studies demonstrate a positive but small overall effect. This finding is based primarily on small samples and postintervention measures or short follow-up periods after the interventions. Carefully implemented and well-dosed multimodal cognitive-behavioral programs targeting high-risk youngsters who already exhibit some behavioral problems seem to be particularly effective. Accordingly, child skills training can be recommended as a promising approach to crime prevention, particularly when it is adequately differentiated. However, more international research is needed based on well-controlled experiments using substantial samples, hard outcome criteria, and long follow-up periods.

REFERENCES

Akhtar, Nameera, and E. Jane Bradley. 1991. Social information processing deficits of aggressive children: Present findings and implications for social skills training. *Clinical Psychology Review* 11: 621–644.

Ang, Rebecca P., and Jan N. Hughes. 2001. Differential benefits of skills training with antisocial youth based on group composition: A meta-analytic investigation. *School Psychology Review* 31: 164–185.

Beelmann, Andreas. 2000. *Prävention dissozialer Entwicklungen: Psychologische Grundlagen und Evaluation früher kind- und familienbezogener Interventionsmaßnahmen. [Prevention of antisocial developments: Psychological foundations and evaluation of early child- and family-oriented interventions].* Unpublished postdoctoral habilitation thesis, University of Erlangen-Nuremberg, Germany.

——, Ulrich Pfingsten, and Friedrich Lösel. 1994. The effects of training social competence in children: A meta-analysis of recent evaluation studies. *Journal of Clinical Child Psychology* 23: 260–271.

Bierman, Karen L., Mark T. Greenberg, and Conduct Problems Prevention Research Group. 1996. Social skills training in the Fast Track Program. In *Preventing childhood disorders, substance abuse, and delinquency* edited by Ray DeV. Peters and Robert J. McMahon. Thousand Oaks, CA: Sage.

Brestan, Elizabeth V., and Sheila M. Eyberg. 1998. Effective psychosocial treatments of conduct-disordered children and adolescents: 29 years, 82 studies, and 5,272 kids. *Journal of Clinical Child Psychology* 27: 180–189.

Bullis, Michael, Hill M. Walker, and Jeffrey R. Sprague. 2001. A promise unfulfilled: Social skills training with at-risk and antisocial children and youth. *Exceptionality* 9: 67–90.

Cohen, Jacob. 1988. *Statistical power analysis for the behavioral sciences.* New York: Academic Press.

Conduct Problems Prevention Research Group. 1999. Initial impact of the Fast Track Prevention Trial for conduct problems: II. Classroom effects. *Journal of Consulting and Clinical Psychology* 67: 648–657.

——. 2002. Evaluation of the first 3 years of the Fast Track Prevention Trial with children at high risk for adolescent conduct problems. *Journal of Abnormal Child Psychology* 19: 553–567.

Crick, Nicki R., and Kenneth A. Dodge. 1994. A review and reformulation of social information-processing mechanisms in children's social adjustment. *Psychological Bulletin* 115: 74–101.

Denham, Susanne A., and M. Connie Almeida. 1987. Children's social problem solving skills, behavioral adjustment, and interventions: A meta-analysis evaluating theory and practice. *Journal of Applied Developmental Psychology* 8: 391–409.

Dishion, Thomas J., and David W. Andrews. 1995. Preventing escalation in problem behaviors with high-risk young adolescents: Immediate and 1-year outcomes. *Journal of Consulting and Clinical Psychology* 63: 538–548.

Durlak, Joseph A., and Anne M. Wells. 1997. Primary prevention mental health programs for children and adolescents: A meta-analytic review. *American Journal of Community Psychology* 25: 115–152.

Erwin, Philip G. 1994. Effectiveness of social skills training with children: A meta-analytic study. *Counseling Psychology Quarterly* 7: 305–310.

Farrington, David P., and Jeremy W. Coid. eds., 2003. *Early prevention of adult antisocial behaviour.* Cambridge, UK: Cambridge University Press.

Farrington, David P., and Anthony Petrosino. 2001. The Campbell Collaboration Crime and Justice Group. *Annals of the American Academy of Political and Social Science* 578: 35–49.

Farrington, David P., and Brandon C. Welsh. 2003. Family-based prevention of offending: A meta-analysis. *Australian and New Zealand Journal of Criminology* 36: 127–151.

Frick, Paul J. 1998. *Conduct disorders and severe antisocial behavior.* New York: Plenum.

Gottfredson, Denise C. 2001. *Schools and delinquency.* Cambridge, UK: Cambridge University Press.

Greenberg, Mark T. 2001. The prevention of mental disorders in school-aged children: Current state of the field. *Prevention & Treatment* 4: 1–57.

Gresham, Frank M. 1998. Social skills training: Should we raze, remodel, or rebuild? *Behavioral Disorders* 24: 19–25.

Grossman, Jean B., and Joseph P. Tierney. 1998. Does mentoring work? An impact study of the big brothers/big sisters program. *Evaluation Review* 22: 403–426.

Hedges, Larry V., and Ingram Olkin. 1985. *Statistical methods for meta-analysis.* New York: Academic Press.

Hundert, Joel, Michael H. Boyle, Charles E. Cunningham, E. Duku, JoAnn Heale, Jan McDonald, David R. Offord, and Yvonne Racine. 1999. Helping children adjust – A tri-ministry study: II. Program effects. *Journal of Child Psychology and Psychiatry* 40: 1061–1073.

Kazdin, Alan E. 1996. Problem solving and parent management in treating aggressive and antisocial behavior. In *Psychosocial treatments for child and adolescent disorders* edited by Euthymia D. Hibbs and Peter S. Jensen. Washington, DC: American Psychological Association.

——, Karen Esveldt-Dawson, Nancy H. French, and Alan S. Unis. 1987. Problem-solving skills training & relationship therapy in the treatment of antisocial child behavior. *Journal of Consulting and Clinical Psychology* 55: 76–85.

Kazdin, Alan E., and Gloria Wassell. 1999. Barriers to treatment participation and therapeutic change among children referred for conduct disorder. *Journal of Clinical Child Psychology* 28: 160–172.

Lahey, Benjamin B., Terri L. Miller, Rachel A. Gordon, and Anne W. Riley. 1999. Developmental epidemiology of the disruptive behavior disorders. In *Handbook of disruptive behavior disorders* edited by Herbert C. Quay and Anne E. Hogan. New York: Kluwer Academic/Plenum.

LeBlanc, Mark. 1998. Screening of serious and violent juvenile offenders: Identification, classification, and prediction. In *Serious and violent juvenile offenders* edited by Rolf Loeber and David P. Farrington. Thousand Oaks, CA: Sage.

Lipsey, Mark W. 2003. Those confounded moderators in meta-analysis: Good, bad, and ugly. *Annals of the American Academy of Political and Social Science* 587: 69–81.

——, and David B. Wilson. 1998. Effective intervention for serious juvenile offenders: A synthesis of research. In *Serious and violent juvenile offenders* edited by Rolf Loeber and David P. Farrington. Thousand Oaks, CA: Sage.

——. 2001. *Practical meta-analysis.* Thousand Oaks, CA: Sage.

Lochmann, John E., John D. Coie, Marion K. Underwood, and Robert Terry. 1993. Effectiveness of a social relations intervention program for aggressive and nonaggressive rejected children. *Journal of Consulting and Clinical Psychology* 61: 1053–1058.

Loeber, Rolf, and David P. Farrington, eds., 1998. *Serious and violent juvenile offenders: Risk factors and successful interventions.* Thousand Oaks, CA: Sage.

—— eds., 2001. *Child delinquents: Development, interventions, and service needs.* Thousand Oaks, CA: Sage.

——, and Daniel A. Waschbusch. 1998. Serious and violent juvenile offenders. In *Serious and violent juvenile offenders* edited by Rolf Loeber and David P. Farrington. Thousand Oaks, CA: Sage.

Lösel, Friedrich. 1995. The efficacy of correctional treatment: A review and synthesis of meta-evaluations. In *What works: Reducing reoffending* edited by James McGuire. Chichester, UK: Wiley.

——. 2001a. Rehabilitation of the offender. In *International encyclopedia of the social and behavioral sciences* edited by Neil J. Smelser and Paul B. Baltes. Oxford, UK: Pergamon.

——. 2001b. Evaluating the effectiveness of correctional programs: Bridging the gap between research and practice. In *Offender rehabilitation in practice* edited by Gary A. Bernfeld, David P. Farrington, and Alan W. Leschied. Chichester, UK: Wiley.

——. 2002. Risk/need assessment and prevention of antisocial development in young people: Basic issues from a perspective of cautionary optimism. In *Multiproblem violent youth* edited Raymond R. Corrado, Ronald Roesch, Stephen D. Hart, and Jozef K. Gierowski. Amsterdam, Netherlands: IOS Press/ NATO Series.

——, and Andreas Beelmann. 2003. Effects of child skills training in preventing antisocial behavior: A systematic review of randomized evaluations. *Annals of the American Academy of Political and Social Science* 587: 84–109.

——, and Doris Bender. 2003. Resilience and protective factors. In *Early prevention of adult antisocial behaviour* edited by David P. Farrington and Jeremy W. Coid. Cambridge, UK: Cambridge University Press.

——, and Thomas Bliesener. 2003. *Aggression und Gewalt unter Jugendlichen: Untersuchungen von sozialen und kognitiven Bedingungen [Aggression and delinquency in adolescents: Studies on cognitive and social origins]*. Neuwied, Germany: Luchterhand.

——, and Werner W. Wittmann. 1989. The relationship of treatment integrity and intensity to outcome criteria. *New Directions for Program Evaluation* 42: 97–108.

Lynam, Donald R. 1996. Early identification of chronic offenders: Who is the fledgling psychopath? *Psychological Bulletin* 120: 209–234.

Magee Quinn, Mary, Kenneth A. Kavale, Sarup R. Mathur, Robert B. Rutherford, and Steven R. Forness. 1999. A meta-analysis of social skills interventions for students with emotional and behavioral disorders. *Journal of Emotional and Behavioral Disorders* 7: 54–64.

McCord, Joan. 1978. A thirty-year follow-up of treatment effects. *American Psychologist* 33: 284–289.

——. 2003. Cures that harm: Unanticipated outcomes of crime prevention programs. *Annals of the American Academy of Political and Social Science* 587: 16–30.

——, and Richard E. Tremblay, eds. 1992. *Preventing antisocial behavior*. New York: Guilford.

McGuire, James. 2002. Integrating findings from research reviews. In *Offender rehabilitation and treatment*, edited by James McGuire. Chichester, UK: Wiley.

Michelson, L., A.P. Mannarino, K.E. Marchione, M. Stern, J. Figueroa, and S. Beck. 1983. A comparative outcome study of behavioral social-skills training, interpersonal problem-solving and nondirective control treatments with child psychiatric outpatients. *BehaviorResearch and Therapy* 21: 545–556.

Moffitt, Terri E. 1993. Adolescence-limited and life-course-persistent antisocial behavior: A developmental taxonomy. *Psychological Review* 100: 674–701.

——, Avshalom Caspi, Nigel Dickson, Phil A. Silva, and Warren Stanton. 1996. Childhood-onset versus adolescent-onset antisocial conduct problems in males: Natural history from ages 3 to 18 years. *Development and Psychopathology* 8: 399–424.

Offord, David R., Helena C. Kraemer, Alan E. Kazdin, Peter S. Jensen, and Richard Harrington. 1998. Lowering the burden of suffering from child psychiatric disorder. Trade-offs among clinical, targeted, and universal interventions. *Journal of the American Academy of Child and Adolescent Psychiatry* 37: 686–694.

Patterson, Gerald R., Marion S. Forgatch, Karen L. Yoerger, and Mike Stoolmiller. 1998. Variables that initiate and maintain an early-onset trajectory for juvenile offending. *Development and Psychopathology* 10: 531–547.

Peters, Ray DeV., and Robert J. McMahon. 1996. *Preventing childhood disorders, substance abuse, and delinquency*. Thousand Oaks, CA: Sage.

Prinz, Ronald J., and Gloria E. Miller. 1994. Family-based treatment for childhood antisocial behavior: Experimental influences on dropout and engagement. *Journal of Consulting and Clinical Psychology* 62: 645–650.

Robins, Lee N., and Rumi K. Price. 1991. Adult disorders predicted by childhood conduct problems: Results from the NIMH epidemiologic catchment area project. *Psychiatry* 54: 116–132.

Schneider, Barry H. 1992. Didactic methods for enhancing children's peer relations: A quantitative review. *Clinical Psychology Review* 12: 363–382.

Sherman, Lawrence W., Denise Gottfredson, Doris MacKenzie, John Eck, Peter Reuter, and Shawn

Bushway. 1997. *Preventing crime: What works, what doesn't, what's promising.* Report to the United States Congress: University of Maryland.

Shure, Myrna B. 1992. *I can problem solve. An interpersonal cognitive problem-solving program.* Champaign, IL: Research Press.

Thornberry, Terence P. 1998. Membership in youth gangs and involvement in serious and violent offending. In *Serious and violent juvenile offenders* edited by Rolf Loeber and David P. Farrington. Thousand Oaks, CA: Sage.

Tremblay, Richard E., and Wendy W. Craig. 1995. Developmental crime prevention. In *Building a safer society: Strategic approaches to crime prevention. Crime and Justice: An Annual Review of Research, Vol. 19,* edited by Michael Tonry and David P. Farrington. Chicago, IL: University of Chicago Press.

Tremblay, Richard E., David LeMarquand, and Frank Vitaro. 1999. The prevention of oppositional defiant disorder and conduct disorder. In *Handbook of disruptive behavior disorders,* edited by Herbert C. Quay and Anne E. Hogan. New York: Kluwer Academic/Plenum.

Wasserman, Gail A., and Laurie S. Miller. 1998. The prevention of serious and violent juvenile offending. In *Serious and violent juvenile offenders,* edited by Rolf Loeber and David P. Farrington. Thousand Oaks, CA: Sage.

Weisburd, David, Cynthia Lum, and Sue-Ming Yang. 2003. When can we conclude that treatments or programs "don't work"? *Annals of the American Academy of Political and Social Science* 587: 31–48.

Weisburd, David, Anthony Petrosino, and Gail Mason. 1993. Design sensitivity in criminal justice experiments. *Crime and Justice* 17: 337–380.

Welsh, Brandon C., and David P. Farrington. 2001. A review of research on the monetary value of preventing crime. In *Costs and benefits of preventing crime,* edited by Brandon C. Welsh, David P. Farrington, and Lawrence W. Sherman. Oxford, UK: Westview Press.

Wilson, David B., Denise C. Gottfredson, and Stacy S. Najaka. 2001. School-based prevention of problem behaviors: A meta-analysis. *Journal of Quantitative Criminology* 17: 247–272.

APPENDIX 1

Primary Studies Included in Meta-Analysis

Barkley, R. A., Shelton, T. L., Crosswait, C., Moorehouse, M., Fletcher, K., Barrett, S., Jenkins, L., & Metevia, L. (2000). Multi-method psycho-educational intervention for preschool children with disruptive behavior: Preliminary results at post-treatment. *Journal of Child Psychology and Psychiatry, 41,* 319–332.

Beelmann, A. (2000). *Prävention dissozialer Entwicklungen: Psychologische Grundlagen und Evaluation früher kind- und familienbezogener Interventionsmaßnahmen. [Prevention of antisocial development: Psychological foundations and evaluation of early child- and family-oriented interventions].* Unpublished postdoctoral habilitation thesis, University of Erlangen-Nuremberg, Germany.

Block, J. (1978). Effects of a rational emotive mental health program on poorly achieving disruptive high school students. *Journal of Counseling Psychology, 25,* 61–65.

Bosworth, K., Espelage, D., DuBay, T., Daytner, G., & Karageorge, K. (2000). Preliminary evaluation of a multimedia violence prevention program for adolescents. *American Journal of Health Behavior, 24,* 268–280.

Camp, B., Blom, C., Herbert, F., & VanDoornick, W. (1977). "Think aloud": A program for developing self-control in young aggressive boys. *Journal of Abnormal Child Psychology, 5,* 157–168.

Coats, K. I. (1979). Cognitive self-instructional training approach for reducing disruptive behavior of young children. *Psychological Reports, 44,* 127–134.

Coie, J., & Krehbiel, G. (1984). Effects of academic tutoring on the social status of low-achieving, socially rejected children. *Child Development, 55,* 1465–1478.

Conduct Problems Prevention Research Group (1999). Initial impact of the fast track prevention trial for conduct problems: II. Classroom effects. *Journal of Consulting and Clinical Psychology, 67*, 648–657.

Dicken, C., Bryson, R., & Kass, N. (1977). Companionship therapy: A replication in experimental community psychology. *Journal of Consulting and Clinical Psychology, 45*, 637–646.

Dishion, T. J., & Andrews, D. W. (1995). Preventing escalation in problem behaviors with high-risk young adolescents: Immediate and 1-year outcomes. *Journal of Consulting and Clinical Psychology, 63*, 538–548.

Dolan, L. J., Kellam, S. G., Werthamer-Larson, L., Rebok, G. W., Mayer, L. S., Laudolff, J., Turkkan, J. S., Ford, C., & Wheeler, L. (1993). The short-term impact of two classroom-based preventive interventions on aggressive and shy behaviors and poor achievement. *Journal of Applied Developmental Psychology, 14*, 317–245.

Downing, C. J. (1977). Teaching children behavior change techniques. *Elementary School Guidance and Counseling, 12*, 227–283.

Durlak, J. A. (1980). Comparative effectiveness of behavioral and relationship group treatment in the secondary prevention of school maladjustment. *American Journal of Community Psychology, 8*, 327–339.

Edelson, J. L., & Rose, S. D. (1981). Investigations into the efficacy of short-term group social skills training for socially isolated children. *Child Behavior Therapy, 3*, 1–16.

Etscheid, S. (1991). Reducing aggressive behavior and improving self-control: A cognitive-behavioral training program for behaviorally disordered adolescents. *Behavioral Disorders, 16*, 107–115.

Factor, D. C., & Schilmoeller, G. L. (1983). Social skills training of preschool children. *Child Study Journal, 13*, 41–56.

Feindler, E. L., Marriott, S. A., & Iwata, M. (1984). Group anger control training for junior high school delinquents. *Cognitive Therapy and Research, 8*, 299–311.

Feis, C. L., & Simons, C. (1985). Training preschool children in interpersonal cognitive problem-solving skills: A replication. *Prevention in Human Services, 3*, 59–70.

Forman, S. (1980). A comparison of cognitive training and response cost procedures in modifying aggressive behavior of elementary school children. *Behavior Therapy, 11*, 594–600.

Fuchs, D., Fuchs, L., & Bahr, M. (1990). Mainstream assistance teams: A scientific basis for the art of consultation. *Exceptional Children, 57*, 128–139.

Garaigordobil, M., & Echebarria, A. (1995). Assessment of a peer-helping game programme on children's development. *Journal of Research in Childhood Education, 10*, 63–69.

Garrison, S. R., & Stolberg, A. L. (1983). Modification of anger in children by affective imagery training. *Journal of Abnormal Child Psychology, 11*, 115–130.

Grant, A. T. (1995). *The effect of social skills training on the self-concept, academic achievement, and discipline of fifth-grade students.* Unpublished doctoral dissertation, University of South Carolina.

Grossman, D. C., Neckerman, H. J., Koepsell, T. D., Liu, P. Y., Asher, K. N., Beland, K., Frey, K., & Rivara, F. P. (1997). Effectiveness of a violence prevention curriculum among children in elementary school. A randomized controlled trial. *Journal of the American Medical Association, 277*, 1605–1611.

Hawkins, J. D., Doueck, H. J., & Lishner, D. M. (1988). Changing teaching practices in mainstream classrooms to improve bonding and behavior of low achievers. *American Educational Research Journal, 25*, 31–50.

Hudley, C., & Graham, S. (1993). An attributional intervention to reduce peer-directed aggression among African-American boys. *Child Development, 64*, 124–138.

Huesmann, L. R., Eron, L. D., Klein, R., Brio, D., & Fisher, P. (1983). Mitigating the imitation of aggressive behaviors by changing children's attitudes about media violence. *Journal of Personality and Social Psychology, 44*, 899–910.

Huey, W. C. & Rank, R. C. (1984). Effects of counselor and peer-led group assertiveness training on black adolescent aggression. *Journal of Counseling Psychology, 31*, 95–98.

Hundert, J., Boyle, M. H., Cunningham, C. E., Duku, E., Heale, J., McDonald, J., Offord, D. R., & Racine, Y. (1999). Helping children adjust – a tri-ministry study: II. Program Effects. *Journal of Child Psychology and Psychiatry, 40*, 1061–1073.

Ialongo, N., Werthamer, L., Kellan, S. G., Brown, C., Wang, S., & Lin, Y. (1999). Proximal impact of two first-grade preventive interventions on the early risk behaviors for later substance abuse, depression, and antisocial behavior. *American Journal of Community Psychology, 27*, 599–641.

Kagey, J. R. (1971). *The adjustment of fourth grade children: A primary prevention approach in behavioral education.* Unpublished doctoral dissertation, Louisiana State University.

Kazdin, A. E., Esveldt-Dawson, K., French, K., & Unis, A. (1987). Problem-solving skills training and relationship therapy in the treatment of antisocial child behavior. *Journal of Consulting and Clinical Psychology, 55*, 76–85.

Kettlewell, P. W., & Kausch, D. F. (1983). The generalization of the effects of a cognitive behavioral treatment program for aggressive children. *Journal of Abnormal Child Psychology, 11*, 101–114.

Larson, J. D. (1992). Anger and aggression management techniques through the Think First curriculum. *Journal of Offender Rehabilitation, 18*, 101–117.

Lee, D. Y., Hallberg, E. T., & Hassard, H. (1979). Effects of assertion training on aggressive behavior of adolescents. *Journal of Counseling Psychology, 26*, 459–461.

Lochmann, J. E., Coie, J. D., Underwood, M. K., & Terry, R. (1993). Effectiveness of a social relations intervention program for aggressive and nonaggressive, rejected children. *Journal of Consulting and Clinical Psychology, 61*, 1053–1058.

Mannarino, A. P., Christy, M., Durlak, J. A., & Magnussen, M. G. (1982). Evaluation of social competence training in the school. *Journal of School Psychology, 20*, 11–19.

Michelson, L., Mannarino, A. P., Marchione, K. E., Stern, M., Figueroa, J., & Beck, S. (1983). A comparative outcome study of behavioral social-skills training, interpersonal problem-solving and non-directive control treatments with child psychiatric outpatients. *Behavior Research and Therapy, 21*, 545–556.

Mize, J., & Ladd, G. W. (1990). A cognitive-social learning approach to social skills training with low-status preschool children. *Developmental Psychology, 26*, 388–397.

Moore, K. J., & Shannon, K. K. (1993). The development of superstitious beliefs in the effectiveness of treatment of anger: Evidence for the importance of experimental program evaluation in applied settings. *Behavioral Residential Treatment, 8*, 147–161.

Newman, M. R. (1989). *Social skills training of emotional/behavioral disordered students: A comparison of coaching and adapted coaching techniques.* Unpublished doctoral dissertation, University of Minnesota.

Oldfield, D. (1986). The effects of the relaxation response on self-concept and acting out behaviors. *Elementary School Guidance and Counseling, 20*, 255–261.

Olexa, D. F., & Forman, S. G. (1984). Effects of social problem-solving training on classroom behavior of urban disadvantaged students. *Journal of School Psychology, 22*, 165–175.

Omizo, M. M., Hershberger, J. M., & Omizo, S. A. (1988). Teaching children to cope with anger. *Elementary School Guidance & Counseling, 22*, 241–245.

Porter, B. A., & Hoedt, K. C. (1985). Differential effects of an Adlerian counseling approach with preadolescent children. *Individual Psychology Journal of Adlerian Theory Research and Practice, 41*, 372–385.

Prinz, R. J., Blechman, E. A., & Dumas, J. E. (1994). An evaluation of peer coping-skills training for childhood aggression. *Journal of Clinical Child Psychology, 23*, 193–203.

Reckless, W. C., & Dinitz, S. (1972). *The prevention of juvenile delinquency: An experiment.* Columbus, OH: Ohio State University Press.

Rickel, A. U., Smith, R. L., & Sharp, K. C. (1979). Description and evaluation of a preventive mental health program for preschoolers. *Journal of Abnormal Child Psychology, 7*, 101–112.

Schneider, B. H., & Byrne, B. M. (1987). Individualized social skills training for behavior-disordered children. *Journal of Consulting and Clinical Psychology, 55*, 444–445.

Sharp, K. C. (1981). Impact of interpersonal problem-solving training on preschoolers' social competency. *Journal of Applied Developmental Psychology, 2*, 129–143.

Shechtman, Z., & Ben-David, M. (1999). Individual and group psychotherapy of childhood aggression: A comparison of outcomes and processes. *Group Dynamics, 3*, 263–274.

Tanner, V. L., & Holliman, W. B. (1988). Effectiveness of assertiveness training in modifying aggressive behaviors of young children. *Psychological Reports, 62*, 39–46.

Tierney, J. P., Grossman, J. B., & Resch, N. L. (1995). *Making a difference: An impact study of Big Brothers/Big Sisters*. Philadelphia, PA: Public/ Private Ventures.

Vaughn, S. R., & Ridley, C. A. (1983). A preschool interpersonal program: Does it affect behavior in the classroom? *Child Study Journal, 13*, 1–11.

Webster-Stratton, C., & Hammond, M. (1997). Treating children with early-onset conduct problems: A comparison of child and parent training interventions. *Journal of Consulting and Clinical Psychology, 65*, 93–109.

PART II: WHAT WORKS FOR OFFENDERS

CHAPTER 4

COGNITIVE-BEHAVIORAL INTERVENTIONS*

Mark W. Lipsey and Nana A. Landenberger

Vanderbilt University

INTRODUCTION

Cognitive-behavioral therapy (CBT) is among the more promising rehabilitative treatments for criminal offenders. Reviews of the comparative effectiveness of different treatment approaches have generally ranked it in the top tier with regard to effects on recidivism (e.g., Andrews et al., 1990; Lipsey and Wilson, 1998). It has a well-developed theoretical basis and explicitly targets "criminal thinking" as a contributing factor to deviant behavior (Beck, 1999; Walters, 1990; Yochelson and Samenow, 1976). And, it can be adapted to a range of juvenile and adult offenders, delivered in institutional or community settings by mental health specialists or paraprofessionals, and administered as part of a multifaceted program or as a stand-alone intervention.

BACKGROUND

In the 1960s and 70s, researchers and clinicians such as Aaron Beck and Albert Ellis outlined the role of dysfunctional thinking and irrational beliefs in psychological disorders. During that same era, Yochelson and Samenow (1976) – and later Walters (1990) – described various cognitive distortions related to dominance and entitlement, self-justification, displacing blame, and unduly optimistic perceptions of reality they believed were contributing factors to criminal behavior. Offenders with such distorted thinking may misperceive benign situations as threats (e.g., be predisposed to perceive harmless remarks as disrespectful or deliberately provocative), demand instant gratification, and confuse wants with needs ("if I want it, I must have it – now").

Criminal thinking is often tied to a profound "victim stance," with offenders viewing themselves as unfairly blamed, if not hated, and cast out from society ("everyone is against me" or "society doesn't give me a chance") while consistently failing to see how their antisocial behavior may have contributed to their problems. These thinking patterns may also be supported by offenders' entrenchment

---

* The research reported in this chapter was funded, in part, by the National Institute of Mental Health (MH39958, MH64485), the Office of Juvenile Justice and Delinquency Prevention (2001-JN-FX-0008), and the Smith Richardson Foundation.

Brandon C. Welsh and David P. Farrington, eds.
Preventing Crime: What Works for Children, Offenders, Victims, and Places, 57–71
© 2007 *Springer.*

in an antisocial subculture (e.g., street or prison codes) where otherwise dysfunctional assumptions about how one should behave (e.g., "you have to punish people for messing with you or they won't respect you") may in fact be adaptive.

Cognitive-behavior therapy is based on the assumption that cognitive deficits and distortions are learned rather than inherent. Programs for offenders, therefore, emphasize individual accountability and attempt to teach offenders to understand the thinking processes and choices that immediately preceded their criminal behavior. Learning to self-monitor thinking is typically the first step, after which the therapeutic techniques seek to help offenders identify and correct biased, risky, or deficient thinking patterns. A crucial aspect of CBT is an emphasis on free choice. Offenders are not told what to think in a specific situation (i.e., there is no assumption of a superior set of values) but, instead, are taught how to consider all aspects of a situation, test whether one's beliefs are accurate and functional, and make choices based on those considerations.

All cognitive-behavioral interventions, therefore, employ a set of structured techniques aimed at building cognitive skills in areas where offenders show deficits and restructuring cognition in areas where offenders' thinking is biased or distorted. These techniques typically involve cognitive skills training, anger management, and various supplementary components related to social skills, moral development, and relapse prevention.

Cognitive skills training aims to teach such thinking skills as interpersonal problem-solving (with information gathering, developing alternative solutions, and evaluating outcomes as crucial steps), abstract thinking, critical reasoning, causal thinking, goal setting, long-term planning, and perspective taking. Often role-play or practice in real situations is used to help consolidate new ways of coping with situations that tend to prompt maladaptive habits and aggressive or criminal behavior.

Anger management training typically focuses on teaching offenders to monitor their patterns of automatic thoughts to situations in which they tend to react with anger or violence. Various strategies are then rehearsed for assessing the validity of those "hot" or "trigger" thoughts. Learning to substitute accurate interpretations for biased ones and to consider non-hostile explanations of others' behavior are the key parts of most anger management programs.

CBT programs differ in their emphasis. For example, programs for batterers are typically geared toward anger control and building relationship skills. For sex offenders, they may center on assuming personal responsibility for crimes (e.g., challenging offenders' tendency to justify their behavior by blaming the victim), and on developing victim empathy (e.g., by correcting their minimization of the harm they caused). Along with these primary emphases, CBT programs often add selected supplementary components such as social skills training, moral reasoning exercises, or relapse prevention planning. Relapse prevention is increasingly popular and is aimed at developing cognitive risk-management strategies along with a set of behavioral contracts for avoiding or deescalating the precursors to offending behavior (e.g., high-risk situations, places, associates, or maladaptive coping responses).

Representative CBT Programs

Prototypical examples of CBT programs for offenders include the following:

- The Reasoning and Rehabilitation program (Ross and Fabiano, 1985) is organized around exercises (e.g., Critical Thinking, Social Perspective-Taking) that focus on "modifying the impulsive, egocentric, illogical and rigid thinking of the offenders and teaching them to stop and think before acting, to consider the consequences of their behavior, to conceptualize alternative ways of responding to interpersonal problems and to consider the impact of their behavior on other people, particularly their victims" (Ross et al., 1988:31).
- Moral Reconation Therapy (Little and Robinson, 1986) is based on Kohlberg's stages of moral development and uses a series of group and workbook exercises designed to raise the moral reasoning level of offenders stepwise through 16 graded moral and cognitive stages.
- Aggression Replacement Training (Goldstein and Glick, 1987; 1994) is comprised of three components- Skillstreaming, Anger Control Training, and Moral Education. Skillstreaming teaches prosocial behaviors through modeling and role-playing. Anger Control Training instructs offenders in self-control by having them record anger-arousing experiences, identify "trigger" thoughts, and apply anger control techniques. Moral Education exposes offenders to moral dilemmas in a discussion format aimed at advancing the level of moral reasoning.
- Thinking for a Change (Bush et al., 1997) consists of 22 sessions of group exercises and homework organized around: (a) understanding that thinking controls behavior; (b) understanding and responding to feelings of self and others; and (c) problem-solving skills.
- Cognitive Interventions Program (National Institute of Corrections, 1996) is a 15 lesson cognitive restructuring curriculum that guides offenders to see their behaviors as the direct result of choices they make. The program leads participants to recognize how distortions and errors in thinking (e.g., victim stance, super-optimism, failure to consider injury to others) and antisocial attitudes influence these choices. Alternative thinking styles are introduced and practiced to create more options from which to choose.
- Relapse prevention approaches to substance abuse (Marlatt and Gordon, 1985) have been adapted for treating aggression and violence (e.g., Cullen and Freeman-Longo, 2001). These programs incorporate cognitive skills and cognitive restructuring elements into a curriculum that builds behavioral strategies to cope with high-risk situations and halt the relapse cycle before lapses turn into full relapses.

Prior Meta-Analytic Reviews

One recent meta-analysis of group-oriented cognitive behavioral programs for offenders examined 20 studies of varying levels of methodological quality and concluded that CBT was effective for reducing criminal behavior (Wilson et al., 2005). Nearly all of the studies showed positive effects and representative CBT programs were found to reduce recidivism by 20–30% compared to untreated control groups. This meta-analysis included studies of a wide range of offenders; some used general samples of offenders, others treated only specialized types of offenders (e.g., sex offenders, drug offenders, DUI cases, or batterers). Wilson et al. (2005) found variability in the effects across studies that may have been due to differences in the response of these different types of offenders, or may have been related to the uneven methodological quality of the studies. However, there were too few studies for them to closely examine these factors.

Pearson et al. (2002) included 69 research studies in a meta-analysis that covered both behavioral (e.g., contingency contracting, token economy) and cognitive-behavioral programs. They found that cognitive-behavioral programs were more effective in reducing recidivism than behavioral programs, with a mean recidivism reduction for treated groups of about 30%. Moreover, studies of higher methodological quality showed the largest effect sizes. The criteria for identifying cognitive-behavioral programs in this meta-analysis were broad, however. They included not only interventions directed specifically toward altering cognitions, but also social skills training and problem-solving programs for which cognitive change was not the main focus.

Lipsey et al. (2001) conducted a meta-analysis of the effectiveness of CBT that aimed to assess recidivism outcomes for a less diverse set of studies than was included in these other efforts. They reported the results of 14 studies that used experimental or strong quasi-experimental research designs, CBT interventions focused centrally on cognitive change, and subject samples from the general offender population (excluding studies of specialized offenders). The overall results showed that, for offenders receiving CBT, the odds of recidivating were only about 55% of those for offenders in the control groups. Further analysis revealed that programs set up as research or demonstration projects produced larger effects than "real world" practice programs. This finding raises questions about what characteristics of the research and demonstration programs account for their greater effectiveness and whether comparable effects can be attained by CBT in routine practice.

The systematic review and meta-analysis reported here is a further exploration of the issues raised by Lipsey et al. (2001). It maintains the focus on recidivism outcomes and programs for general offender populations that are clearly identifiable as CBT. Its primary purpose, however, is to examine the effectiveness of research and demonstration programs in comparison with routine practice programs. In particular, it aims to better identify the characteristics of research and demonstration programs that may account for their better outcomes. To minimize variation in results associated with differing quality of research design, this systematic review and meta-analysis was restricted to randomized controlled studies so as to have the best available estimates of the actual effects of CBT on offenders' recidivism. Also, recent studies that have become available since the previous meta-analysis have been added to increase the body of evidence relevant to these purposes.

SUMMARY OF RESEARCH METHODS

Criteria for Inclusion of Evaluation Studies

Studies were selected for inclusion in this systematic review and meta-analysis based on the following criteria:

1. The treatment under investigation must be directed primarily toward changing participants' distorted or dysfunctional cognitions or teaching new cognitive skills. The therapeutic techniques should involve specific, relatively structured lessons designed to affect such cognitive processes as monitoring "self-talk," identifying trigger thoughts, assessing the accuracy of interpretations of events, evaluating the impact of behavior on others, generating alternative solutions, and self-coaching statements for high-risk situations.
2. The recipients of the intervention must be criminal offenders, either juveniles or adults, who are drawn from a general offender population and not selected for, or restricted to, those committing specific types of offenses.
3. The study must report subsequent delinquent or criminal offending as an outcome variable in a form that permits estimation of an effect size statistic representing the contrast between the recidivism of treated versus untreated offenders.
4. The study must use a design in which participants are randomly assigned to intervention and control conditions. Control groups can represent placebo, wait-list, no treatment, or "treatment as usual" conditions, with the latter restricted to cases of clearly routine probation, institutional, or aftercare/parole practices.
5. Eligible studies may be either published or unpublished.

Identification and Coding of Relevant Studies

Computerized bibliography searches were conducted in a wide range of electronic databases for the period from 1970, which was prior to the first reported application of CBT to offenders (Yochelson and Samenow, 1976), through mid-year 2003. The Campbell Collaboration Social, Psychological, Educational and Criminological Trials Register (C2-SPECTR) was also searched and search engines were used on the Internet. The references in relevant review articles and meta-analyses were scanned for candidate studies, as were the reference lists of all the candidate studies retrieved and screened for eligibility. Finally, major journals in criminology and related fields likely to publish relevant studies were scanned for promising studies that were then screened more closely for eligibility.

Information from each eligible study was coded into a computerized database by one of the authors. The items in the coding form encompassed bibliographic information, research methods and procedures, sample characteristics, a wide range of treatment characteristics, and recidivism outcomes.

Statistical Procedures

The eligible studies reported recidivism outcomes in several different forms. Most commonly, this was the proportions or percentages of offenders in each research condition that recidivated. In some cases the outcomes were presented as mean number of offenses or as summary statistics (e.g., t-test results). To encompass this diversity, the standardized mean difference was used as the effect size statistic for representing all outcomes. This statistic is defined as the difference between the treatment and control group means on an outcome variable divided by their pooled standard deviations (Lipsey and Wilson, 2001). As such, it is interpretable as the treatment-control difference in outcome expressed in standard deviation units, with positive values indicating better outcomes for the treatment group and negative values favoring the control group.

The statistical analysis was conducted using conventional meta-analysis techniques (Lipsey and Wilson, 2001) with each effect size weighted by its inverse variance in all analyses involving multiple effect sizes to give studies based on larger samples more influence in the results. For one study with an exceptionally large sample (Robinson, 1995), the weight was recoded a less extreme value when its effect size was analyzed with those from other studies to keep it from dominating the results. Because of the small number of studies involved in this meta-analysis and the associated low statistical power for detecting effects, all statistical tests were conducted with alpha = .10, somewhat relaxed from the conventional .05 standard.

RESULTS

Overall, 14 studies were found that met the stipulated eligibility criteria, all conducted in the United States or Canada. As this is a work in progress, the search for qualifying studies continues, but we do not expect to locate many more studies that meet the stringent criteria we have set. Table 1 summarizes the characteristics of these 14 studies. Several features of this body of research are notable. As required by the selection criteria, of course, all the studies used randomized designs. In addition, 10 of the 14 involved research or demonstration projects rather than evaluation of cognitive-behavioral treatment in routine practice. Most of the studies were based on relatively small samples (under 100 total) and all but two used only male subjects. Treatment was administered while the offenders were incarcerated in a correctional institution in about half the studies, and while they were in the community in the other half. In most instances, the treatment providers had little or no evident mental health background and had received relatively minimal training in cognitive behavioral therapy.

*TABLE 1.   Characteristics of the Eligible Studies and Their Correlations with the
Selected Best Recidivism Effect Size*

	N		N
Publication type ($-.58*$)		**Risk level (.46*)**	
journal	5	low-moderate	4
chapter	5	medium	3
technical report	2	medium-high	4
other	2	high	3
Date of publication ($-.67*$)		**Treatment setting (.58*)**	
1973	1	correctional institution	8
1988–90	7	community-probation	4
1995–98	5	community- no CJ supervision	2
2001	1	**Cog-behavioral treatment (ns[a])**	
Country ($-.14$)		generic cognitive behavioral	2
USA	10	aggression replacement therapy	2
Canada	4	interpersonal problem solving therapy	2
		reasoning and rehabilitation	6
Type of study (.63*)		moral reconation therapy	2
practice	4		
demonstration	4	**Treatment fidelity check (.53*)**	
research	6	observed low	1
		not assessed/reported	4
Sample size ($-.46*$)		attendance	5
18–28	3	monitored	4
33–45	3		
57–84	4	**Treatment length (weeks) (.44)**	
134–212	3	7–13	7
2125	1	17–26	6
		63	1
Attrition (.02)			
.00	9	**Treatment hours/week ($-.26$)**	
.17–.27	3	1–2	4
.33	2	3–4	7
		6	2
Sample age ($-.32$)		15	1
juvenile	6		
adult	8	**Total hours of treatment ($-.11$)**	
		8–11	3
Percent male (.01)		30–44	3
50	2	63–80	6
100	10	169–240	2
not reported	2		
		CBT training/supervision for providers (.47*)	
Percent minority (.44)		minimal	10
12	1	moderate-high	4
34	1		
60–74	4	**Mental health background of providers (.26)**	
94	1	none or little	10
not reported	7	some or more	3

[a] No significant difference in mean effect sizes for cognitive-behavior treatment types shown by Q-test
(Q-between = 6.2, $df = 4$, $p = .18$).
* $p < .10$ for correlation between characteristic and recidivism effect size.

TABLE 2.   *Mean Effect Sizes for Recidivism Outcomes*

Type of Recidivism Event	N of Studies	Mean[a] Effect Size	Months At-Risk: Mean (Range)
Violation, revocation, etc.	5	.06	6.4 (3–12)
Arrest	9	.29*	10.3 (3–18)
Conviction	3	.19*	13.0 (9–18)
Incarceration	4	.22*	13.5 (9–18)

[a] Inverse-variance weighted means.
*$p < .05$.

Recidivism Outcomes

The recidivism outcomes reported in these studies were of four different types: (a) violations and revocations of probation or parole (reported in five studies); (b) arrests or police contacts (reported in nine studies); (c) court convictions (reported in three studies); and (d) incarceration (reported in four studies). The at-risk intervals over which these measures were taken ranged from three months to 18 months. As Table 2 shows, the mean effect sizes for all these outcomes were positive and, for three of the four, were statistically significant. The exception was recidivism measured as parole or probation violations, which showed a notably lower mean than the outcomes in the other categories. This low value is some-what misleading, however, because it results entirely from one study that produced an exceptionally small effect size heavily weighted because of an exceptionally large sample. Without that one case, the mean effect size for violations/revocations is in the same range as the others shown in Table 2.

Subsequent arrest was the most commonly reported recidivism outcome, available in nine of the 14 studies. Furthermore, the confidence intervals around the mean effect sizes for the other outcomes all overlapped that of the mean effect size for arrests. We, therefore, selected arrest recidivism as the main outcome for further analysis for those studies that reported it. For the five studies that did not report arrest recidivism, one of the other recidivism types was substituted. For two of the studies, the only available outcome was violations/revocations, but neither involved the discrepant value mentioned above. The remaining three studies provided data on both subsequent convictions and incarcerations. In these cases, convictions were judged more similar to arrests than incarcerations and were selected. This procedure resulted in one selected "best available" recidivism effect size for each of the 14 studies.

Further analysis showed that there were no significant differences among the selected effect sizes with regard to the type of recidivism represented. The at-risk interval over which the selected recidivism outcomes were measured ranged from three to 18 months with a mean of 10.2 months. Despite this wide range, the correlation between the at-risk intervals and the recidivism effect sizes was small (.05) and nonsignificant. No further account was therefore taken of the varying intervals in computing the overall mean effect size.

FIGURE 1. Cognitive Behavioral Therapy: Recidivism Outcomes

Citation	Effect Size (ES)	ES and 95% Confidence Interval
Armstrong (2000)	.14	
Chandler (1973)	.87	
Corr Serv Canada (1990)	.40	
Finn (1998)	.19	
Goldstein et al.(1989)	.63	
Guerra & Slaby (1990)	.24	
Johnson & Hunter (1995)	.20	
Kownacki (1995)	.71	
Larson (1989)	1.26	
Leeman et al. (1993)	.36	
Pullen (1996)	.00	
Robinson (1995)	.08	
Ross et al. (1988)	1.07	
Shivrattan (1988)	.42	
Overall Mean	**.25**	

```
          -2.00    -1.00    0.00    1.00    2.00
          Favors Control           Favors Treatment
```

The selected recidivism effect sizes for the 14 studies are shown with their confidence intervals and the overall mean in Figure 1. The study-level effect sizes ranged from .00 to 1.26. None were negative but, as the confidence intervals that overlap zero in Figure 1 indicate, few of their positive values were statistically significant at the individual study level. However, the overall mean of .25 was significantly different from zero. On average, therefore, cognitive behavioral therapy for offenders has significant positive effects on their subsequent recidivism.

The .25 mean effect size is represented in standard deviation units for analytic convenience. The magnitude of the corresponding treatment effect, however, can be more easily understood in terms of the recidivism rate of the offenders who received treatment relative to that of the controls who did not receive treatment. Thirteen of the studies reported recidivism as a rate and, for those, the mean control group recidivism was 45%. Relative to that, the rate for the treatment group represented by the overall effect size mean is 33%. Thus the mean effect of cognitive behavioral therapy on offenders found in these 14 randomized controlled studies was a 12 percentage-point reduction in recidivism from 45% to 33%. It is worth noting that a reduction of 12 points from a baseline of 45 is itself a 27% decrease in the recidivism rate.

Factors Related to CBT Effects

A Q-test of the homogeneity of the recidivism effect sizes was conducted to determine if there was significant variation among them, though it had little statistical power because of the small number of effect sizes involved. Despite that, the results were statistically significant at alpha = .10 (Q = 21.8, df = 13, p = .06), indicating sufficient heterogeneity to justify consideration of factors that might be related to larger or smaller treatment effects.

Along with a descriptive summary of the characteristics of the studies, Table 1 (presented earlier) reported the correlation of each characteristic with recidivism effect sizes. A number of those correlations are relatively large though, given the small numbers, fewer reach statistical significance. The largest of the correlations with substantive implications is with the coding of the type of study as practice, demonstration, or research. Research studies were defined as those in which the treatment, as well as offender intake and progress assessments, were designed and administered by the researcher mainly for research purposes. Demonstration projects included those with treatments that were also administered under research auspices and largely for research purposes, but which involved providers and procedures that were more representative of criminal justice settings. In demonstration projects, for instance, the researchers had limited say over the selection of treatment providers, but had the opportunity to train and supervise them for treatment, assessment, and administration related tasks. Practice projects were those implemented by criminal justice agencies as relatively routine practice and evaluated by a researcher who had little or nothing to do with their design and administration. In practice projects, the researcher had no contact with the offenders in treatment and was not in a supervisory position over providers.

As the correlation of .63 with effect size shown in Table 1 indicates, treatments that were implemented as research or demonstration projects had larger effects on recidivism than those implemented as routine practice. In particular, the mean recidivism effect size was .47 for the six research studies (Chandler, 1973; Guerra and Slaby, 1990; Johnson and Hunter, 1995; Kownacki, 1995; Larson, 1989; Ross et al., 1988). For the four demonstration studies, it was .48 (Correctional Service Canada, 1990; Goldstein et al., 1989; Leeman et al., 1993; and Shivrattan, 1988). By contrast, for the four practice programs, the mean effect size was only .11 (Armstrong, 2000; Finn, 1998; Pullen, 1996; Robinson, 1995).

In comparison with the 45% average recidivism in the control groups, these mean effect sizes translate into 23% recidivism for offenders receiving CBT treatment in research and demonstration projects and 40% recidivism for those receiving CBT in practice projects. Expressed as recidivism reductions, the treatment-control difference in the research and demonstration projects represents a decrease of 49% in the recidivism rate while that in the practice projects is a decrease of 11%.

Table 3 shows that the practice/demonstration/research status of the treatment is itself correlated with various other study characteristics. In particular, studies with interventions implemented as research are more likely to be published in journals and at earlier dates, involve fewer treatment hours per week, and utilize providers with more mental health background. Though short of statistical significance with such small numbers, the correlations also showed some tendency for

*TABLE 3. Correlations of Study Characteristics with Type of Study
(Practice, Demonstration, Research)*

Study Characteristic[a]	Correlation	N
Publication type	−.76*	14
Date of publication	−.56*	14
Country	−.11	14
Sample size	−.43	14
Attrition	.10	14
Sample age	−.03	14
Percent male	−.42	12
Percent minority	.40	7
Risk level	.33	14
Treatment setting	.43	14
Treatment fidelity check	.45	14
Treatment length	.24	14
Treatment hours/week	−.55*	14
Total hours of treatment	−.42	14
CBT training/supervision for providers	.08	14
Mental health background of providers	.54*	13

[a] The study characteristics represented in these correlations are coded and sequenced as shown in Table 1.
*$p < .10$.

research-oriented studies to use smaller samples of mixed gender and more minorities, treatment in community settings, monitored treatment implementation, and fewer total hours of treatment.

Research-oriented studies, in contrast to studies of treatment practice, therefore, have a number of distinctive characteristics that may account for their greater effects on recidivism. Among the intervention characteristics significantly associated with recidivism effect sizes (see Table 1) and *not* very strongly associated with the practice vs. research nature of the intervention (see Table 3), were the risk level of the sample and CBT training and supervision for providers. These variables, therefore, have the greatest potential to account for differences in study effects beyond those associated with the practice-research factor. Sample size, sample age (juvenile/adult), percent minority, length of treatment in weeks, treatment fidelity check, and treatment setting also showed somewhat stronger associations with effect size than with the practice-research factor, thus indicating they might also have some potential to account for further differences in study effects.

To examine the relationship of variables other than those associated with practice-research to the recidivism effect sizes, a regression analysis was conducted with three predictors of effect size: practice-research, risk level, and CBT training/supervision for providers. As shown in Table 4, all three of these variables had independent and relatively equal relationships to effect size. Moreover, none of the other variables mentioned above as candidates had such relationships. The largest independent effects on recidivism, therefore, are associated with research-oriented interventions with higher risk offenders that are administered

TABLE 4. Regression Model for Recidivism Effect Sizes

Variables in the Model[a]	B	z	p	Beta
Constant	−.07	−.25	.80	
Practice-research	.21	3.16	.001	.68
Risk level	.23	2.68	.007	.58
CBT training	.32	2.41	.016	.52
Model Summary				
R-Square	.94	N = 14	$p < .001$	

[a] Weighted multiple regression analysis with inverse-variance weights.

by providers with moderate to high amounts of CBT training and supervision. The three studies of the 14 that have this combination of characteristics (Goldstein et al., 1989; Larson, 1989; Ross et al., 1988) have a mean effect size of .84. In recidivism rates, this is equivalent to a reduction for high-risk offenders from 70% recidivism to 29%, a substantial decrease of nearly 60%.

CONCLUSIONS AND POLICY IMPLICATIONS

This systematic review and meta-analysis gathered all the published and unpublished studies using a rigorous random assignment research design to assess the effects of cognitive-behavioral treatment on the recidivism of general offenders that could be located with a thorough search. The overall results showed that, on average, CBT reduced recidivism rates by 27%, confirming the findings of prior meta-analyses of the effects of CBT that have shown recidivism reductions of 20% to 30%.

The implications of this finding for correctional practice, however, must be tempered by the further finding that these positive results were largely the product of research and demonstration (R&D) projects that were not fully representative of routine correctional practice. The average recidivism reduction shown in studies of the application of CBT in practice projects was 11%, compared with 49% in the R&D projects. While a decrease of 11% in the recidivism of treated offenders is not trivial, it clearly falls well short of the effects CBT has the potential to produce, as indicated by the results of the R&D projects.

The key question for practice and policy, therefore, is how to implement this promising program approach in a manner that will attain the best possible results in routine correctional practice. For clues, we examined the characteristics of the R&D projects in hopes of identifying those that might be carried into practice. The defining characteristic of such projects – being set up and implemented largely for research purposes under the guidance of researchers – has no realistic potential for translation into routine practice. The manner in which CBT treatment is designed, delivered, and monitored in R&D, however, does have some characteristics that could be emulated in practice in ways that might increase its effectiveness in practice.

It is worth noting right off that no significant differences were found in the effectiveness of the different types or "brand names" of CBT, though the number of studies of each is so small that this result is not definitive. In this collection of studies, however, the generic forms of CBT were as effective as the packaged programs. It thus appears to be the general CBT approach, and not any specific version, that is responsible for the overall positive effects. Moreover, the CBT treatment implemented in the R&D projects generally involved fewer treatment hours per week and fewer total contact hours than in the practice projects. Though they employed somewhat longer periods of treatment, this pattern of results suggests that it is not larger amounts of treatment that account for the greater effects in the R&D projects. There is thus little indication that practice would be improved by picking one or another brand of CBT or by greatly increasing the number of contact hours.

Other than researcher involvement, what most characterizes the R&D projects are smaller sample sizes, greater monitoring of offender attendance and adherence to the intervention plan (treatment fidelity checks), and providers with mental health backgrounds. These factors suggest that treatment effectiveness is mainly a function of the quality of the CBT provided. This is an encouraging possibility from the standpoint of practice. It suggests that any representative CBT program delivered in typical amounts might have results in practice that approached those produced in R&D projects if they were implemented well by appropriately qualified personnel and closely monitored. The importance of the qualifications of personnel is further emphasized by the finding that the amount of training specifically in CBT that was given to the treatment providers was associated with more positive outcomes above and beyond the factors generally associated with R&D programs.

Two additional findings of this systematic review and meta-analysis may bear on the question of how to optimize the effects of CBT in routine practice. First, one of the characteristics of the R&D programs that was correlated with effect size was the treatment setting, with CBT provided in the community, e.g., to probationers or parolees, showing larger recidivism effects than CBT provided in prison settings. Second, a significant predictor of positive effects was the risk level of the offenders, with larger effects appearing for higher risk offenders in both practice and R&D projects. This pattern shows that CBT can be effective with relatively serious offenders, where there is the greatest potential for recidivism. It also indicates that it will be most effective when the participating offenders are in circumstances where they are directly at risk for recidivism rather than when they are incarcerated and not yet fully exposed to the factors that provoke reoffending.

In short, there is ample indication from research that CBT is an effective rehabilitative treatment for offenders. However, the amount of high quality research evidence is not yet sufficient to permit the most critical factors for effective practical implementation of CBT to be definitively identified. What the best research does show, however, is that R&D projects produce impressively large reductions in recidivism and that many of the characteristics of the implementation of CBT in those projects should be replicable in routine practice. In particular, it appears that well-implemented and supervised programs administered by well-trained personnel to offenders with significant recidivism risk account for much of the success of the most effective R&D projects. These characteristics are not unique to R&D projects and there is little apparent reason why they should not also characterize routine correctional program practice.

REFERENCES

Andrews, Don A., Ivan Zinger, Robert D. Hoge, James Bonta, Paul Gendreau, and Francis T. Cullen. 1990. Does Correctional Treatment Work? A Clinically-Relevant and Psychologically Informed Meta-Analysis. *Criminology* 28: 369–404.

Armstrong, Todd. 2000. *Treating Youthful Offenders with Moral Reconation Therapy: A Survival Analysis.* Unpublished manuscript. Montgomery County, MD: Montgomery County Detention Center. Available from: http://www.asc41.com/www/2000/abscr213.htm.

Beck, Aaron T. 1999. *Prisoners of Hate: The Cognitive Basis of Anger, Hostility, and Violence.* New York: Harper Collins.

Bush, Jack, Barry Glick, and Juliana Taymans. 1997 (revised 1998). *Thinking For a Change: Integrated Cognitive Behavior Change Program.* Washington DC: National Institute of Corrections, U.S. Department of Justice.

Chandler, Michael J. 1973. Egocentrism and Antisocial Behavior: The Assessment and Training of Social Perspective-Taking Skills. *Developmental Psychology* 9: 326–332.

Correctional Service Canada. 1990. *Results of a Pilot Study.* Reported in Ross, Robert R. 1995. "The Reasoning and Rehabilitation Program for High-Risk Probationers and Prisoners." In *Going Straight: Effective Delinquency Prevention and Offender Rehabilitation,* edited by Robert R. Ross, Daniel H. Antonowicz, and Gurmeet K. Dhaliwal, 195–222. Ottawa, Canada: Air Training and Publications.

Cullen, Murray, and Robert E. Freeman-Longo. 2001. *Men & Anger: Understanding and Managing Your Anger.* Holyoke, MA: NEARI Press.

Finn, Peter. 1998. *The Delaware Department of Correction Life Skills Program.* Washington, DC: Office of Justice Programs, U.S. Department of Justice.

Goldstein, Arnold. P., and Barry Glick. 1987. *Aggression Replacement Training: A Comprehensive Intervention for Aggressive Youth.* Champaign, IL: Research Press.

———. 1994. *The Prosocial Gang: Implementing Aggression Replacement Training.* Thousand Oaks, CA: Sage.

Goldstein, Arnold P., Barry Glick, Mary J. Irwin, Claudia Pask-McCartney, and Ibrahim Rubama. 1989. *Reducing Delinquency: Intervention in the Community.* First ed. New York: Pergamon Press.

Guerra, Nancy G., and Ronald G. Slaby. 1990. Cognitive Mediators of Aggression in Adolescent Offenders: 2. Intervention. *Developmental Psychology* 26: 269–277.

Johnson, Grant, and Robert M. Hunter. 1995. "Evaluation of the Specialized Drug Offender Program." In *Thinking Straight: The Reasoning and Rehabilitation Program for Delinquency Prevention and Offender Rehabilitation,* edited by Robert R. Ross and Roslyn D. Ross, 215–234. Ottawa, Canada: Air Training and Publications.

Kownacki, Richard J. 1995. "The Effectiveness of a Brief Cognitive-Behavioral Program on the Reduction of Antisocial Behaviour in High-Risk Adult Probationers in a Texas Community. In *Thinking Straight: The Reasoning and Rehabilitation Program for Delinquency Prevention and Offender Rehabilitation,* edited by Robert R. Ross and Roslyn D. Ross, 249–257. Ottawa, Canada: Air Training and Publications.

Larson, Kathrine A. 1989. "Problem-Solving Training and Parole Adjustment in High-Risk Young Adult Offenders." In *Yearbook of Correctional Education 1989,* edited by Stephen Duguid, 279–299. Burnaby, Canada: Simon Fraser University.

Leeman, Leonard W., John C. Gibbs, and Dick Fuller. 1993. Evaluation of a Multi-Component Group Treatment Program for Juvenile Delinquents. *Aggressive Behavior* 19: 281–292.

Lipsey, Mark W., and David B. Wilson. 2001. *Practical Meta-Analysis.* Thousand Oaks, CA: Sage.

Lipsey, Mark W., and David B. Wilson. 1998. "Effective Intervention for Serious Juvenile Offenders: A Synthesis of Research." In *Serious and Violent Juvenile Offenders: Risk Factors and Successful Interventions*, edited by Rolf Loeber and David P. Farrington, 313–345. Thousand Oaks, CA: Sage.

Lipsey, Mark W., Gabrielle Chapman, and Nana A. Landenberger. 2001. Cognitive-Behavioral Programs for Offenders. *Annals of the American Academy of Political and Social Science* 578: 144–157.

Little, Gregory L., and Kenneth D. Robinson. 1986. *How to Escape Your Prison.* Memphis, TN: Eagle Wing Books.

Marlatt, G. Alan, and Judith R. Gordon. 1985. "Relapse Prevention: Theoretical Rationale and Overview of the Model. In *Relapse Prevention: Maintenance Strategies in the Treatment of Addictive Behaviors*, edited by G. Alan Marlatt and Judith R. Gordon, 3–70. New York: Guilford.

National Institute of Corrections. 1996. *Cognitive Interventions Program: Think.* Washington, DC: National Institute of Corrections Information Center, U.S. Department of Justice.

Pearson, Frank S., Douglas S. Lipton, Charles M. Cleland, and Dorline S. Yee. 2002. The Effects of Behavioral/Cognitive-Behavioral Programs on Recidivism. *Crime & Delinquency* 48: 476–496.

Pullen, Suzanne. 1996. *Evaluation of the Reasoning and Rehabilitation Cognitive Skills Development Program as Implemented in Juvenile ISP in Colorado.* Boulder, CO: Division of Criminal Justice.

Robinson, David. 1995. *The Impact of Cognitive Skills Training on Post-Release Recidivism Among Canadian Federal Offenders.* Research Report, No. R-41. Ottawa, Canada: Correctional Service Canada.

Ross, Robert R., and Elizabeth A. Fabiano. 1985. *Time to Think: A Cognitive Model of Delinquency Prevention and Offender Rehabilitation.* Johnson City, TN: Institute of Social Sciences and Arts.

Ross, Robert R., Elizabeth A. Fabiano, and Crystal D. Ewles. 1988. Reasoning and Rehabilitation. *International Journal of Offender Therapy and Comparative Criminology* 32: 29–35.

Shivrattan, Jacob L. 1988. Social Interactional Training and Incarcerated Juvenile Delinquents. *Canadian Journal of Criminology* 30: 145–163.

Walters, Glenn D. 1990. *The Criminal Lifestyle: Patterns of Serious Criminal Conduct.* Newbury Park, CA: Sage.

Wilson, David B., Leana C. Allen, and Doris Layton MacKenzie. 2005. A Quantitative Review of Structured, Group-Oriented, Cognitive-Behavioral Programs for Offenders. *Journal of Criminal Justice and Behavior* 32: 172–204.

Yochelson, Samuel, and Stanton E. Samenow. 1976. *The Criminal Personality: Vol I. A Profile for Change.* New York: Aronson.

CHAPTER 5

BOOT CAMPS*

David B. Wilson
George Mason University

Doris Layton MacKenzie
University of Maryland

INTRODUCTION

Discipline is one of the first words that come to mind when one hears the phrase "boot camps." Boot camps have a long history within the United States military (officially called basic training) and have been used to indoctrinate recruits into the culture of the military. The military boot camp is replete with strict discipline, grueling physical activity, and instruction in the basics of military life. Boot camps have been romanticized as an environment that changes boys into men and many men who served in the military reflect nostalgically on their boot camp experience (Simon, 1995).

The marriage of the military style boot camp and correctional programming is intuitively appealing. Juvenile delinquents and young adult offenders are often considered to be lacking in discipline. A leading criminological theory places self-control, a cousin of discipline, at the center of a causal framework for criminal behavior (Gottfredson and Hirschi, 1990). It seems natural that if juvenile and young adult offenders lack discipline, then a program based on discipline should be beneficial.

Boot camps' intuitive appeal has lead to their rapid proliferation since first emerging in 1983 in Georgia and Oklahoma. Their growth first occurred in the adult correctional systems and later in juvenile corrections. Boot camps appear to represent the next step in the evolution of Western penology. There is nothing new, however, in boot camps as a method of punishment and correction. One of the early United States prisons was constructed in Auburn, Pennsylvania, in 1817. The Auburn model of punishment was developed during the 1820s by an individual with a military background and was structured around a belief in the value of strict discipline, a regimented routine, and corporal punishment (Colvin,

---

* This chapter updates our systematic review on the effects of correctional boot camps on offending (see MacKenzie et al., 2001), including the addition of a few new studies and the refinement of study coding. This project was supported, in part, by funding from the Jerry Lee Foundation. We thank Suzanne Kider and Fawn Ngo for their work retrieving and coding studies.

Brandon C. Welsh and David P. Farrington, eds.
Preventing Crime: What Works for Children, Offenders, Victims, and Places, 73–86
© 2007 *Springer.*

1997), a strikingly similar philosophy to the modern boot camp. The boot camp is simply a repackaging of an old idea for punishment and rehabilitation (Simon, 1995).

Despite intuitive appeal and widespread adoption, boot camps are controversial within the field of criminal justice. Debate revolves around questions of the impact on the adjustment and behavior of offenders both during and after incarceration in the boot camps. According to advocates, the atmosphere of the camps is conducive to positive growth and change (Clark and Aziz, 1996; MacKenzie and Hebert, 1996). In contrast, critics argue that many of the components of the camps are in direct opposition to the type of relationships and supportive conditions that are needed for quality therapeutic programming and rehabilitation (Andrews et al., 1990; Gendreau et al., 1996; Morash and Rucker, 1990; Sechrest, 1989).

This systematic review of boot camps will critically examine the extant empirical evidence on the effect of these programs on future criminal activity. Deterring future crime, protecting the public, and rehabilitating offenders are major goals of boot camps according to advocates and a survey of state correctional officials (Gowdy, 1996). The starting point for deciding whether or not boot camps should continue as a form of corrections is determining the effect of these programs on criminal behavior. Thus, we apply meta-analytic methods to all available boot camp evaluations with recidivism as an outcome. As a result, we do not summarize the studies that examine other effects of these programs, such as impact on attitudes, attachment to the community, or impulsivity (e.g., MacKenzie et al., 2001; MacKenzie and Shaw, 1990; MacKenzie and Souryal, 1995). Before reviewing the evidence regarding effectiveness, we provide background information on the nature of boot camps.

BACKGROUND

Correctional boot camps are short-term incarceration programs modeled after basic training in the military (MacKenzie and Parent, 1992; MacKenzie and Hebert, 1996). Participants are required to follow a rigorous daily schedule of activities, including drill, ceremony, and physical training. They rise early each morning and are kept busy most of the day. Correctional officers are given military titles, and participants are required to use these titles when addressing staff. Staff and inmates are required to wear uniforms. Punishment for misbehavior is immediate and usually involves some type of physical activity like push-ups. Frequently, groups of inmates enter the boot camps as cohorts, called squads or platoons. There is often an elaborate intake ceremony where inmates are immediately required to follow the rules, respond to staff in a subordinate manner, stand at attention, and have their heads shaved. Many programs have graduation ceremonies for those who successfully complete the program. Frequently, family members and others from the public attend the graduation ceremonies.

While there are some basic similarities among the correctional boot camps, the programs vary in many aspects (MacKenzie and Hebert, 1996). For example, the camps differ in the amount of focus given to the physical training and hard labor required in the program versus therapeutic elements, such as academic education, drug treatment, or cognitive skills building. Some camps emphasize the therapeutic programming, while others focus on discipline and rigorous physical training. Programs also differ in their points of departure from the justice system. Some are designed to be an alternative to probation; others as an alternative to prison. In some jurisdictions judges sentence participants to the camps; in others, participants are identified by department of corrections personnel from those serving terms of incarceration. Another difference among programs is the presence or absence of an aftercare or reentry program designed to assist the participants with adjustment to the community following the residential phase.

SUMMARY OF RESEARCH METHODS

To be eligible for this systematic review, a study must have: (1) examined a residential program that incorporated a militaristic environment (the programs were called by various names such as boot camp, shock incarceration, intensive incarceration, etc.); (2) included a comparison group that received either community supervision (e.g., probation) or incarceration in an alternative facility such as jail, prison, or juvenile residential facility; (3) included participants who were convicted or adjudicated; and (4) reported a post-program measure of criminal behavior, such as arrest or conviction. The measure may have been based on official records or self-report and may have been reported on a dichotomous or continuous scale. Note that this criteria allowed for the inclusion of studies ranging in methodological quality. The consequence of this decision to include weak studies will be addressed in the results section.

The strategies used to identify all studies that met these criteria included a keyword search of computerized databases and contact with researchers working in this area. The following databases were searched: Criminal Justice Periodical Index, Dissertation Abstracts Online, Government Publications Office Monthly Catalog, Government Publications Reference File, National Criminal Justice Reference Service Abstracts Database, PsychINFO, Sociological Abstracts, Social SciSearch, and U.S. Political Science Documents. The keywords used were "boot camp(s)," "intensive incarceration," and "shock incarceration." Several of the searched databases index unpublished as well as published works. This identified 771 unique documents and a review of the title and abstracts suggested that 152 might meet the above criteria or were a relevant review article that might contain additional references. Of these 152, 144 were obtained and evaluated for eligibility, resulting in 32 eligible studies reported in 43 documents. Three of these studies evaluated multiple cohorts or jurisdictions. These distinctions were maintained in the analyses presented below and resulted in 43 unique samples comparing a boot camp program to a comparison group. Most of these studies evaluated boot camp programs in the U.S., with only one evaluating a Canadian program and another evaluating a British program.

Information was extracted from each study regarding characteristics of the boot camp program and comparison condition, sample characteristics, and features of the research methodology. The primary outcome of interest was recidivism or a return to criminal activity on the part of the offender after leaving the program. Recidivism data were reported dichotomously across all studies and were based on official records, generally indicated as arrest, conviction, or institutionalization. As such, the natural index of effectiveness is the odds-ratio (see Fleiss, 1994; Lipsey and Wilson, 2001) and was the index of effect used below. The odds-ratio can be difficult to interpret and therefore all results were translated into event rates (average percentage of boot camp and comparison group samples recidivating).

Studies typically reported multiple outcomes, resulting in a total of 142 recidivism effects sizes, excluding effect sizes based solely on technical violations. The recidivism effects were examined in two ways. First, multiple recidivism effects from a single study and sample were averaged prior to synthesis, producing a set of 43 recidivism effect sizes for the analysis. The second set of analyses used arrest as the measure of recidivism if it was available; if not, conviction was used as the measure; and, if neither of these were available, institutionalization was used. The results from the two approaches for measuring recidivism were compared and did not yield any significant differences in the results. Therefore, results based on the second method of measuring recidivism are reported in the following analyses.

RESULTS

The analysis of the effects of boot camps on criminal activity following release first examined the general pattern of results across the studies and then examined the relationship between study features and effectiveness. The distribution of recidivism effects across the 43 boot camp versus comparison group samples is shown in Figure 1. Each row of this forest plot represents a distinct sample, identified by the label in the left column. The recidivism odds-ratio is represented by the small diamond, and the horizontal line spans the 95 percent confidence interval around the odds-ratio (the longer the line, the less precise the effect for a given study). The samples are sorted with the largest positive effect at the top and the smallest negative effect on the bottom. At the very bottom of the plot is the average odds-ratio across all 43 comparisons (computed under the assumptions of a random effects model; see Lipsey and Wilson, 2001).

The effects across these studies ranged from large reductions to large increases in the risk of criminal activity for the boot camp participants relative to the comparison participants. The average effect across studies was near 1 (1.02) suggesting that the odds of a boot camp participant recidivating is roughly equal to the odds of a comparison participant recidivating. As an aid to interpretation, we determined the "average" success rate for the boot camp participants using the overall odds-ratio and the success rate for the comparison participants. From

FIGURE 1.   Forrest Plot of Odds-Ratio and 95% Confidence Interval for Each Sample

Author and Year	N
Fl. Dept. of JJ (Martin Co.), 1997	110
Fl. Dept. of JJ (Polk Co., Boys), 1997	128
Farrington et al. (Thron Cross), 2001	314
MacKenzie & Souryal (Louisiana), 1994	404
MacKenzie & Souryal (Illinois), 1994	294
MacKenzie & Souryal (Florida), 1994	289
Marcus-Mendoza (Men), 1995	4032
Aloisi & Lebaron, 2001	609
Farrington et al. (Colchester), 2001	175
Kempinem & Kurlychek, 2001	1040
MacKenzie & Souryal (S.C., Old), 1994	217
Peters (Mobile, AL), 1996b	363
Flowers, Carr, & Ruback 1991	2468
CA Dept. of the Youth Authority, 1997	642
MacKenzie & Souryal (Oklahoma), 1994	311
Fl. Dept. of JJ (Leon Co.), 1996	129
T3 Associates, 2000	294
MacKenzie & Souryal (New York), 1994	286
Zhang (unmatched comparison), 2000	200
Camp & Sandhu, 1995	508
NY DCS (88-99 Releases), 2003	59136
Jones, 1996	307
Jones (FY91-93), 1998	19099
Stinchcomb & Terry, 2001	479
Zhang (matched comparison), 2000	854
Harer & Klein-Saffran, 1996	310
Austin, Jones, & Bolyard, 1993	760
Burns & Vito, 1995	375
Gransky & Jones, 1995	8496
NY DCS (99-00 Releases), 2003	5365
Peters (Denver, CO), 1996a	240
Mackenzie, et al. 1997	694
Fl. Dept. of JJ (Bay Co.), 1997	121
NY DCS (00-01 Releases), 2003	5369
Fl. Dept. of JJ (Pinellas Co.), 1996	109
Fl. Dept. of JJ (Manatee Co.), 1996	121
Wright & Mays, 1998	1937
Thomas & Peters, 1996	364
Jones, 1997	700
Boyles, Bokenkamp, & Madura, 1996	735
MacKenzie & Souryal (S.C., New), 1994	218
Fl. Dept. of JJ (Polk Co., Girls), 1997	60
MacKenzie & Souryal (Georgia), 1994	164

this data, the average comparison success rate is 60% (40% recidivating); whereas, the boot camp average success rate is 60.5% (39.5% recidivating), a trivial difference. Thus, the evidence suggests that boot camp programs do not reduce the risk of recidivism relative to other existing criminal justice system options.

This average may mask meaningful positive effects in some studies and meaningful negative effects in others. It is evident from the forest plot that some studies observed large positive effects favoring the boot camp and other studies observed large negative effects favoring the comparison. From a statistical perspective, the distribution was highly heterogeneous ($Q = 141.91$, $df = 42$, $p < .0001$), suggesting that some boot camps may be effective whereas others may be harmful. This raises the question: Are there circumstances under which boot camps are effective? Similarly, are there circumstances under which the boot camps are harmful? We explore the relationship between the findings across studies and the studies' methodology, sample, and program characteristics.

Methodological Characteristics

The inclusion criteria for this systematic review were intentionally inclusive with respect to research design, resulting in a collection of studies, many of which have clear methodological weaknesses. Might the variation in research methods across studies account for the differences in odds-ratios? Do the weaker studies consistently under- or over-estimate the effectiveness of boot camps?

Table 1 shows the mean odds-ratio by several method features, such as whether the study used random assignment to conditions and whether it included program dropouts in the analysis. At issue is whether the overall conclusion of no effect is robust to the method differences across studies. Studies that used random assignment observed a smaller overall effect, although the effect is not statistically significantly different from the overall effect for those studies not using random assignment to condition and the difference is trivial. It is important to note that three of these four random assignment studies suffered methodological weaknesses that undermined the random assignment, such as excluding boot camp program dropouts from the analysis (three of the four) or severe overall or differential attrition (two of the four). The exclusion of dropouts for three of the four randomized designs should have upwardly biased the results. Thus, the negative overall effect was surprising and gives weight to the conclusion that boot

TABLE 1.   Mean Odds-Ratio and 95% Percent Confidence Interval by Method Variables

Method Variable	Mean Odds-Ratio	Boot Camp/ Comparison Recidivism Rate[a]	95% Confidence Interval	k[b]
Random Assignment to Conditions				
Yes	0.99	40/40	0.67–1.44	4
No	1.03	39/40	0.91–1.16	39
Used Group Level Matching or Statistical Controls[c]				
Yes	1.03	39/40	0.87–1.22	27
No	1.02	40/40	0.83–1.25	12
Boot Camp Dropouts in Analysis				
Yes	1.07	38/40	0.91–1.26	18
No	0.94	41/40	0.79–1.11	24
Overall Attrition Apparent				
Yes	0.87	43/40	0.65–1.20	7
No	1.05	39/40	0.93–1.18	36
Differential Attrition Apparent*				
Yes	0.76	47/40	0.58–0.99	8
No	1.09	38/40	0.97–1.23	35

*$p < .05$ for test of difference between mean odds-ratios.
[a] Comparison recidivism rate set at 40%, roughly the meta-analytic average across studies. The boot camp recidivism rate is computed as (odds-ratio $*p$)/(1 + odds-ratio $*p - p$), where p is the comparison recidivism rate. Because we coded the odds-ratio such that larger values indicated reduced recidivism, the inverse of the odds-ratio was used in this formula to reverse the direction of effect.
[b] Number of odds-ratios (i.e., number of distinct samples).
[c] Excludes random assignment studies.

camp programs are ineffective relative to the existing alternatives to which they were compared.

Examining the remaining methodological features shows only slight variation in effects by method. Higher quality quasi-experimental studies that either matched boot camp and control offenders or that incorporated statistical controls for baseline differences produced results that were comparable on average to those of lower quality quasi-experimental studies. Attrition, both overall and differential, appeared to relate to observed effects. Studies that experienced high levels of overall study attrition (loss of cases from the start of the study to the point of measuring recidivism), had a negative mean effect. Similarly, studies with differential attrition (greater attrition in one condition than the other) had a smaller and negative mean effect than studies that did not suffer from differential attrition. In all of these analyses, the higher quality studies had average effects near zero (i.e., an odds-ratio of 1). Differential attrition reduces the comparability of the conditions, weakening the inferences that can be drawn. Taken together, the finding of the ineffectiveness of boot camps at reducing recidivism appears robust to methodological differences across studies.

Offender Characteristics

Studies typically provided limited information regarding the characteristics of the offenders in the boot camp and comparison programs. Most of the samples were exclusively male, with only two studies examining the effects of female only boot camps, and five studies evaluating mixed gender boot camps. The average effect for these studies was similar to that for the full collection of studies. The existing evidence, therefore, does not provide a basis for concluding that boot camps are differentially effective based on sex.

Correctional boot camps were initially created for adult offenders with juvenile boot camps developing later. Thus, it was not surprising that there were more evaluations of adult boot camps than juvenile programs. The overall effect for juvenile boot camps was slightly lower than for adult boot camps, although the difference was not statistically significant (see Table 2). Juvenile boot camps that restricted their population to non-violent/non-property offenders observed slightly larger effects than boot camps with a more diverse and mixed offender population (broader range of offense types and more extensive criminal histories), although the difference was small.

Boot Camp Characteristics

Dominant features of boot camps are physical exercise, military drill, and ceremony, all carried out in the context of strict discipline. The distribution of effects across studies suggests that there is no general positive effect of boot camps; that is, the common features of boot camps do not appear beneficial. Many boot camps, however, incorporate other traditional rehabilitative programs, such as drug abuse counseling, vocational education, and aftercare transition assistance.

TABLE 2.   Mean Odds-Ratio and 95% Percent Confidence Interval by Offender Characteristics

Offender Characteristics	Mean Odds-Ratio	Boot Camp/ Comparison Recidivism Rate[a]	95% Confidence Interval	k[b]
Juveniles				
Non-violent/non-person crimes	1.08	38/40	0.81–1.46	5
Mixed (violent and non-violent)	0.91	42/40	0.72–1.15	12
Total	0.98	40/40	0.81–1.17	17
Adults				
Non-violent/non-person crimes	1.06	39/40	0.83–1.35	9
Mixed (violent and non-violent)	1.05	39/40	0.86–1.27	17
Total	1.05	39/40	0.90–1.22	26

[a] Comparison recidivism rate set at 40%, roughly the meta-analytic average across studies. The boot camp recidivism rate is computed as (odds-ratio $*p$)/(1 + odds-ratio $*p-p$), where p is the comparison recidivism rate. Because we coded the odds-ratio such that larger values indicated reduced recidivism, the inverse of the odds-ratio was used in this formula to reverse the direction of effect.
[b] Number of odds-ratios (i.e., number of distinct samples).

These expressly rehabilitative components may add value to a boot camp program, producing a beneficial effect for the offenders. Table 3 shows the mean odds-ratio by features of the boot camp program and does so separately for juvenile and adult boot camps.

Of the six program characteristics examined, only counseling as an integral component of the boot camp program was appreciably related to the mean odds-ratio. This difference was statistically significant for the juvenile boot camp programs. Juvenile boot camp programs without a counseling component had a negative overall impact (higher rates of recidivism). This difference was reduced when statistically adjusting for methodological features using a meta-analytic regression model, suggesting that the finding might not be robust to methodological variation across studies. Small differences in the expected direction were also observed for the incorporation of an aftercare component, drug treatment, and academic programming (adult only).

It was not possible to cleanly disentangle the various effects of program components given that boot camp programs tend to include a mix of vocational, educational, and psychosocial programming. To try to better assess the potential effectiveness of incorporating these therapeutic elements into a boot camp, we rated boot camps as having either a primary or secondary emphasis on treatment. The results show that studies evaluating boot camp programs with a strong treatment focus had a larger mean odds-ratio (1.12) than studies evaluating boot camps with a weak treatment focus (0.89). This difference is statistically significant ($p = 0.05$) and remains so after adjusting for methodological features using a meta-analytic regression model. Thus, the evidence suggests that while the essential features of a boot camp do not appear to be effective in reducing future offending, traditional rehabilitative type programming may be beneficial or at least may counteract any negative effects of the boot camp environment.

TABLE 3.   Mean Odds-Ratio and 95% Percent Confidence Interval by Program Characteristics

Program Characteristic	Mean Odds-Ratio	Boot Camp/ Comparison Recidivism Rate[a]	95% Confidence Interval	k[b]
Aftercare Treatment Component				
Juveniles				
Yes	0.98	40/40	0.81–1.17	17
No				0
Adults				
Yes	1.08	38/40	0.91–1.28	20
No	0.96	41/40	0.69–1.32	6
Academic Education				
Juveniles				
Yes	0.98	40/40	0.81–1.17	17
No				0
Adults				
Yes	1.09	38/40	0.92–1.28	22
No	0.88	43/40	0.60–1.29	4
Vocational Education				
Juveniles				
Yes	0.92	42/40	0.71–1.19	11
No	1.04	39/40	0.79–1.36	6
Adults				
Yes	1.02	40/40	0.76–1.38	8
No	1.06	39/40	0.89–1.27	18
Drug Treatment				
Juveniles				
Yes	1.01	40/40	0.81–1.26	13
No	0.89	43/40	0.63–1.26	4
Adults				
Yes	1.06	39/40	0.90–1.24	22
No	1.02	40/40	0.67–1.55	4
Counseling (Group and Individual)[†]				
Juveniles				
Yes	1.07	38/40	0.90–1.28	14
No*	0.72	48/40	0.51–1.00	3
Adults				
Yes	1.17	36/40	0.96–1.43	14
No	0.93	42/40	0.75–1.15	12
Manual labor				
Juveniles				
Yes	0.96	41/40	0.69–1.32	7
No	0.99	40/40	0.78–1.25	10
Adults				
Yes	1.04	39/40	0.87–1.24	19
No	1.09	38/40	0.80–1.47	7

*$p < .05$ for test of mean odds-ratio = 1 (no effect). [†]$p < .05$ for test of difference between mean odds-ratios.

[a] Comparison recidivism rate set at 40%, roughly the meta-analytic average across studies. The boot camp recidivism rate is computed as (odds-ratio *p)/(1 + odds-ratio *$p - p$), where p is the comparison recidivism rate. Because we coded the odds-ratio such that larger values indicated reduced recidivism, the inverse of the odds-ratio was used in this formula to reverse the direction of effect.

[b] Number of odds-ratios (i.e., number of distinct samples).

CONCLUSIONS AND POLICY IMPLICATIONS

This systematic review addressed the question: Are correctional boot camps effective at reducing criminal behavior among offenders? It should be clear from the discussion thus far that boot camp is a general term for a category of correctional programs that vary substantially from one-to-another. All boot camps, however, do have a common set of features that include the militaristic atmosphere, a rigorous and rigid daily schedule that includes physical training or labor, and strict discipline. We believe it is meaningful to ask whether this common component of boot camps is effective and should inform the policy debate regarding the continued funding, use, and proliferation of these programs.

Advocates and critics of boot camps are likely to be disappointed by this review. Advocates of the program expect the programs to successfully reduce the future criminal activities of adults and juveniles. Critics argue that boot camps are poorly conceived as therapeutic programs and they will not reduce recidivism and may actually have the opposite effect by increasing criminal activities. Our results do not support either side of this argument. Correctional boot camps are neither as good as the advocates expect nor as bad as the critics hypothesize.

Although the overall effect appears to be that of "no difference," some studies found that boot camp participants did better than the comparison, while others found that comparison samples did better. There are many plausible reasons for these differences, including methodological variation across studies, differential effectiveness for various offender groups, and differences in the nature of the boot camps themselves. Our examination of the methodological variables showed that no single methodological feature accounted for much variation in effect, and there was no clear bias across method features. Therefore, the failure to establish that boot camps were effective or harmful does not appear to be the result of the inclusion of methodologically weak studies.

Our examination of the offender characteristics was unfortunately limited due to the dearth of reported information that would have enabled us to code and analyze the possible impact of these characteristics on study outcomes. The only variables we were able to examine were: (1) whether the studies focused on adult offenders or adjudicated juveniles, and (2) whether the participants were limited to those convicted or adjudicated for non-violent/non-person crimes or mixed violent and non-violent crimes. Again, we found no evidence that differences in these characteristics explained the differences in the results, although the average effect for nonviolent juvenile offenders was slightly better than for mixed offender juvenile boot camps.

Advocates for boot camps will point out that not all boot camps are alike. We were able to code and analyze the impact of six program boot camp characteristics. These characteristics were limited to general information about the presence or absence of a programmatic component, such as aftercare treatment. We assume the quality and intensity of these components may differ greatly and data was insufficient to permit coding of such distinctions. For example, some programs consider Narcotics Anonymous (NA) or Alcoholics Anonymous (AA) meetings to be drug treatment, whereas others provided a more intensive drug treatment experience using a Therapeutic Community-type model.

The potential impact of the programmatic differences discussed above on recidivism cannot be overlooked. Our ability to disentangle these potential effects was limited. We did find, however, larger positive effects for boot camp programs that incorporated counseling and more generally for programs that had a primary focus on therapeutic programming beyond discipline, physical training, and military drill and ceremony.

What do these findings mean? All of these studies had the common element of a militaristic boot camp program for offenders. We reason that if this common component across studies is truly effective at reducing the future criminal behavior among offenders, then we would expect to see a distribution of effects that is positive, on average. That is, if a militaristic atmosphere, strict discipline, and rigorous physical exercise are beneficial, then the boot camp samples would have shown lower rates of recidivism than the comparison samples, even though the effects may have varied substantially due to other programmatic elements incorporated into the boot camp programs. This is not what we found. Thus, the extant evidence suggests that the military component of boot camps is not effective in reducing post boot camp offending. Discipline and physical exercise by themselves do not appear to be the solution to our crime problem.

Should boot camps be abolished? Although this review questions the effectiveness of boot camps as a correctional practice, the evidence also suggests that they are no worse than the alternatives examined in these studies (e.g., probation or jail/prison time). The large variation in the distribution of effects suggests that effective treatment components, such as those identified by other meta-analyses (Andrews and Bonta, 1998; Gendreau and Ross, 1979; 1987; Lipsey, 1992), may be added to boot camps, resulting in an effective program. We do not know whether effective correctional programming is more effective within the boot camp environment than when provided within a prison or as an adjunct to probation. Furthermore, boot camps may have other benefits, such as reduced need for prison beds (e.g., MacKenzie and Piquero, 1994; MacKenzie and Parent, 1991) or improved prosocial attitudes, attachment to community or reduced impulsivity (MacKenzie et al., 2001; MacKenzie and Shaw, 1990; MacKenzie and Souryal, 1995). Justifying the adoption or continued use of boot camps should not, however, be made on claims of their potential to reduce crime within a community.

REFERENCES

References marked with an asterisk (*) are primary sources included in the systematic review. References marked with two asterisks (**) are secondary sources.

*Aloisi, Michael, and Jennifer LeBaron. 2001. *The Juvenile Justice Commission's Stabilization and Reintegration Program: An Updated Recidivism Analysis.* New Jersey: New Jersey Department of Law and Public Safety Research and Evaluation Unit.

Andrews, Donald A., and James Bonta. 1998. *The Psychology of Criminal Conduct.* Second ed. Cincinnati, OH: Anderson.

Andrews, Donald A., Ivan Zinger, Robert D. Hoge, James Bonta, Paul Gendreau, and Francis T. Cullen. 1990. Does Correctional Treatment Work? A Clinically Relevant and Psychologically Informed Meta-Analysis. *Criminology* 28: 369–404.

*Austin, James, Michael Jones, and Melissa Bolyard. 1993. *Assessing the Impact of a County Operated Boot Camp: Evaluation of the Los Angeles County Regimented Inmate Diversion Program.* San Francisco, CA: National Council on Crime and Delinquency. (NCJRS Document Reproduction Service No. 154401.)

**Bottcher, Jean, and Michael E. Ezell. 2004. *Examining the Effectiveness of Boot Camps: A Randomized Experiment with a Long-term Follow-up.* Unpublished manuscript, Western Oregon University, Monmouth, OR.

*Boyles, Cecilia E., Eric Bokenkamp, and William Madura. 1996. *Evaluation of the Colorado Juvenile Regimented Training Program.* Golden, CO: Colorado Department of Human Services, Division of Youth Corrections.

**Burns, Jerald C. 1994. *A Comparative Analysis of the Alabama Department of Corrections Boot Camp Program.* Unpublished Ph.D. dissertation. Tuscaloosa, AL: Department of Political Science, University of Alabama at Tuscaloosa.

*———, and Gennaro F. Vito. 1995. An Impact Analysis of the Alabama Boot Camp Program. *Federal Probation* 59: 63–67.

** Burton, Velmer S., James W. Marguart, Steve J. Cuvelier, Leanne F. Alarid, and Robert J. Hunter. 1993. A Study of Attitudinal Change Among Boot Camp Participants. *Federal Probation* 57: 46–52.

*California Department of the Youth Authority. 1997. *LEAD: A Boot Camp and Intensive Parole Program; The Final Impact Evaluation.* Report to the California Legislature. Sacramento, CA: Author.

*Camp, David A., and Harjit S. Sandhu. 1995. Evaluation of Female Offender Regimented Treatment Program (FORT). *Journal of the Oklahoma Criminal Justice Research Consortium* 2: 50–57.

Clark, Cheryl L., and David W. Aziz. 1996. "Shock Incarceration in New York State: Philosophy, Results, and Limitations." In *Correctional Boot Camps: A Tough Intermediate Sanction*, edited by Doris Layton MacKenzie and Eugene E. Hebert, 39–69. Washington, DC: National Institute of Justice, U. S. Department of Justice.

Colvin, Mark. 1997. *Penitentiaries, Reformatories, and Chain Gangs: Social Theory and the History of Punishment in Nineteenth-Century America.* New York: St. Martin's Press.

**Courtright, Kevin E. 1991. An Overview and Evaluation of Shock Incarceration in New York State. Unpublished M.A. thesis. Erie, PA: Department of Administration of Justice, Mercyhurst College.

*Farrington, David P., John Ditchfield, Gareth Hancock, Philip Howard, Darrick Jolliffe, Mark S. Livingston, and Kate A. Painter. 2002. *Evaluation of Two Intensive Regimes for Young Offenders.* Home Office Research Study, No. 239. London: Research, Development, and Statistics Directorate, Home Office.

**———, Gareth Hancock, Mark S. Livingston, Kate A. Painter, and G. J. Towl. 2000. *Evaluation of Intensive Regimes for Young Offenders* (Home Office Research Findings). London, UK: Home Office Research, Development and Statistics Directorate.

Fleiss, Joseph L. 1994. "Measures of Effect Size for Categorical Data." In *The Handbook of Research Synthesis*, edited by Harris Cooper and Larry V. Hedges, 245–260. New York: Russell Sage Foundation.

*Florida Department of Juvenile Justice. 1996. *Manatee County Sheriff's Boot Camp: A Follow-Up Study of the First Four Platoons.* Tallahassee, FL: Bureau of Data and Research, Author.

*———. 1996. *Pinellas County Boot Camp: A Follow-Up Study of the First Five Platoons.* Research Report, No. 33. Tallahassee, FL: Bureau of Data and Research, Author.

*———. 1997. *Polk County Juvenile Boot Camp: A Follow-Up Study of the First Four Platoons.* Tallahassee, FL: Bureau of Data and Research, Author.

*——. 1997. *Martin County Sheriff's Office Boot Camp: A Follow-Up of the First Four Platoons*. Research Rep. No. 43. Martin County, FL: Bureau of Data and Research, Author.

*——. 1997. *Bay County Sheriff's Office Boot Camp: A Follow-Up Study of the First Seven Platoons*. Research Rep. No. 44. Bay County, FL: Bureau of Data and Research, Author.

*——. 1997. *Polk County Juvenile Boot Camp-Female Program: A Follow-Up Study of the First Seven Platoons*. Polk County, FL: Bureau of Data and Research, Author.

*Florida Department of Juvenile Justice. 1996. *Leon County Sheriff's Department Boot Camp: A Follow-Up Study of the First Five Platoons*. Tallahassee, FL: Bureau of Data and Research, Author.

*Flowers, Gerald T., Timothy S. Carr, and R. Barry Ruback. 1991. *Special Alternative Incarceration Evaluation*. Atlanta, GA: Georgia Department of Corrections.

Gendreau, Paul, Tracy Little, and Claire E. Groggin. 1996. A Meta-analysis of the Predictors of Adult Offender Recidivism: What Works! *Criminology* 34: 575–607.

Gendreau Paul, and Robert R. Ross. 1979. Effective Correctional Treatment: Bibliotherapy for Cynics. *Crime & Delinquency* 25: 463–489.

——. 1987. Revivication of Rehabilitation: Evidence from the 1980s. *Justice Quarterly* 4: 349–408.

Gottfredson, Michael R., and Travis Hirschi. 1990. *A General Theory of Crime*. Stanford, CA: Stanford University Press.

Gowdy, Voncile B. 1996. "Historical Perspective." In *Correctional Boot Camps: A Tough Intermediate Sanction*, edited by Doris Layton MacKenzie and Eugene E. Hebert, 1–15. Washington, DC: National Institute of Justice, U.S. Department of Justice.

*Gransky, Laura A., and Robert J. Jones. 1995. *Evaluation of the Post-release Status of Substance Abuse Program Participants* (September 1995). Chicago, IL: Illinois Criminal Justice Information Authority.

*Harer, Miles D., and Jody Klein-Saffran. 1996. *An Evaluation of the Federal Bureau of Prisons Lewisburg Intensive Confinement Center*. Unpublished manuscript. Washington, DC: Research and Evaluation, Federal Bureau of Prisons, U.S. Department of Justice.

**Holley, Philip D., and David E. Wright. 1995. Oklahoma's Regimented Inmate Discipline Program for Males: Its Impact on Recidivism. *Journal of the Oklahoma Criminal Justice Research Consortium* 2: 58–70.

*Jones, Mark. 1996. Do Boot Camp Graduates Make Better Probationers? *Journal of Crime and Justice* 19: 1–14.

*——. 1997. Is Less Better? Boot Camp, Regular Probation and Rearrest in North Carolina. *American Journal of Criminal Justice* 21: 147–161.

*Jones, Robert J. 1998. *Annual Report to the Governor and the General Assembly: Impact Incarceration Program*. Springfield, IL: Illinois Department of Corrections.

*Kempinen, Cynthia A. and Megan C. Kurlychek. 2003. An Outcome Evaluation of Pennsylvania's Boot Camp: Does Rehabilitative Programming Within a Disciplinary Setting Reduce Recidivism? *Crime & Delinquency* 49: 581–602.

**——. 2001. *Pennsylvania's Motivational Boot Camp*. 2000 Report to the Legislature. Quehanna, PA.: Pennsylvania Commission on Sentencing.

Lipsey, Mark W. 1992. "Juvenile Delinquency Treatment: A Meta-Analytic Inquiry Into the Variability of Effects." In *Meta-Analysis for Explanation: A Casebook*, edited by Thomas Cook, Harris Cooper, David S. Cordray, Heidi Hartmann, Larry V. Hedges, Richard J. Light, Thomas A. Louis, and Frederick Mosteller, 83–127. New York: Russell Sage Foundation.

——, and David B. Wilson. 2001. *Practical Meta-Analysis*. Thousand Oaks, CA: Sage.

**Mackenzie, Doris Layton, Robert Brame, David McDowall, and Claire Souryal. 1995. Boot Camp Prisons and Recidivism in Eight States. *Criminology* 33: 327–357.

MacKenzie, Doris Layton, and Eugene E. Hebert, eds. 1996. *Correctional Boot Camps: A Tough Intermediate Sanction*. Washington, DC: National Institute of Justice, U.S. Department of Justice.

MacKenzie, Doris Layton, and Dale G. Parent. 1991. Shock Incarceration and Prison Crowding in Louisiana. *Journal of Criminal Justice* 19: 225–237.

——. 1992. "Boot Camp Prisons for Young Offenders." In *Smart Sentencing: The Emergence of*

Intermediate Sanctions, edited by James M. Byrne, Arthur J. Lurigio, and Joan Petersilia, 103–119. Newbury Park, CA: Sage.

MacKenzie, Doris Layton, and Alex Piquero. 1994. The Impact of Shock Incarceration Programs on Prison Crowding. *Crime & Delinquency* 40: 222–249.

MacKenzie, Doris Layton, and James W. Shaw. 1990. Inmate Adjustment and Change During Shock Incarceration. *Justice Quarterly* 7: 125–150.

*Mackenzie, Doris Layton, and Claire Souryal. 1994. *Multi-Site Evaluation of Shock Incarceration: Executive Summary*. Washington, DC: National Institute of Justice, U.S. Department of Justice.

——. 1995. Inmate Attitude Change During Incarceration: A Comparison of Boot Camp with Traditional Prison. *Justice Quarterly* 12: 325–354.

*——, Miriam Sealock, and Mohammed Bin Kashem. 1997. *Outcome Study of the Sergeant Henry Johnson Youth Leadership Academy (YLA)*. Washington, DC: University of Maryland and National Institute of Justice, U.S. Department of Justice.

MacKenzie, Doris Layton, David B. Wilson, Gaylene S. Armstrong, and Angela R. Gover. 2001. The Impact of Boot Camps and Traditional Institutions on Juvenile Residents: Perception, Adjustment, and Change. *Journal on Research in Crime and Delinquency* 38: 279–313.

MacKenzie, Doris Layton, David B. Wilson, and Suzanne B. Kider. 2001. Effects of Correctional Boot Camps on Offending. *Annals of the American Academy of Political and Social Science* 578: 126–141.

*Marcus-Mendoza, Susan T. 1995. Preliminary Investigation of Oklahoma's Shock Incarceration Program. *Journal of the Oklahoma Criminal Justice Research Consortium* 2: 44–49.

Morash, Merry, and Lila Rucker. 1990. A Critical Look at the Idea of Boot Camp As a Correctional Reform. *Crime & Delinquency* 36: 204–222.

*Peters, Michael. 1996. *Evaluation of the Impact of Boot Camps for Juvenile Offenders: Denver Interim Report*. Fairfax, VA: Office of Juvenile Justice and Delinquency Prevention, U.S. Department of Justice.

*——. 1996. *Evaluation of the Impact of Boot Camps for Juvenile Offenders: Mobile Interim Report*. Fairfax, VA: Office of Juvenile Justice and Delinquency Prevention, U.S. Department of Justice.

**——, David Thomas, and Christopher Zamberlan. 1997. *Boot Camps for Juvenile Offenders: Program Summary*. Rockville, MD: National Institute of Justice, U.S. Department of Justice.

Sechrest, Dale D. 1989. Prison 'Boot Camps' Do Not Measure Up. *Federal Probation* 53: 15–20.

Simon, Jonathan. 1995. They Died with Their Boots On: The Boot Camp and the Limits of Modern Penality. *Social Justice* 22: 25–48.

*State of New York Department of Correctional Services Division of Parole. 2003. *The Fifteenth Annual Shock Legislative Report*. Albany, New York: Division of Parole.

**——. 2000. *The Twelfth Annual Shock Legislative Report (Shock Incarceration and Shock Parole Supervision)*. Albany, NY: Division of Parole.

**——. 1996. *The Eighth Annual Shock Legislative Report*. Albany, New York: Division of Parole.

*Stinchcomb, Jeanne B., and Clinton W. Terry, III. 2001. Predicting the Likelihood of Rearrest Among Shock Incarceration Graduates: Moving Beyond Another Anil in the Boot Camp Coffin. *Crime & Delinquency* 47: 221–242.

*T3 Associates Training and Consulting. 2000. *Project Turnaround Outcome Evaluation. Final Report*. Ottawa, Canada: Author.

*Thomas, David, and Michael Peters. 1996. *Evaluation of the Impact of Boot Camps for Juvenile Offenders: Cleveland Interim Report*. Fairfax, VA: Office of Juvenile Justice and Delinquency Prevention, U.S. Department of Justice.

*Wright, Dionne T., and G. Larry Mays. 1998. Correctional Boot Camps, Attitudes, and Recidivism: Tthe Oklahoma Experience. *Journal of Offender Rehabilitation* 28: 71–87.

*Zhang, Sheldon X. 2000. *An Evaluation of the Los Angeles County Juvenile Drug Treatment Boot Camp: Final Report*. Washington, DC: National Institute of Justice, U.S. Department of Justice.

CHAPTER 6

SCARED STRAIGHT AND OTHER JUVENILE AWARENESS PROGRAMS*

Anthony Petrosino

Research Consultant, Amherst, NH

Carolyn-Turpin Petrosino

Bridgewater State College

John Buehler

Harvard University

INTRODUCTION

On August 18, 2003, Illinois Governor Rod Blagojevich signed a bill into law that mandated the Chicago Public School system to identify students at risk for committing future crime and set up a program to give them "tours of state prison" to discourage any future criminal conduct (Long and Chase, 2003). As the news article makes clear, policymakers had good reasons for passing the law. Parents of young children were desperate to find ways to deter their kids from a life of crime. With some youth (even at ages 11 and 12) getting involved early in gangs, there was mounting pressure on policymakers to intervene early in their lives to dissuade them from potentially more serious behavior. The Governor himself is quoted as saying that the law is intended to "give some kids a chance to see what

---

* This review was a pilot test for the Campbell Collaboration (C2) using the existing infrastructure of the Cochrane Collaboration Development, Psychosocial, and Learning Disorders Editorial Group. The full text of this review was published in the *Cochrane Library* (beginning in 2002, issue 2) and will also be made available in the *Campbell Collaboration Reviews of Interventions and Policy Effects (C2-RIPE)* database. Parts of this paper are also published in the September 2003 issue of the *Annals of the American Academy of Political and Social Science*. Support was received from the Smith-Richardson Foundation, the Mellon Foundation, and the UK Home Office. Phyllis Schultze of the Criminal Justice Collection at Rutgers University and Carla Lillvik of the Harvard Graduate School of Education Library greatly facilitated interlibrary loan requests. We appreciate the assistance of the Cochrane Developmental, Psychosocial, and Learning Disorders Group team: Jane Dennis, Geraldine MacDonald, Stuart Logan and the other Editorial Group members, Celia Almedia, Jo Abbott, and Julian Higgins. Comments by Robert Boruch, Iain Chalmers, Phoebe Cottingham, Lyn Feder, and Joan McCord on earlier drafts of this work also helped.

Brandon C. Welsh and David P. Farrington, eds.
Preventing Crime: What Works for Children, Offenders, Victims, and Places, 87–101
© 2007 *Springer.*

happens if they don't follow the rules, follow the law, and what's ahead for them if they don't do that" (Long and Chase, 2003:1).

This is only the surface of the discussion that was briskly reported in this *Chicago Tribune* article. There was certainly some opposition to it, and some of this criticism reflected upon prior research about similar programs. Indeed, one opponent said that the prison tours were an attempt to resurrect "Scared Straight" type programs, which had been found to be ineffective in curbing delinquency (Long and Chase, 2003). Is this true? Or is the Illinois government right on target by introducing this law?

The latter is a difficult question to answer without looking at the evidence. In this chapter, we report the results of a systematic review of the nine randomized experiments of Scared Straight and other prison tour programs (also referred to as juvenile awareness or prison awareness programs). Of course, prior research is no guarantee that interventions will work (or not work) in a future setting. But a reader might ask oneself the following question upon reading the results of a systematic review: Would I want a doctor to prescribe a drug for my children that has the same track record of research results?

BACKGROUND

In the 1970s, inmates serving life sentences at a New Jersey prison began a program to "scare" at-risk or delinquent children from a future life of crime. The program, known as "Scared Straight," featured as its main component an aggressive presentation by inmates to juveniles visiting the prison facility. The presentation brutally depicted life in adult prisons, and often included exaggerated stories of rape and murder (Finckenauer, 1982). A television documentary on the program aired in 1979 and provided evidence that 16 of the 17 delinquents interviewed in the film remained law abiding for three months after attending "Scared Straight," a 94% success rate (Finckenauer, 1982). The program received considerable and favorable media attention and was soon replicated in over 30 jurisdictions nationwide, resulting in special Congressional hearings on the program and film by the United States House Subcommittee on Human Resources (U.S. House Committee on Education and Labor, 1979).

The underlying theory of programs like "Scared Straight" is deterrence. Program advocates and others believe that realistic depictions of life in prison and presentations by inmates will deter juvenile offenders (or children at risk of becoming delinquent) from further involvement with crime. Although the harsh presentation in the earlier New Jersey version is the most famous, inmate presentations are now sometimes designed to be more educational than confrontational but with a similar crime prevention goal (Finckenauer and Gavin, 1999). It is not surprising why such programs are popular: They fit with common notions by some on how to prevent or reduce crime (by "getting tough"); they are very inexpensive (a Maryland program was estimated to cost less than $1 per participant); and they provide one way for incarcerated offenders to contribute productively to society by preventing youngsters from following down the same path (Finckenauer, 1982).

A randomized controlled trial of the New Jersey program in 1982, however, reported no effect on the criminal behavior of participants in comparison with a no-treatment control group (Finckenauer, 1982). In fact, Finckenauer reported that participants in the experimental program were more likely to be arrested. Yet, beliefs in the program's efficacy continued. Finckenauer called the process by which policymakers, practitioners, media reporters and others sometimes latch onto quick, short-term and inexpensive cures to solve difficult social problems the "Panacea Phenomenon." Other randomized trials reported in the U.S. also questioned the effectiveness of Scared Straight-type programs in reducing subsequent criminality, including one in Illinois (Greater Egypt Regional Planning and Development Commission, 1979). Consistent with these findings, reviewers of research on the effects of crime prevention programs have not found deterrence-oriented programs like Scared Straight effective (Sherman et al., 2002).

Despite this seeming convergence of evidence, Scared Straight-type programs remain popular and continue to be used (Finckenauer and Gavin, 1999). For example, a program in Carson City, Nevada, brings juvenile delinquents on a tour of an adult Nevada State Prison (Scripps, 1999). The United Community Action Network has its own program called "Wisetalk" in which at-risk youth are locked in a jail cell for over an hour with four to five parolees. They claim that only ten of 300 youngsters exposed to this intervention have been re-arrested (United Community Action Network, 2001). In 2001, a group of guards – apparently without the knowledge of administrators – strip-searched Washington, DC, students during their tours of a local jail under the guise that they were using "a sound strategy to turn around the lives of wayward kids" – claiming the prior success of Scared Straight (Blum and Woodlee, 2001).

Scared Straight and other "kids visit prison" programs have been used in several other nations. For example, it is called the "day in prison" or "day in gaol" in Australia (O'Malley et al., 1993), "day visits" in the U.K. (Lloyd, 1995), and the "Ullersmo Project" in Norway (Storvoll and Hovland, 1998). Hall (1999) reports positively on a program in Germany designed to scare straight young offenders with ties to Neo-Nazi and other organized hate groups. In a different variant in the U.K., a program was initiated that employed ex-prison guards to recreate a prison atmosphere in public schools, with the goal of deterring any potential lawbreakers (Middleton et al., 2001).

In 1999, "Scared Straight: 20 Years Later" was shown on U.S. television and reported similar results as the 1979 film (UPN, 1999; Muhammed, 1999). The 1999 version reports that ten of the 12 juveniles attending the program have remained crime free in the three months follow-up (Muhammed, 1999). As in the 1979 television program, no data on a control or comparison group of young people were presented.

More recently, Petrosino and his colleagues (2000a) reported on a preliminary analysis of a systematic review, drawing on the raw percentage differences in each study. They found that Scared Straight and like interventions generally *increased* crime between 1% and 28% when compared to a no-treatment control group. This paper updates that review, and utilizes more sophisticated meta-analytic techniques to analyze the data.

SUMMARY OF RESEARCH METHODS

The goal of this review was to assess the effects of programs comprising organized visits to prisons of juvenile delinquents (officially adjudicated or convicted by a juvenile court) or pre-delinquents (children in trouble but not officially adjudicated as delinquents), aimed at deterring them from criminal activity.

Eligibility Criteria

We included only randomized or quasi-randomized (i.e., alternation assignment procedures, such as assigning every other case to treatment) controlled trials, provided they had a no-treatment control group. Only studies involving juveniles (i.e., children 17 years of age or younger) were included. Participants were delinquents or pre-delinquents. Studies that contain overlapping samples of juveniles and young adults (e.g., ages 13–21) were also included. The intervention had to feature a visit by program participants to a prison facility as its main component. The interest of citizens, policy and practice decision-makers, media, and the research community is in whether Scared Straight and other "kids visit prison" programs have any crime deterrent effect on the kids participating in them. We, therefore, focused on crime measures: Each eligible study reported on at least one outcome measure of subsequent criminality (e.g., arrest, conviction, police contact, self-reported criminality).

Search Strategy for Identification of Studies

In order to minimize publication bias or the possibility journals are more likely to publish findings that reject the null hypothesis (and find programs to be more effective than unpublished literature generally does), we conducted a search strategy designed to identify published and unpublished studies. First, randomized experiments were identified from a larger review of field trials in crime reduction conducted by the first author. These search methods are described in detail elsewhere (Petrosino, 1997; 1995). The citations found in Petrosino (1997) covered literature with a publication date between 1945 and 1993, inclusive. Seven randomized trials meeting the eligibility criteria were identified from this sample.

Second, we augmented this work with searches designed to find experiments possibly overlooked by this earlier work and to cover more recent literature (1994–2001). These methods included: (1) broad searches of the Campbell Collaboration Social, Psychological, Educational and Criminological Trials Register, also known as C2-SPECTR (Petrosino et al., 2000b); (2) check of citations from more recent reviews (e.g., Sherman et al., 1997); (3) citation checking of studies and other reports on the program (e.g., Finckenauer and Gavin,

1999); (4) email correspondence with selected researchers; and (5) broad searches of the Cochrane Controlled Trials Register. By broad searches, we mean that we tried to first identify studies relevant to crime or delinquency and then we visually scanned the citations and abstracts to see if any were relevant.

Third, we decided to conduct a more specific search of fourteen available electronic databases relevant to the topic area. Many of these include published and unpublished literature (e.g., dissertations or government reports). The bibliographic data bases and the years searched are described in detail in Petrosino et al. (2002).

We anticipated that the amount of literature on Scared Straight would be of moderate size, and that our best course of action would be to identify all citations relevant to the program and screen them for potential leads to eligible studies. This removed the need to include keywords for identifying randomized trials (e.g., "random assignment") in our searches. After several trial runs, we found that nearly all documents used phrases like "Scared Straight" or "juvenile awareness" in the title or abstract of the citation. We used various combinations of keywords to identify relevant citations (Petrosino et al., 2002; 2003). Finally, we conducted searches of the Internet and World Wide Web using the above terms in two popular search engines: *Hotbot* and *Altavista* and later updated this with another search using *Google*.

Selection of Trials

The search methods above generated over 500 citations (most had abstracts). The first author of this chapter screened these citations, determining that 30 were evaluation reports. The first and second authors then independently examined these citations and were in agreement that 11 were leads to potential randomized trials. Seven had already been retrieved in an earlier review (Petrosino, 1997). We determined that the full text reports for four should be pursued. Upon inspection of the full text reports, we determined that two studies should be excluded (Dean, 1982; Chesney-Lind, 1981). After all exclusions, we were left with nine randomized trials for analysis.[1]

Data Management and Extraction

The first author extracted data from each of the nine main study reports using a specially designed instrument. The data collection instrument was adapted from Petrosino (1997) and is described in detail in Petrosino et al. (2003). In cases in which outcome information was missing from the original reports, we made attempts via email and regular mail correspondence to retrieve the data for the

---

[1]   The more detailed version of this review was published in the *Cochrane Library* (Petrosino et al., 2002) and is forthcoming in *C2-RIPE*. Readers are invited to consult these publications for more details on the nine included studies, including methodological features. It includes a full list of studies excluded from this synthesis and the rationale for such exclusions.

analysis from the original investigators. (We were unsuccessful in obtaining any additional data from investigators.) We ran statistical analyses using Cochrane Collaboration's MetaView statistical software, a component of *Review Manager* Version 4.1 (*RevMan*). These were repeated, and additional analyses run, using *Meta Analyst* software created by Dr. Joseph Lau of the New England Cochrane Center. One of us (John Buehler) also created meta-analytic formulae in *Excel* to double-check three of the analyses. Results were identical.

RESULTS

Collectively, the nine studies were conducted in eight different states, with Michigan the site for two studies (Yarborough, 1979; Michigan Department of Corrections, 1967). No set of researchers conducted more than one experiment. The studies span the years 1967–1992. The first five studies located were unpublished and were disseminated in government documents or dissertations; the remaining four were found in academic journal or book publications. The average age of the juvenile participants in each study ranged from 15 to 17. Only the New Jersey study included girls (Finckenauer, 1982). Racial composition across the nine experiments was diverse, ranging from 36% to 84% white. Most of the studies dealt with delinquent youths already in contact with the juvenile justice system. Nearly 1,000 (946) juveniles or young adults participated in the nine randomized studies.

All of the experiments were straightforward two-group experiments except the evaluation of the Texas Face-to-Face program (Vreeland, 1981). Only one study used quasi-random alternation techniques to assign participants (Cook and Spirrison, 1992). The remaining studies claimed to use randomization although not all were explicit about how such assignment was conducted. Only the Texas study (Vreeland, 1981) included data on self-report measures. In two studies (Cook and Spirrison, 1992; Locke et al., 1986) no prevalence rates were reported. Some of the studies that did include average or mean rates did not include standard deviations to make it possible to compute the weighted mean effect sizes. Also, the follow-up periods were diverse and included measurements at three, six, nine, 12 and 24 months.

Narrative Findings

Whether relying on the actual data reported or measures of statistical significance, the nine trials do not yield evidence for a positive effect for Scared Straight and other juvenile awareness programs on subsequent delinquency. For example, in an internal, unpublished government document, the Michigan Department of Corrections (1967) reported on a trial testing a program that involved taking adjudicated juvenile boys on a tour of a state reformatory. Unfortunately, the report is remarkably brief. Sixty juvenile delinquent boys were randomly assigned to attend two tours of a state reformatory or to a no-treatment control group. Tours included 15 juveniles at a time. No other part of the program is described.

Recidivism was measured as either a petition in juvenile court for either a new offense or a violation of existing probation order. The Michigan Department of Corrections (1967) reported that 43% of the experimental group recidivated, compared to only 17% of the control group. No statistical test is reported. Curiously, more attention is not provided to this large negative result in the original document.

The Scared Straight program at the Menard Correctional Facility in Illinois started in 1978 and is described as a frank and realistic portrayal of adult prison life (Greater Egypt Regional Planning and Development Commission, 1979). The researchers randomly assigned 161 youths aged 13–18 to attend the program or to a no-treatment control group. Program participants were a mix of delinquents or children at-risk of becoming delinquent. The outcomes are statistically insignificant but negative in direction, with 17% of the experimental participants being re-contacted by police in contrast to 12% of the controls (Greater Egypt Regional Planning and Development Commission, 1979). The report concluded that, "Based on all available findings one would be ill advised to recommend continuation or expansion of the juvenile prison tours. All empirical findings indicate little positive outcome, indeed, they may actually indicate negative effects" (19). Researchers report no effect for the program on attitudinal measures. In contrast, interview and mail surveys of participants and their parents and teachers indicated unanimous support for the program. Researchers also note how positive and enthusiastic the adult inmates were about their efforts.

In the Juvenile Offenders Learn Truth (JOLT) program, juvenile delinquents in contact with one of four Michigan county courts participated (Yarborough, 1979). Each juvenile spent five total hours (half of that time in the rap session) in the facility. After a tour of the facility, they were escorted to the cell, subjected to interaction with inmates (e.g., taunting), and then taken to a confrontational rap session with inmates. In the evaluation, 227 youngsters were randomly assigned to JOLT or to a no-treatment control group. Participants were compared on a variety of crime outcomes collected from participating courts at three and six month follow-ups. This second Michigan study also reported very little difference between the intervention and control groups (Yarborough, 1979). The average offense rate for program participants, however, was .69 compared to .47 for the control group. Yarborough concluded that, "... the inescapable conclusion was that youngsters who participated in the program, undergoing the JOLT experience, did no better then their control counterparts" (1979:14).

The Insiders program in Virginia was described as an inmate-run, confrontational intervention with verbal intimidation and graphic descriptions of adult prison life (Orchowsky and Taylor, 1981). Juveniles were locked in a cell 15 at a time and told about the daily routine by a guard. They then participated in a two-hour confrontational rap session with inmates. Juvenile delinquents from three court service units in Virginia participated in the study. The investigators randomly assigned 80 juveniles ages 13–20 with two or more prior adjudications for delinquency to the Insiders program or a no-treatment control group. Orchowsky and Taylor (1981) reported on a variety of crime outcome measures at six-, nine-, and 12-month intervals; though statistically insignificant, the only positive results of this systematic review were reported in this study. At six months, the results slightly favored the control group (39% of controls had new court intakes versus 41% of experimental participants), but they favored the experimental participants at nine and twelve months. The investigators noted, however, that the attrition rates in their experiment were dramatic. At nine months, 42% of the original sample dropped out, and at twelve months, 55% dropped out. The investigators conducted analyses that seemed to indicate that the constituted groups were still comparable on selected factors.

The Face-to-Face program in Texas included a 13-hour orientation session in which the juvenile lived as an inmate. Counseling followed. Participants were 15–17 years of age, on probation from Dallas County Juvenile Court, and most averaged two to three offenses before the study. Participants (160 boys) were randomly assigned to one of four conditions: prison orientation and counseling, orientation only, counseling only, or a no-treatment control group. Vreeland (1981) examined official court records and self-reported delinquency at six months. He reported that the control participants outperformed the three treatment groups on official delinquency (28% delinquent versus 39% for the prison orientation plus counseling, 36% for the prison only, and 39% for the counseling only). The self-report measure, however, showed the reverse. None of these findings were statistically significant. There were discrepancies between the self-report and official data; some who were officially charged did not self-report the offense and vice-versa. Viewing all the data, Vreeland (1981) concluded that there was no evidence that Face-to-Face was an effective delinquency prevention program. He also found no effect for Face-to-Face on several attitudinal measures.

The New Jersey Lifers' program began in 1975 and stressed confrontation with groups of juveniles, ages 11–18, who participated in a rap session. Finckenauer (1982) randomly assigned 82 juveniles, some of who were not delinquents, to the program or to a no-treatment control group. He then followed them for six months in the community, using official court records to assess their behavior. Finckenauer (1982) reported that 41% of the kids who attended the Scared Straight program in New Jersey committed new offenses, while only 11% of controls did, a difference that was statistically significant. He also reported that the program participants committed more serious offenses. He also reported no impact of the program on nine attitude measures except one: Experimental participants do much worse on a measure called "attitudes toward crime." His concerns about randomization integrity are dealt with in a sensitivity analysis (see below).

The California San Quentin Utilization of Inmate Resources, Experience and Studies (SQUIRES) program was the oldest such program in the U.S., beginning in 1964. The SQUIRES program included male juvenile delinquents from two California counties between the ages of 14–18, most with multiple prior arrests. The intervention included confrontational rap sessions with rough language, guided tours of prison with personal interaction with prisoners, and a review of pictures depicting prison violence. The intervention took place one day per week over three weeks. The rap session was three hours long, and normally included 20 youngsters at a time. In the study, 108 participants were randomly assigned to treatment or to a no-treatment control group. Lewis (1983) compared them on seven crime outcomes at 12 months post-intervention. He reported that 81% of the program participants were arrested compared to 67% of the controls. He also found that the program did worse with seriously delinquent youths, leading him to conclude that such kids could not be "turned around by short-term programs such as SQUIRES ... a pattern for higher risk youth suggested that the SQUIRES program may have been detrimental" (Lewis, 1983:222). The only data supporting a deterrent effect for the program was the average length of time it took to be rearrested: 4.1 months for experimental participants and 3.3 months for controls. Data were reported on eight attitudinal measures, and Lewis (1983) reported that the program favored the experimental group on all of them.

The Kansas Juvenile Education Program (JEP) was an intervention to educate children about the law and the consequences of violating it (Locke et al., 1986). The program also tried to roughly match juveniles with inmates based on personality types. Fifty-two juvenile delinquents ages 14 to 19 from three Kansas counties were randomly assigned while on probation to JEP or a no-treatment control group. The investigators examined official (from police and court sources) and self-report crime outcomes at six months for program attendees and a no-treatment control group. Locke and his colleagues also reported little effect of the Juvenile Education Program in the Kansas State Prison (Locke et al., 1986). Both groups improved from pretest to posttest, but the investigators concluded that there were no differences between experimental and control groups on any of the crime outcomes measured. Investigators also reported no effect for the program on psychological tests.

The Mississippi Project Aware was a non-confrontational, educational program comprising one five-hour session run by prisoners (Cook and Spirrison, 1992). The intervention was delivered to juveniles in groups numbering from six to 30. In the study, 176 juveniles (between the ages of 12 and 16 and under the jurisdiction of the county youth court) were randomly assigned to the program or to a no-treatment control group. The experimental and control groups were compared on a variety of crime outcomes retrieved from court records at 12 and 24 months. Little difference was again found between experimental and control participants in the study. For example, the mean offending rate for controls at 12 months was 1.25 versus 1.32 for Project Aware participants. Both groups improved from 12 to 24 months, but the control mean offending rate was still lower than the experimental group. The investigators concluded that, "attending the treatment program had no significant effect on the frequency or severity of subsequent offenses" (Cook and Spirrison, 1992:97). The investigators also reported on two educational measures: School attendance and dropouts. Curiously, they reported that Project Aware reduced school dropouts, but noted that "... it is not clear how the program succeeded in reducing dropout rates ..." (97).

Should We Believe These Studies?

There are many factors in which to grade the quality of studies. Complicating any assessment of methods is that review teams, by and large, must rely on written reports by investigators. In some cases, methodology sections may be briskly written (sometimes due to journal space requirements) and key features of design and analysis may be deleted or considerably condensed. We determined that four were most critical to criminological experiments and practical to extract from the experimental reports. These were: (1) randomization integrity; (2) attrition from initial sample; (3) blinding of outcome assessors; and (4) fidelity of program implementation. Blinding of outcome assessors was reported in only one study (Michigan Department of Corrections, 1967), but given that most outcome data were collected from state or federal criminal history data bases (and not by program designers), it would seem that this was not a threat to the results. As these programs were relatively simple, none of the evaluators reported problems with implementation of the program (i.e., the subjects received what they were supposed to get).

Our review, however, found three studies with reported methodological problems that should be taken into account, with two having implications for our statistical analysis. The New Jersey study reported problems with randomization, and they were dramatic (Finckenauer, 1982). Only eight of the 11 participating agencies that referred troubled or delinquent boys to the program correctly assigned their cases. Finckenauer (1982) did conduct additional analyses in an attempt to compensate for violation of randomization, but the program still had criminogenic effects. We conducted sensitivity analyses (i.e., dropped this study from the meta-analysis) to determine its impact on the results (see below).

The Virginia Insiders study reported a major loss of participants from the initial randomization sample (Orchowsky and Taylor, 1981). They reported this, however, at the second and third follow-up intervals (not the first, at six months). Because there was a paucity of data beyond the first follow-up interval across studies, we only conducted a pooled analysis using the "first-effect." Therefore, a sensitivity analysis of the impact of this later attrition was not performed.

The Michigan JOLT study did report a large number of no-shows, but they were deleted from the analysis. The problem is that we do not know how many participants were initially assigned and we have no assurances from investigators that the remaining sample was similar to the initial sample. We also dropped the JOLT study in a sensitivity analysis to determine its influence on the pooled analysis (see below).

Meta-Analysis

Given that few outcome measures and time intervals using crime data were reported in the studies, we were limited to a single meta-analysis. We report the crime outcomes for official measures at "first-effect" (and usually the only effect reported). Each of the analyses focuses on the prevalence data, as the outcomes

FIGURE 1.   First Effect of Intervention, Official Crime Measures, Random Effects Model

Study	Treatment nM	Control nM	OR (94% CI Random)	Weight %	OR (95% CI Random)
Frickenauer 1982	19/46	4/35		9.8	5.45 (1.65, 18.02)
GERP & DC 1979	16/94	8/67		14.7	1.51 (0.61, 3.77)
Lewis 1983	43/53	37/55		15.3	2.09 (0.86, 5.09)
Michigan D.O.C. 1967	12/28	5/30		9.5	3.75 (1.11, 12.67)
Orchowsky & Taylor 1981	16/39	16/41		15.2	1.09 (0.44, 2.66)
Vreeland 1981	14/39	11/40		13.9	1.48 (0.57, 3.83)
Yarborough 1979	27/137	17/90		21.6	1.05 (0.54, 2.07)
Total (95% CI)	147/436	98/358		100.0	1.72 (1.13, 2.62)

Test for heterogeneity chi-square = 8.50 df = 6 p = 0.2

Test for overall effect z = 2.55 p = 0.01

.1   .2   1   5   10

Favors treatment   Favors control

Notes: n = number of participants re-offending; N = number assigned to group; OR = odds ratio; CI = confidence intervals; weight = amount of weight given to study in analysis.

reporting means or averages is sparse and often does not include the standard deviations. Thus, because the data rely on dichotomous outcomes, both analyses report odds ratios (OR) for each study, and their 95% confidence intervals (CI). Because there is some disagreement in the literature about this, we tested the data assuming both random and fixed effects models for weighting the treatment effects across the studies.

Figure 1 plots the odds ratios for the seven studies reporting prevalence rates. We assume a random effects model (i.e., the studies do not come from some single underlying population). Figure 1 shows that intervention increases the crime or delinquency outcomes at the first follow-up period. The mean odds ratio is 1.72 (CI 1.13–2.62) and is statistically significant.[2] The intervention increases the odds of offending about 1.7:1 (1.7 treatment participants offend for every control participant who offends).

There is always a question about whether or not the results are being driven by experiments that reported methodological problems. To test for this, we conducted a sensitivity analysis. Specifically we excluded the two studies identified in our methodological assessment as having potentially threatening flaws: The

---

[2]   Assuming a fixed effects model (i.e., the studies come from one underlying population) did not change these findings. The mean odds ratio was 1.68, and this was also statistically significant.

Finckenauer (1982) experiment because of concerns about randomization break-down and the Yarborough (1979) study because of the deletion of no-shows (which could indicate a potential for large attrition from the initial study sample). We again ran analyses assuming both random and fixed effects models (which did not differ). The deletion of these studies did not alter the results (see Petrosino et al., 2003).

CONCLUSIONS AND POLICY IMPLICATIONS

These randomized trials, conducted over a quarter-century in eight different jurisdictions and involving nearly 1,000 participants, provide evidence that Scared Straight and other juvenile awareness programs are not effective as a stand-alone crime prevention strategy. More importantly, they provide empirical evidence – under experimental conditions – that these programs likely increase the odds that children exposed to them will commit another delinquent offense. Despite the variability in the type of intervention used, on average, these pro-grams result in an increase in criminality in the experimental group when com-pared to a no-treatment control group. According to these experiments, doing nothing would have been better than exposing juveniles to the program. We would argue that the evidence is not good that the Illinois law will reduce delinquency and, on the contrary, might very well make things worse in the short-term. Readers might well object if a medical treatment or drug with the same record of results was used with their own children.

These data here are supported by a range of other scientific evidence. For example, the other two trials in our review that did not report prevalence data for the meta-analysis also reported no effect for the intervention (Cook and Spirrison, 1992; Locke et al., 1986). A meta-analysis of juvenile prevention and treatment programs by Lipsey (1992) indicated that the effect size for 11 "shock incarceration and Scared Straight programs" was $-.14$ (or produced about 7% higher recidivism rates in experimental participants than controls, assuming a 50% baseline).

Given the strong suggestion here that these programs have a harmful effect, they raise a dilemma for policymakers. Criminological interventions, when they cause harm, are not just toxic to the participants; they result in increased misery to ordinary citizens that come from the "extra" criminal victimization they create when compared to just doing nothing at all. Policymakers in Illinois and else-where should take steps to build the kind of research infrastructure within their jurisdiction that could rigorously evaluate criminological interventions to ensure they are not harmful to the very citizens they aim to help.

We note the following irony. Despite the gloomy findings reported here and elsewhere, Scared Straight and its derivatives continue in use, although a random-ized trial has not been reported since 1992. As Finckenauer and Gavin (1999) noted, when the negative results from the California SQUIRES study came out, the response was to end evaluation, not the program. Today the SQUIRES program continues, evaluated by the testimonials of prisoners and participants alike. Some may argue that these trials, with the most recent reported in 1992, do not apply to the "newer" Scared Straight-type programs. We believe that our review places the onus on every jurisdiction to show how their current or proposed program is different than the ones reviewed here. Given that, they should then put in place rigorous evaluation to ensure that no harm is caused by the intervention.

Despite these findings here and our earlier report (Petrosino et al., 2000a), the first author still get inquiries about how to get someone's son, daughter, or friend into a Scared Straight program. Many of these people are understandably looking for any program than can help "turn around" a wayward or anti-social youth. Unfortunately, we found no evidence that would support using this program for a particular type of kid with a special constellation of personality or other characteristics. Illinois officials may very well find a set of characteristics to identify kids at-risk for future delinquency, but they would have to identify particular youths in such a high-risk group who would benefit and not be harmed by the tours. This would be an incredible task.

One of the critical questions raised by this review is *why* the program has a criminogenic effect. Some investigators presented theories for such results, but we did not find any of the theory-driven evaluations that would have provided clues as to why Scared Straight fails. Future research studies, including experimental trials, ought to formulate a causal model diagramming how the program is theorized to work – and then test critical variables that can be operationalized, measured, and tested (Petrosino, 2000).

REFERENCES

References marked with an asterisk (*) were included in the systematic review.

Blum, Justin, and Yolanda Woodlee. 2001. "Trying to Give Kids a Good Scare." *Washington Post*, 3 June, p. C1.
Chesney-Lind, Meda. 1981. *'Ike Na Pa'ahao: The Experience of the Prisoners. A Juvenile Awareness Program. Report No. 258.* Manao, Hawaii: Youth Development and Research Center, University of Hawaii at Manoa.
*Cook, David D., and Charles L. Spirrison. 1992. Effects of a Prisoner-Operated Delinquency Deterrence Program: Mississippi's Project Aware. *Journal of Offender Rehabilitation* 17: 89–99.
Dean, Douglas G. 1982. The Impact of a Juvenile Awareness Program on Select Personality Traits of Male Clients. *Journal of Offender Counseling, Services and Rehabilitation* 6: 73–85.
*Finckenauer, James O. 1982. *Scared Straight and the Panacea Phenomenon.* Englewood Cliffs, NJ: Prentice-Hall.
Finckenauer, James O., and Patricia W. Gavin. 1999. *Scared Straight: The Panacea Phenomenon Revisited.* Prospect Heights, IL: Waveland Press.
*Greater Egypt Regional Planning and Development Commission. 1979. *Menard Correctional Center: Juvenile Tours Impact Study.* Carbondale, IL: Author.
Hall, Allan. 1999. "Jailhouse Shock Aims to Scare Youths Straight." *The Scotsman*, 26 October, p. 12.
*Lewis, Roy V. 1983. Scared Straight–California Style: Evaluation of the San Quentin SQUIRES Program. *Criminal Justice and Behavior* 10: 209–226.
Lipsey, Mark W. 1992. "Juvenile Delinquency Treatment: A Meta-Analytic Inquiry into the Variability of Effects." In *Meta-Analysis for Explanation: A Casebook*, edited by Thomas Cook,

Harris Cooper, David S. Cordray, Heidi Hartmann, Larry V. Hedges, Richard J. Light, Thomas A. Louis, and Frederick M. Mosteller, 83–127. New York: Russell Sage Foundation.

Lloyd, Charles. 1995. *To Scare Straight or Educate? The British Experience of Day Visits to Prison for Young People.* Home Office Research Study, No. 149. London: Home Office.

*Locke, Thomas P., Glenn M. Johnson, Kathryn Kirigin-Ramp, Jay D. Atwater, and Meg Gerrard. 1986. An Evaluation of a Juvenile Education Program in a State Penitentiary. *Evaluation Review* 10: 281–298.

Long, Ray, and John Chase. 2003. "Schools to Target 'bad' Kids for Prison – But Law to Scare Youths Has Critics." *Chicago Tribune*, 19 August, p. 1.

*Michigan Department of Corrections. 1967. *A Six Month Follow-Up of Juvenile Delinquents Visiting the Ionia Reformatory.* Research Report, No. 4. Lansing: MI: Author.

Middleton, John, Richard Lilford, and Chris Hyde. 2001. Applying Campbell Principles: Letter to the Editor. *British Medical Journal* 323: 1252.

Muhammed, Lawrence. 1999. "Kids and Crooks Revisited: Some Were 'Scared Straight!'." *USA Today* 12 April, p. 4D.

O'Malley, Pat, Gerry Coventry, and Reece Walters. 1993. Victoria's Day in Prison Program: An Evaluation and Critique. *Australian and New Zealand Journal of Criminology* 26: 171–183.

*Orchowsky, Stan, and K. Taylor. 1981. *The Insiders Juvenile Crime Prevention Program.* Richmond, VA: Virginia Department of Corrections.

Petrosino, Anthony. 2000. Answering the Why Question in Evaluation: The Causal-Model Approach. *Canadian Journal of Program Evaluation* 15: 1–24.

Petrosino, Anthony. 1997. *'What Works?' Revisited Again: A Meta-Analysis of Randomized Experiments in Rehabilitation, Deterrence and Delinquency Prevention.* Unpublished Ph.D. Dissertation. Newark, NJ: Rutgers University.

Petrosino, Anthony. 1995. The Hunt for Experimental Reports: Document Search and Efforts for A 'What Works?' Meta-Analysis. *Journal of Crime and Justice* 18: 63–80.

Petrosino, Anthony, Carolyn Turpin-Petrosino, and John Buehler. 2003. 'Scared Straight' and Other Juvenile Awareness Programs for Preventing Juvenile Delinquency: A Systematic Review of the Randomized Experimental Evidence. *Annals of the American Academy of Political and Social Science* 589: 41–62.

Petrosino, Anthony, Carolyn Turpin-Petrosino, and John Buehler. 2002. The Effect of 'Scared Straight' and Other 'Kids Visit Prison' Programmes on Juvenile Delinquency. *Cochrane Library* Issue 2 (May). Oxford, UK: Update Software.

Petrosino, Anthony J., Robert F. Boruch, Catherine Rounding, Steve McDonald, and Iain Chalmers. 2000b. The Campbell Collaboration Social, Psychological, Educational and Criminological Trials Register (C2-SPECTR) to Facilitate the Preparation and Maintenance of Systematic Reviews of Social and Educational Interventions. *Evaluation Research in Education* 14: 293–307.

Petrosino Anthony, Carolyn Turpin-Petrosino, and James O. Finckenauer. 2000a. Well-Meaning Programs Can Have Harmful Effects!: Lessons from Experiments in Scared Straight and Other Like Programs. *Crime & Delinquency* 47: 354–379.

Scripps, J. 1999. "Prison Tour Serves As A Wake-Up Call." *The Forum* 27 October, p. 1.

Sherman, Lawrence W., David P. Farrington, Brandon C. Welsh, and Doris Layton MacKenzie, eds. 2002. *Evidence-Based Crime Prevention.* New York: Routledge.

Sherman, Lawrence W., Denise C. Gottfredson, Doris Layton MacKenzie, John E. Eck, Peter Reuter, and Shawn D. Bushway. 1997. *Preventing Crime: What Works, What Doesn't, What's Promising.* A Report to the United States Congress. Washington, DC: National Institute of Justice, U.S. Department of Justice.

Storvall, Elisabet, and Arid Hovland. 1998. Ullersmoprosjecktet: 'Scared Straight' I Norge 1992–1996 [The Ullersmo Project: Scared Straight in Norway 1992–1996]. *Nodisk Trddskrift for Kriminalvidenskab* 2: 122–135.

United Community Action Network. 2001. "Services: Wisetalk (Scared Straight)." Retrieved April 26, 2001, from www.ucan.av.org/services.htm.

UPN. 1999. "Scared Straight! 20 Years Later." Television program hosted by Danny Glover.

Retrieved April 15, 1999, from http://www.contrib.andrew.cmu.edu/~aaron2/upn/upn-specials.html.

U.S. House Committee on Education and Labor. 1979. *Oversight on Scared Straight – Hearings Before the House Subcommittee on Human Resources, 96th Congress, 1st Session, June 4th.* Washington, DC: General Printing Office.

*Vreeland, Allan D. 1981. *Evaluation of Face-to-Face: A Juvenile Aversion Program.* Unpublished Ph.D. Dissertation. Dallas, TX: University of Texas at Dallas.

*Yarborough, James C. 1979. *Evaluation of JOLT As A Deterrence Program.* Lansing, MI: Michigan Department of Corrections.

CHAPTER 7

INCARCERATION-BASED DRUG TREATMENT*

Ojmarrh Mitchell
University of Cincinnati

Doris Layton MacKenzie
University of Maryland

David B. Wilson
George Mason University

INTRODUCTION

America's continuing "war on drugs" has flooded the criminal justice system with substance abusers (Lipton, 1995; 1998). A 1997 Bureau of Justice Statistics survey of incarcerated offenders found that 57% of state inmates and 45% of federal inmates reported drug use in the month prior to their offense. These rates are increases of 14% and 40%, respectively, over 1991 levels (Mumola, 1999). During the same period drug use among the general U.S. population was declining or holding steady (SAMHSA, 1998). Moreover, many of these drug using offenders are serious substance abusers, not casual users. Peters and his colleagues (1998), for example, reported that 56% of a sample of Texas inmates were diagnosed as having a substance abuse or dependence disorder during the 30 days prior to their incarceration. Similarly, a survey of jail inmates in Ohio found that 51% were currently drug dependent (Lo and Stephens, 2000). In all, a large body of accumulated evidence points to the substantial treatment need for a considerable proportion of offenders under criminal justice supervision (Belenko et al., 1998; Lo and Stephens, 2000). In fact, it is estimated that about 40% of all Americans who clearly need drug treatment are under the supervision of the criminal justice system (Gerstein and Harwood, 1990:7).

Without effective substance abuse treatment, a high-proportion of these incarcerated offenders will resume their patterns of illicit drug use, and in all likelihood their patterns of criminal offending, once released from prison. As such, the period of time when an offender is incarcerated represents a crucial opportunity to prevent crime by intervening in this cycle of drug abuse and crime. Several aspects of correctional facilities (i.e., prisons, jails) make incarceration-based substance

* This research was graciously supported in part by the Jerry Lee Foundation.

Brandon C. Welsh and David P. Farrington, eds.
Preventing Crime: What Works for Children, Offenders, Victims, and Places, 103–116
© 2007 *Springer.*

abuse treatment attractive. Perhaps most importantly, these facilities have the capacity to mobilize considerable coercive force to encourage substance abusing offenders to engage in treatment; many of whom otherwise would not do so. Additionally, the reduced availability of illicit substances facilitates detoxification and the isolated environments of many of these programs allow participants to focus on their substance abuse problems, in an environment typically more safe and clean than the environment in the general population.

While the potential of incarceration-based drug treatment programs is clear, their effectiveness is much less so. Many evaluations of these programs have been conducted; however, methodological shortcomings prevalent in this body of research make it difficult to determine whether the observed effects are actually due to the program, or to methodological flaws in the evaluation. This chapter reviews this body of research utilizing meta-analytic techniques in an attempt to determine whether participation in these programs is associated with reduced drug use and other criminal behavior. More specifically, this systematic review focuses on addressing the following research questions: Are incarceration-based drug treatment programs effective in reducing recidivism and drug use? Approximately how effective are these programs? Is the estimated magnitude of a program's effect associated with attributes of the research method, research sample, or intervention? Are there particular types of drug treatment that are especially effective or ineffective?

BACKGROUND

Incarceration-based drug treatment includes a broad range of treatment programs, including group and individual psychotherapy, 12-step programs, methadone maintenance and punitive interventions, such as boot camps for drug abusing offenders. For our purposes, the defining features of these programs were that they targeted substance abusers, intended to reduce recidivism or substance abuse, and that the intervention was based in a correctional facility. Evaluations of incarceration-based drug treatment programs predominantly have focused on evaluations of therapeutic communities (TCs) and group counseling programs (e.g., drug education, 12-step programs, such as Alcoholics Anonymous [AA] or Narcotics Anonymous [NA]). A considerably smaller number of evaluations have considered the effects of boot camp or methadone maintenance programs on drug users' behavior.

The individual components of TCs vary widely; yet, most commonly, residents in therapeutic communities are housed in a separate, distinct treatment unit away from non-participating inmates, in order to create an environment conducive to rehabilitation. Residents are instrumentally involved in running the therapeutic community, including leading treatment sessions, monitoring other residents for rule compliance, maintaining the treatment unit, and resolving disputes. Staff and residents of TCs tend to be confrontational with rule violators, but residents also are supportive of each other's struggles to maintain sobriety. The guiding philosophy of TCs is that drug use is symptomatic of more general personal disorders, thus the focus of the treatment is on the underlying disorders and not drug abuse per se.

Counseling/drug education programs are somewhat harder to characterize. Generally these programs incorporate elements of group counseling programs (e.g., 12-step programs, such as AA or NA), life skills training, cognitive skills training, drug education, and adult basic (academic) education. The commonality among these programs is their reliance on group-based therapies, in which substance abuse and other problems are discussed among group members in an effort to solve these problems.

Boot camps are modeled after military basic training. Inmates participate in rigorous exercise regimens, learn military drill and ceremony, wear uniforms, and take on challenge courses. Boot camps are highly structured – from the moment residents wake in the morning until lights out they are constantly engaged in scheduled activities. Boots camps also involve considerable confrontation, but unlike most TC programs confrontations most often occur between correctional staff and inmates – with drill instructors disciplining any deviation from established codes of conduct. Boot camps are designed to prevent future crime by instilling self-discipline, and the punitive nature of boot camps theoretically deters future criminal conduct.

Methadone maintenance programs are very different than other types of incarceration-based drug treatment programs, in that these programs attempt to solve the problems associated with heroin dependency (e.g., disease transmission, criminal activity) by prescribing methadone, a synthetic opiate. Unlike heroin, methadone does not produce a euphoric high; instead, methadone supplies a controlled amount of opiates into the client's blood stream that reduces opiate cravings. Furthermore, methadone blocks the euphoric high produced by heroin use. Long term methadone treatments gradually reduce the amount of methadone administered to the client until the opiate dependence is relieved.

SUMMARY OF RESEARCH METHODS

Search Strategy and Eligibility Criteria

The present systematic review conducted a search for published and unpublished studies that evaluated substance abuse treatment interventions located in secure correctional facilities (e.g., prisons, jails, work release, secure in-patient facilities). Bibliographic databases (i.e., PsychLit, MedLine, NCJRS, Criminal Justice Abstracts, Dissertation Abstracts, Sociological Abstracts, Social Science Citation Index, SocioFile, Conference Papers Index, and UnCover), reference lists from literature reviews, and conference proceedings were searched for potentially eligible evaluations using a list of key words. Potentially eligible evaluations were retrieved and closely scrutinized to determine eligibility for this review.

The eligibility criteria were that: (1) the study evaluated an incarceration-based substance abuse intervention (i.e., the intervention was administered in a secure correctional facility); (2) the intervention was primarily focused on substance users; (3) the intervention was delivered since 1979 in North America or Western Europe (to increase generalizability to current programs operating in these areas); (4) the evaluation used an experimental or two-group quasi-experimental research design (i.e., the research design must have included either a no treatment or a minimal treatment comparison group); (5) the study reported an outcome measure relating to criminal behavior or drug use; and (6) the study was reported in the English language.

Coding

Key features of the research methodology (e.g., random assignment, extent of attrition, use of multivariate data analysis), nature of the treatment (e.g., type of program, length of program, presence of aftercare), and of the treatment and comparison groups participants (e.g., age, gender mix, violent vs. non-violent offenders) were rated by two coders for each study.[1] The overall internal validity of each study also was rated by two coders, using a four-point scale. This four-point categorization was similar to the University of Maryland's Scientific Methods Scale (see Farrington et al., 2002). The highest level on this internal validity scale was reserved for studies utilizing randomized experimental designs with low levels of attrition. The next highest level denotes rigorous quasi-experimental designs (i.e., studies with carefully matched comparison groups or statistically equated groups by controlling for important pre-intervention differences) or experimental designs with more than minimal attrition. The two lowest levels of this scale distinguished standard quasi-experimental and weak quasi-experimental research designs. Standard quasi-experimental studies were characterized by comparison groups of questionable similarity to the treatment condition and these differences between groups were not statistically equated via multivariate analyses or other methods. Weak quasi-experiments utilized clearly non-comparable comparison groups.

The primary measure of recidivism utilized in this review is re-arrest (59%). In studies not reporting an arrest measure of recidivism, we substituted conviction (19%), incarceration (9%), or other measures of recidivism (e.g., revocation, 13%), in that order. The primary measure of drug use was self-reported drug relapse rate. A few studies, however, measured drug relapse using urinalysis results.

From each study, an odds-ratio effect size was computed for each recidivism and drug use outcome. We chose the odds-ratio effect size because the majority of the studies reported outcomes as dichotomies (e.g., recidivists vs. non-recidivists).[2] Effect sizes were coded such that larger effect sizes indicated greater treatment benefits. Thus, odds-ratios greater than 1 indicated that the treatment

---

1 Any coding differences were resolved by a senior project member.
2 For outcomes measured as continuous variables we calculated standardized mean difference effect sizes and then transformed these effect sizes into the odds-ratio scale (see Hasselblad and Hedges, 1995; Lipsey and Wilson, 2001).

group had a lower level of recidivism or drug use than the comparison group with larger odds ratios denoting larger treatment benefits; whereas odds-ratios less than 1 indicated that the treatment group had a higher level of recidivism or drug use.[3]

It is important to note that whenever possible effect sizes were coded in a manner that encompassed the overall impact of an intervention. Often evaluators reported the results of the outcome analysis separately for program completers, non-completers, and a comparison group (see e.g., Eisenberg 2001; Eisenberg and Fabelo, 1996; Hughey and Klemke, 1996). These evaluators often interpret differences between program completers and comparison group as being due to the program; however, such conclusions are likely to be tainted by selection bias. As we are interested in the overall effect of each program, in those instances where outcomes were reported separately for completers, non-completers, and a comparison group, we collapsed the outcomes of program completers and non-completers into an overall treatment group and compared this group to the comparison group.

RESULTS

Drug Treatment and Recidivism

Twenty-six independent studies meeting our eligibility criteria were located. A few of these studies assessed more than one drug treatment program. As a result, these 26 studies represented 31 independent evaluations.[4] Three of these program evaluations reported their results separately for men and women. Because we were interested in the possible differential effect of these programs by gender, we coded these samples separately. Thus, a total of 34 recidivism treatment-comparison contrasts were examined in this review. Preliminary effect size analyses, however, showed that two studies (Field, 1985; 1989) that used program dropouts as a comparison group had unusually large effect sizes. These two studies were excluded from all analyses; reducing the number of effect sizes to 32, and thus no studies using dropouts as a comparison group were included.

Only half (16) of the coded recidivism effect sizes came from published documents. The other half of the effect sizes were derived from government documents (7) or unpublished manuscripts (9). Given the high proportion of effect sizes from

---

3   In a few instances, evaluators reported the results of a program at multiple follow-up periods in separate studies; e.g., Wexler and his colleagues have produced a series of evaluations reporting the results of a prison-based therapeutic community at 12, 24, and 36 months (Wexler et al., 1995; 1999a; 1999b). In order to maintain statistical independence, we combined the results of each of these studies into one study with repeated measures. We then averaged these repeated measures into one effect size that was included in the analysis of effect sizes. Similarly, if the results included multiple arrest or drug use measures (e.g., frequency and prevalence of arrest), these measures were averaged into one effect size.

4   One evaluation, Zhang (2000), reported the results from two independent samples from the same program, thus 30 separate programs are actually evaluated.

FIGURE 1.   Forest Plot of Recidivism Odds Ratios (k = 32)

Author and Year	N	Favors Comparison	Favors Treatment
PRENDERGAST ET AL 1996	64		
HARTMANN ET AL 1997	244		
TUNIS ET AL (DEUCE) 1995	264		
TUNIS ET AL (JET) 1995	150		
INCIARDI ET AL (CREST) 1997	359		
TUNIS ET AL (REACH) 1995	159		
WEXLER ET AL (MALES) 1990	594		
WEXLER ET AL 1999A & B	715		
TAXMAN & SPINNER 1996	528		
PETERS ET AL 1993	420		
KNIGHT ET AL (ITC) 1999	396		
SMITH 1996	495		
HUGHEY & KLEMKE 1996	394		
WEXLER ET AL (FEMALES) 1990	285		
WA STATE DOC 1988	676		
LITTLE ET AL 1991	152		
EISENBERG & FABELO 1996	1067		
ZHANG ('97 COHORT) 2000	200		
PELISSIER ET AL (MALES) 2000	1842		
PELISSIER ET AL (FEMALES) 2000	473		
TUNIS ET AL (SAID) 1995	374		
ZHANG ('92-93 COHORT) 2000	854		
OREGON DOC 1994	240		
GRANSKY & JONES 1995	415		
TUNIS ET AL (NEW BEGIN) 1995	166		
EISENBERG 2001	5746		
SEALOCK ET AL 1997	520		
DUGAN & EVERETT 1998	117		
MAGURA ET AL (MALES) 1993	149		
SHAW & MACKENZIE 1992	256		
SIEGAL ET AL 1997	726		
MAGURA ET AL (FEMALES) 1993	100		

Overall Mean Odds-Ratio

.1   .25   .50 .75 1   2   5   10   25
Odds-Ratio

Notes:

JET = Jail Education and Treatment

DEUCE = Deciding, Evaluating, Understanding, Counseling, and Evaluation

REACH = Rebuilding, Educating, Awareness, Counseling, and Hope

SAID = Substance Abuse Intervention Division

NEW BEGIN = New Beginnings

ITC = In-prison Therapeutic Community

unpublished sources, it appears unlikely that publication bias meaningfully influenced the results of the following analyses.

Figure 1 is a forest plot of the distribution of the odds ratios. In this figure, each treatment-comparison contrast is identified on the far left and on the right is the odds ratio for that study represented by a diamond and the 95% confidence interval represented by the horizontal line. The overall mean random-effects odds ratio effect size and confidence interval is displayed at the very bottom of the forest plot. Those confidence intervals that do not cross the centerline (an odds ratio of 1) are statistically significant.

From this plot it is apparent that 24 of the 32 (75%) effect sizes favored the treatment group over the comparison group. Fourteen of the effect sizes (44%) favoring the treatment group were statistically significant, whereas only two effect sizes (6%) favoring the comparison group were statistically significant. The overall mean odds ratio was 1.25, with the 95% confidence interval ranging from a lower bound of 1.07 to an upper bound of 1.45, indicating that, on average, participation in these drug treatment programs was associated with a small reduction in post-treatment offending. A more intuitive sense of this effect size can be gained by transforming this effect size into a percentage. If we assume a 50% recidivism rate for the comparison group, the overall mean odds ratio translates into a recidivism rate of 44.5% for the treatment group; thus, a mean effect size of this magnitude translates into an 11% reduction in recidivism.[5]

The distribution displayed in Figure 1 shows considerable variability in the effect of the drug treatment programs ($Q = 198.34$, $df = 31$, $p < 0.001$). This suggests that features of the treatment programs, research methodology, and/or characteristics of the sample may moderate the size of the observed treatment effect. The following analyses investigated whether these features were systematically related to the magnitude of effects.

Table 1 presents a bivariate analysis of the magnitude of recidivism effect sizes with coded methodological features. Perhaps the most striking aspect of these analyses is the overall methodological weakness of this body of research. The majority of the effect sizes were generated by standard quasi-experimental evaluations (14 effect sizes) or weak quasi-experimental evaluations (7 effect sizes). Only three of the effect sizes came from evaluations using randomized experimental designs, and eight other effect sizes were obtained from rigorous quasi-experimental designs. Yet, even when only the results from these 11 more rigorous ones are considered, participation in incarceration-based drug treatment is associated with a statistically significant reduction in recidivism. This is important as it indicates that the general finding of a benefit of drug treatment was not confined to studies with methodologically weak research designs.

Only two of the eight methodological features were associated with treatment effectiveness. Specifically, estimates of program effectiveness were influenced by the type of recidivism measure utilized by the evaluators: evaluations that measured recidivism in terms of convictions produced larger estimates of treatment effectiveness and studies that used "other" measures of recidivism (such as probation or parole revocation) were associated with smaller effect sizes. As previously stated, studies with considerable overall attrition (i.e., attrition from both groups) were associated with smaller effect sizes.

There is widespread belief that treatment works differentially for different people (National Institute of Drug Abuse, 1999). We failed to find evidence of this notion. None of the participant characteristics were statistically associated with treatment effectiveness. Table 2 presents the results of a bivariate analysis similar to the above analysis of methodological features. Only four characteristics of study participants were consistently reported by evaluators: age, gender, race, and type of sample (violent or non-violent offenders). From this table it is evident that none of the participant characteristics were found to have a substantively meaningful or statistically significant relationship with effect size magnitude. This finding holds regardless of whether age or gender are measured by ordinal variables (as shown in Table 2) or as continuous variables (not shown).

---

5 It should be noted that, because of the non-linearity of the odds ratio, assuming a 50% recidivism rate for the comparison group maximizes the percentage difference in recidivism rates for the treatment and comparison groups. That is, if we assumed any other recidivism rate for the comparison group, the percentage difference between the two groups would be smaller. This translation is for heuristic purposes only.

TABLE 1.   *Recidivism Odds Ratio and 95% Confidence Interval by Method Variables*

Method variable	Mean odds ratio	95% confidence interval		k^a
		Lower	Upper	
Overall Method Quality				
Experimental design, low attrition	1.46	0.86	2.46	3
Rigorous quasi-experiment	1.17	0.85	1.60	8
Standard Quasi-experiment	1.25	0.96	1.61	14
Weak quasi-experiment	1.25	0.89	1.76	7
Randomly assigned to conditions				
Yes	1.46	0.86	2.46	3
No	1.22*	1.03	1.46	29
Used group-level matching				
Yes	1.37	0.99	1.91	9
No	1.20	0.99	1.46	23
Used multivariate data analysis				
Yes	1.14	0.92	1.42	19
No	1.40*	1.09	1.79	13
Used statistical significance testing				
Yes	1.27	1.07	1.51	29
No	1.27	0.63	1.72	3
Overall attrition apparent[†]				
Yes	0.97	0.70	1.34	9
No	1.34*	1.09	1.65	20
Differential attrition apparent				
Yes	0.94	1.07	1.58	6
No	1.30*	0.62	1.41	23
Recidivism measure[†]				
Arrest	1.29*	1.07	1.56	19
Conviction	1.53*	1.04	2.56	6
Re-incarceration	1.26	0.81	1.98	3
Other (e.g., revocation)	0.69	0.42	1.12	4

[a] k = number of effect sizes included in analysis.
* $p < .05$ for test of mean odds ratio is equal to 1; i.e., rejects hypothesis of equality of mean odds ratios (recidivism rates) between treatment and comparison samples.
[†] $p < .05$ for test of difference between mean odds ratios; i.e., rejects hypothesis of equality of mean odds ratios between levels of moderator variable.

Characteristics of each intervention were also coded. Selected results are shown in Table 3. From this table it is apparent that the magnitude of effect sizes varied significantly by type of intervention (TC, group counseling, boot camp, or methadone maintenance), with TCs having the largest mean effect size and methadone maintenance programs having the smallest mean effect size. In fact, TC and group counseling interventions were both found to be associated with statistically significant positive effect sizes; the observed mean odds ratio of TC programs was substantial, suggesting that participation in such programs was associated with a 20% reduction in recidivism (if we assume a 50% recidivism rate in comparison samples). In contrast, participants in methadone maintenance programs were

TABLE 2. *Recidivism Odds Ratio and 95% Confidence Interval by Sample Characteristics*

Sample characteristics	Mean odds ratio	95% confidence interval		k^a
		Lower	Upper	
Age group of sample				
Juveniles	1.08	0.69	1.70	3
Adults	1.27*	1.08	1.49	29
Gender mix				
All male	1.35*	1.02	1.79	13
Mixed (male and female)	1.17	0.82	1.67	8
All female	1.05	0.67	1.66	6
Race				
50% or less non-white	1.36	0.87	2.12	5
51%–70% non-white	1.53*	1.13	2.08	11
More than 70% non-white	1.06	0.76	1.47	9
Offender type				
Non-violent offenders	1.28*	1.00	1.63	13
Mixed (violent and non-violent)	1.27*	1.02	1.57	16

[a] k = number of effect sizes included in analysis.

*$p < .05$ for test of mean odds ratio is equal to 1; i.e., rejects hypothesis of equality of mean odds ratios (recidivism rates) between treatment and comparison samples.

found to have statistically significantly greater rates of recidivism than non-participants. Further, boot camp programs did not appear to provide any rehabilitative benefits with respect to future criminal behavior.

Table 3 also reveals that none of the other intervention characteristics were meaningfully related to effect size. Contrary to conventional wisdom (see e.g., MacKenzie, 2002), programs that included aftercare components were not associated with larger effect sizes. While this finding is interesting, many of the programs incorporating an aftercare component did not adequately describe the aftercare treatment, which leaves open the possibility that some of these aftercare programs may be minimal interventions. In concordance with principles of drug addiction treatment (National Institute of Drug Abuse, 1999), treatment programs of short duration (less than three months) were not associated with positive outcomes; however, longer interventions were statistically associated with reduced recidivism.

Drug Treatment and Post-Program Drug Use

Only 11 of the 31 independent program evaluations included in this review reported on drug use as an outcome, roughly half of which were TC evaluations. Only one group counseling/drug education intervention reported a drug use outcome and only two boot camps evaluations and two jail-based methadone maintenance programs did so. Nine of the 11 effect sizes (82%) favored the treatment group over the comparison group. The overall mean odds ratio from the 11 drug use effect sizes was 1.39, which was statistically significant and in

TABLE 3.   Recidivism Odds Ratio and 95% Confidence Interval by Program Characteristics

| Program characteristics | Mean odds ratio | 95% confidence interval | | k^a |
		Lower	Upper	
Type of program[†]				
Therapeutic community	1.47*	1.22	1.77	17
Group counseling	1.25*	1.00	1.56	10
Boot camp	1.00	0.66	1.52	3
Methadone maintenance	0.31*	0.17	0.59	2
Aftercare component				
Yes	1.16	0.99	1.62	15
No	1.26	0.99	1.47	15
Treatment location				
Jail	1.12	0.84	1.51	11
Prison	1.43*	1.13	1.81	14
Other (e.g., work release)	1.09	0.79	1.51	7
Program maturity				
New Program	1.40*	1.06	1.84	11
Developing Program	0.99	0.71	1.38	9
Established Program	1.46*	1.05	2.05	8
Treatment Length[†]				
Less than 3 months	1.06	0.81	1.38	11
Greater than 3 months	1.39	1.12	1.72	17

[a] k = number of effect sizes included in analysis.
* $p < .05$ for test of mean odds ratio is equal to 1; i.e., rejects hypothesis of equality of mean odds ratios (recidivism rates) between treatment and comparison samples.
[†] $p < .05$ for test of difference between mean odds ratios; i.e., rejects hypothesis of equality of mean odds ratios between levels of moderator variable.

favor of the treatment group. If we assume a 50% drug use rate for comparison participants, this mean odds ratio effect size translates into a 42% drug use rate for treatment participants. Once again, however, the effectiveness of the various programs included in this analysis varied widely, from modest positive effects to modest negative effects. This suggests that there may be moderator variables that can account for this excess variability in treatment effects.

The small number of drug use effect sizes necessitates that all findings be interpreted as only suggestive. In agreement with the analysis of the recidivism effect sizes, type of treatment program was strongly related to treatment effect. Once again, TC programs had the largest positive treatment effect, with a mean odds ratio of 1.83. In fact, the apparent effect of TC programs was substantial; if we continue to assume a 50% failure rate for comparison samples, the observed mean odds ratio translates into a drug relapse rate of 35% for participants of TCs. Also in agreement with the results from the recidivism analysis, participation in boot camp programs was not associated with reductions in drug use in comparison to standard criminal justice treatment. However, in contrast to the recidivism analysis, participation in methadone maintenance programs was associated with reductions in drug use.

CONCLUSIONS AND POLICY IMPLICATIONS

The above findings suggest that offenders with substance abuse problems who participate in incarceration-based drug treatment programs are less likely to reoffend and relapse into drug use than drug using offenders who do not participate in these programs. Based on the mean odds ratios from the above analyses, participation in incarceration-based drug treatment is expected to reduce recidivism by approximately 11% and drug use by 16% (if we assume a 50% failure rate for comparison samples). Methodologically rigorous evaluations produced similar mean estimates of treatment effectiveness as less rigorous evaluations, suggesting that findings of treatment benefits were not confined to methodologically weak evaluations. The generally weak methodology of these studies, however, allows for the possibility that the positive findings are affected by selection bias, reinforcing a need for more methodologically rigorous studies.

The incarceration-based drug treatment programs reviewed here varied substantially in effectiveness by type of treatment. The available evidence suggests that more intensive programs, such as TCs (which immerse participants in a treatment oriented environment), are more effective in reducing criminal behavior than the other programs examined here. These programs exhibited substantial reductions in recidivism and drug use; in fact, participants in TC programs were 20% less likely to recidivate and 30% less likely to relapse into drug use than samples of non-participants. Participation in less intensive drug treatment programs, such as group counseling, was also associated with reductions in criminal behavior; these observed effects, however, were considerably smaller than those observed in evaluations of TCs. By contrast, correctional boot camps with their focus on physical activity and discipline were not found to be effective in reducing criminal behavior.

These findings suggest that drug treatment programs that are intensive and focused at the multiple personal problems underlying drug use are more likely to be effective. Because of methodological shortcomings in the existing research and gaps in our knowledge regarding which components of drug treatment programs are actually responsible for the observed treatment benefits, this conclusion is necessarily tentative. Before more firm conclusions can be drawn, both the number and quality of research studies must be increased. Future research should not simply test for differences in recidivism between participants and non-participants; rather, it should carefully construct groups of non-participants to closely match participants or use random assignment to conditions. These evaluations should also examine intervening processes hypothesized to lead to reductions in criminal behavior. For example, treatment programs including a cognitive behavioral component should assess change in anti-social attitudes, beliefs, and cognitions. Furthermore, future evaluations need to determine which program aspects are the active ingredients in successful treatment outcomes; for instance, TC programs could determine whether treatment sessions led by clients or professional staff are most effective by varying this component. Other programs could similarly add, remove, or vary components thought to be important in order to determine these components' influences on treatment outcomes.

In spite of the limits of our current knowledge, the strength and consistency of existing findings indicate that policymakers seeking effective interventions for incarcerated substance abusers are most likely to find success with programs intensively focused on the multiple problems of substance abusers, such as TC programs. Policymakers should expect smaller treatment benefits from less intensive drug treatment programs. Further, correctional boot camps targeted at substance abusers, at least in their present form, cannot reasonably be expected to reduce criminal behavior or drug use. The continued existence and proliferation of boot camps must be justified on other grounds.

REFERENCES

*References marked with an asterisk (*) were included in the systematic review.

Belenko, Steven, Jordon. Peugh, and Joseph A. Califano. 1998. *Behind Bars: Substance Abuse and America's Prison Population.* New York: National Center on Addiction and Substance Abuse at Columbia University.

*Dugan, John R., and Ronald S. Everett. 1998. An Experimental Test of Chemical Dependency Therapy for Jail Inmates. *International Journal of Offender Therapy and Comparative Criminology* 42: 360–368.

*Eisenberg, Michael. 2001. *The Substance Abuse Felony Punishment Program: Evaluation and Recommendations.* Austin, TX: Criminal Justice Policy Council.

*Eisenberg, Michael, and Tony Fabelo. 1996. Evaluation of the Texas Correctional Substance Abuse Treatment Initiative: The Impact of Policy Research. *Crime & Delinquency* 42: 296–308.

Farrington, David P., Denise C. Gottfredson, Lawrence W. Sherman, and Brandon C. Welsh. 2002. "The Maryland Scientific Methods Scale." In *Evidence-Based Crime Prevention*, edited by Lawrence W. Sherman, David P. Farrington, Brandon C. Welsh, and Doris Layton MacKenzie, 13–21. New York, NY: Routledge.

Field, Gary. 1985. The Cornerstone Program: A Client Outcome Study. *Federal Probation* 49: 50–55.

———. 1989. *A Study of the Effects of Intensive Treatment on Reducing the Criminal Recidivism of Addicted Offenders.* Unpublished manuscript. Salem, OR: Oregon Correctional Treatment Programs.

Gerstein, Dean R., and Hernick J. Harwood, eds. 1990. *Treating Drug Problems: A Study of the Evolution, Effectiveness, and Financing of Public and Private Drug Treatment Systems.* Washington, DC: National Academy Press.

*Gransky, Laura A., and Robert J. Jones. 1995. *Evaluation of the Post-Release Status of Substance Abuse Program Participants.* Chicago: Illinois Criminal Justice Information Authority.

*Hartmann, David J., James L. Wolk, L. Scott Johnston, and Corey J. Colyer. 1997. Recidivism and Substance Abuse Outcomes in a Prison-Based Therapeutic Community. *Federal Probation* 61: 18–25.

Hasselblad, Vic, and Larry V. Hedges. 1995. Meta-Analysis of Screening and Diagnostic Tests. *Psychological Bulletin* 117: 167–178.

*Hughey, Ray, and Lloyd W. Klemke. 1996. Evaluation of a Jail-Based Substance Abuse Treatment Program. *Federal Probation* 60: 40–44.

*Inciardi, James A., Steven S. Martin, Clifford A. Butzin, Robert M. Hooper, and Lana D. Harrison. 1997. An Effective Model of Prison-Based Treatment for Drug-Involved Offenders. *Journal of Drug Issues* 27: 261–279.

*Knight, Kevin, D. Dwayne Simpson, and Matthew Hiller. 1999. Three-Year Reincarceration

Outcomes for In-Prison Therapeutic Community Treatment in Texas. *Prison Journal* 79: 337–351.

Lipsey, Mark W., and David B. Wilson. 2001. *Practical Meta-Analysis.* Thousand Oaks, CA: Sage.

Lipton, Douglas S. 1995. *The Effectiveness of Treatment for Drug Abusers Under Criminal Justice Supervision.* Washington, DC: National Institute of Justice, U.S. Department of Justice.

——. 1998. Treatment for Drug Abusing Offenders During Correctional Supervision: A Nationwide Overview. *Journal of Offender Rehabilitation* 26: 1–45.

*Little, Gregory L., Kenneth D. Robinson, and Katherine D. Burnette. 1991. Treating Drug Offenders with Moral Reconation Therapy: A Three-Year Recidivism Report. *Psychological Reports* 69: 1151–1154.

Lo, Celia C., and Richard C. Stephens. 2000. Drugs and Prisoners: Treatment Needs on Entering Prison. *American Journal of Drug and Alcohol Abuse* 26: 229–245.

MacKenzie, Doris Layton. 2002. "Reducing the Criminal Activities of Known Offenders and Delinquents: Crime Prevention in the Courts and Corrections. In *Evidence-Based Crime Prevention,* edited by Lawrence W. Sherman, David P. Farrington, Brandon C. Welsh, and Doris Layton MacKenzie, 330–404. New York: Routledge.

*Magura, Stephen, Andrew Lewis, Carla Rosenblum, and Herman Joseph. 1993. The Effectiveness of In-Jail Methadone Maintenance. *Journal of Drug Issues* 23: 75–99.

Mumola, Christopher J. 1999. *Substance Abuse and Treatment, State and Federal Prisoners, 1997.* Washington, DC: Bureau of Justice Statistics, U.S. Department of Justice.

National Institute of Drug Abuse. 1999. *Principles of Drug Addiction Treatment: A Research-Based Guide.* Washington, DC: National Institutes of Health.

*Oregon Department of Corrections. 1994. *Comparison of Outcomes and Costs: Residential and Outpatient Treatment Programs for Inmates: Alcohol and Drug, Mental Health, Sex Offender, and Social Skills Treatment.* Salem, OR: Oregon Department of Corrections.

*Pelissier, Bernadette, William Rhodes, William Saylor, Gerry Gaes, Scott D. Camp, Suzy D. Vanyur, and Sue Wallace. 2000. *TRIAD Drug Treatment Evaluation Project Final Report of Three-Year Outcomes: Part I.* Washington, DC: Office of Research and Evaluation, Federal Bureau of Prisons, U.S. Department of Justice.

Peters, Roger H., Paul E. Greenbaum, John F. Edens, Chris R. Carter, and Madeline M. Ortiz. 1998. Prevalence of DSM-IV Substance Abuse and Dependence Disorders Among Prison Inmates. *American Journal of Drug and Alcohol Abuse* 24: 573–587.

*Peters, Roger H., William D. Kearns, Mary R. Murrin, Addis S. Dolente, and Robert L. May II. 1993. Examining the Effectiveness of In-Jail Substance Abuse Treatment. *Journal of Offender Rehabilitation* 19: 1–39.

Prendergast, Michael L., Jean Wellisch, and Mamie Mee Wong. 1996. Residential Treatment for Women Parolees Following Prison-Based Drug Treatment Experiences, Needs and Services, and Outcomes. *Prison Journal* 76: 253–274.

*Sealock, Miriam D., Denise C. Gottfredson, and Catherine A. Gallagher. 1997. Drug Treatment for Juvenile Offenders: Some Good and Bad News. *Journal of Research in Crime and Delinquency* 34: 210–236.

*Shaw, James W., and Doris L. MacKenzie. 1992. The One-Year Community Supervision Performance of Drug Offenders and Louisiana DOC-Identified Substance Abusers Graduating from Shock Incarceration. *Journal of Criminal Justice* 20: 501–516.

*Siegal, Harvey A., Jichuan Wang, Russel S. Falck, Ahmmed M. Rahman, and Robert G. Carlson. 1997. *An Evaluation of Ohio's Prison-Based Therapeutic Community Treatment Programs for Substance Abusers: Final Report.* Dayton, OH: School of Medicine, Wright State University.

*Smith, Cindy J. 1996. *The California Civil Addict Program: An Evaluation of Implementation and Effectiveness.* Unpublished Ph.D. dissertation. Irvine, CA: University of California, Irvine.

Substance Abuse and Mental Health Services Administration Office of Applied Studies (SAMSHA). 1998. *Preliminary Results from the 1997 National Household Survey on Drug Abuse.* Rockville, MD: Office of Applied Studies, Substance Abuse and Mental Health Services Administration.

*Taxman, Faye S., and David L. Spinner. 1996. *The Jail Addiction Services (JAS) Project in Montgomery County, Maryland.* College Park, MD: University of Maryland.

*Tunis, Sandra, James Austin, Mark Morris, Patricia Hardyman, and Melissa Bolyard. 1995. *Evaluation of Drug Treatment in Local Corrections: Final Report*. San Francisco, CA: National Council on Crime and Delinquency.

*Washington State Department of Corrections. 1988. *Substance Abuse Treatment Program Evaluation of Outcomes and Management Report*. Olympia, WA: Author.

*Wexler, Harry K., Gregory P. Falkin, and Douglas S. Lipton. 1990. Outcome Evaluation of a Prison Therapeutic Community for Substance Abuse Treatment. *Criminal Justice and Behavior* 17: 71–92.

*Wexler, Harry K., Wendy F. Graham, Renee Koronkowski, and Lois Lowe. 1995. *Amity Therapeutic Community Substance Abuse Program: Preliminary Return to Custody Data – May 1995*. Laguna Beach, CA: National Development and Research Institutes.

*Wexler, Harry W., George DeLeon, George Thomas, David Kressell, and Jean Peters. 1999a. The Amity Prison TC Evaluation: Reincarceration Outcomes. *Criminal Justice and Behavior* 26: 147–167.

*Wexler, Harry K., Gerald Melnick, Lois Lowe, and Jean Peters. 1999b. Three-Year Reincarceration Outcomes for Amity In-Prison Therapeutic Community and Aftercare in California. *Prison Journal* 79: 321–336.

*Zhang, Sheldon. 2000. *An Evaluation of the Los Angeles County Juvenile Drug Treatment Boot Camp: Final Report*. San Marcos, CA: California State University.

CHAPTER 8

COSTS AND BENEFITS OF SENTENCING

Cynthia McDougall
University of York

Mark A. Cohen
Vanderbilt University

Amanda Perry
University of York

Raymond Swaray
University of York

INTRODUCTION

Since the early 1990's there has been a move towards an evidence-based criminal justice policy internationally and in the United Kingdom. The development of 'what works' programs has provided a model for the evaluation of the effectiveness of current criminal justice interventions on the basis of research evidence. More recently, it has also become necessary to evaluate programs based on their relative costs and benefits, providing information not only on 'what works' with 'which offenders', but also 'at what cost' and with 'what benefits.'

Evaluating the cost of criminal justice programs is not new to the criminal justice field, since virtually all programs require the support of a funding agency that is likely to request budget information. Government agencies routinely report on annual expenditures on police, courts, prisons, and various program interventions. Until recently, however, there have been few attempts to ask the related question of what these programs are actually buying in terms of crime control or public safety. Such analyses are termed 'cost-effectiveness' studies since they ask how much crime reduction (or other social benefit) is obtained per dollar spent. Even fewer studies have gone beyond this question to ask whether the benefits of the program exceed its costs, that is, by conducting a 'cost-benefit' study.

The differences between cost-effectiveness and cost-benefit analyses are not well understood. One such definition provided by Barnett and Escobar (1990) suggests that cost-effectiveness is an 'incomplete' form of cost-benefit analysis because it fails to assign monetary values to the outcomes involved (i.e., benefits

Brandon C. Welsh and David P. Farrington, eds.
Preventing Crime: What Works for Children, Offenders, Victims, and Places, 117–127
© 2007 *Springer.*

and/or dis-benefits), but focuses only on the costs (resources) used. A cost-effectiveness study provides information on the cost of X dollars needed to prevent Y crimes. A cost-benefit analysis evaluates both the costs and benefits of a program or intervention, providing a complete analysis of a program or sentencing option in terms of monetary tangible and intangible costs and benefits. The product of such an analysis is a benefit-cost ratio, which provides a single measurement of the monetary benefit derived from one monetary dollar. This is a much more sensitive measure of benefit than simple reconviction data, as it takes into account levels of seriousness of the offense, numbers of offenses in a time period, and in particular takes a victim perspective in terms of costs of an offense to the victim, both tangible and intangible. When these factors are related to the amount of resource required to achieve the benefits of crime averted, the benefit-cost ratio becomes a very powerful measure.

To date, very few studies have attempted to systematically review the literature on the economic costs and benefits of crime control programs. One exception is the recent review conducted by Welsh and Farrington (2000), which examined correctional interventions such as drug treatment, educational programs, and other forms of interventions in the context of corrections. The authors identified only seven published studies that met the criteria of their review. One reason that so few cost-benefit studies have been conducted is the dearth of evidence on the cost of crime, as endured by victims. Tangible costs for victims may be their out-of-pocket losses, such as medical costs or lost wages; however, the largest component of victim costs is the intangible losses such as pain, suffering, and lost quality of life. More recently, there has been a growing body of literature attempting to fill in that gap by estimating intangible losses.

While conducting the current systematic review of the costs and benefits of sentencing, it became evident that there was a need for an economic scale against which to measure the quality of the cost-benefit methodologies applied to the studies. A new rating scale, the Cost-Benefit Validity Scale (Cohen et al., 2002) has therefore been developed to assess the quality of cost-benefit studies and to assist future researchers in structuring their studies so that a valid benefit-cost ratio can be estimated.

The Cost-Benefit Validity Scale (see Figure 1) was developed using an approach similar to the University of Maryland Scientific Methods Scale (SMS; Sherman et al., 1997). The purpose of the scale is to measure the extent to which the methodology employed in a cost-benefit study is sufficiently comprehensive for conclusions to be drawn about a program's costs and benefits. A higher score on the Cost-Benefit Validity Scale indicates that the cost and benefit information is generally of higher quality and can be used for more policy analysis purposes than a lower number.

BACKGROUND

There is an ongoing debate about the effectiveness of sentencing, and in recent years has been of special interest in the UK, where a review of sentencing policy

FIGURE 1.   Cost-Benefit Validity Scale

Level 1   Cost Studies
          Relevant program costs (or averted program costs) are fully assessed in monetary terms.
Level 2   Cost-Effectiveness Studies
          Relevant program costs (or averted program costs) and effectiveness measures are included,
          but the effectiveness measures are not monetized.
Level 3   Partial Cost-Benefit Analysis
          A cost-benefit ratio is included in the study, but costs and benefits are incomplete, hence
          there is lack of confidence in the direction of the ratio.
Level 4   Valid Cost-Benefit Analysis
          A cost-benefit ratio is included, with sufficient costs and benefits information to rate a valid
          analysis, with confidence in the direction of the ratio.
Level 5   Complete Cost-Benefit Analysis
          A cost-benefit ratio is included, based on calculation of all appropriate costs and benefits,
          giving a complete analysis, with confidence in the direction and the size of the ratio.

(Halliday, 2001) led to a Government White Paper and a proposed new Criminal Justice Bill, intended to bring about major changes in sentencing legislation. The systematic review of the costs and benefits of sentencing (McDougall et al., 2003) was carried out at the request of the Economic Resource and Analysis Unit in the UK Home Office. Although it was known that many studies had been conducted on the effectiveness of sentencing, less was known about how much international research was available providing costs and benefits information on sentencing. This review was conducted to answer that specific question, and it should be noted that the review does not therefore cover the large body of research evidence on effectiveness of sentencing, but has only concentrated on those studies which applied cost and benefit methodologies to sentencing processes.

SUMMARY OF RESEARCH METHODS

The methods applied followed closely those described in the guidelines of the Centre for Reviews and Dissemination (1996). Seven databases of research studies, abstracts, and citations were searched for publications that were related to sentencing in the period between 1980 and 2001. In addition, the grey literature and the World Wide Web were searched for further reports, conference papers, and web-sites that might hold additional information. Full details of the searches are included in McDougall et al. (2003). Studies were screened for inclusion in the review using the Cost-Benefit Validity Scale. Only those studies that received a level 3 or higher were included. As a secondary rating, the SMS was used to measure the level of scientific quality in each of the reviewed studies, but was not used to exclude studies.

Following a thorough search of the international literature, only nine studies satisfied our designated criteria for inclusion in the final review. Key elements of these nine studies are described in the next section.

Of the nine studies identified, only six were considered to have either a 'complete' or 'valid' cost-benefit analysis. Two studies were rated 5 on the Cost-Benefit Validity Scale, each providing a 'complete' cost-benefit analysis. Four studies were rated 4, a 'valid' cost-benefit analysis, and three studies scored 3 on the Cost-Benefit Validity Scale, described as a 'partial' cost-benefit analysis.

RESULTS

Since the number of studies included in the present systematic review is small, these are discussed in terms of related international findings on effectiveness in sentencing.

As noted above, the Cost-Benefit Validity Scale was the primary method of evaluating the economic quality of studies. In some of these studies, however, the scientific rigor of the research design was not strong. Results of such studies should therefore be treated with caution, even though the cost-benefit analysis may have been 'complete' or 'valid'.

What Is Cost-Beneficial?

Five program types were found to be cost-beneficial:

- Sex offender treatment in prison (two studies: Donato and Shanahan, 1999;);
- Drug treatment pre-trial diversion;
- Imprisonment for high-risk repeat offenders – but with diminishing returns;
- Intensive supervision following shock incarceration; and
- Family and juvenile offender treatment programs compared to parole.

Sex Offender Treatment. Only two of the cost-beneficial studies covered the same sentencing option – sex offender treatment programs. The Donato and Shanahan (1999) study was a review of existing studies. They looked at a range of studies of child sex offenders that demonstrated reduced recidivism through cognitive-behavioral sex-offender treatment programs, and on that basis calculated the costs of programs against the benefits of crimes averted by reduced recidivism.

While the Donato and Shanahan (1999) study was not in itself a program evaluation, and would thus rate low on the SMS, it is of considerable value as a cost-benefit study. Donato and Shanahan (1999) found that the increased cost of in-prison sex offender treatment programs was outweighed by the additional benefits in reduced recidivism.

The other study by Prentky and Burgess (1990) presented a 'valid' cost-benefit analysis of treatment for child sex offenders in a maximum-security residential facility, but there was no control group and recidivism rates were based only on treated residents on release. Data for untreated offenders was taken from a study by Marshall and Barbaree (1988).

Prentky and Burgess (1990) found that sex offender treatment program benefits exceeded their costs, as did Donato and Shanahan (1999), lending some degree of confidence in this finding, especially once it is coupled with the fact that MacKenzie (1997; 2002) found cognitive behavioral programs generally to work.

The MacKenzie (1997; 2002) reviews of 'effectiveness' research support sex offender treatment programs as being effective in reducing reconvictions, both in prison and in the community.

Drug Treatment Pre-Trial Diversion.   Mauser et al. (1994) evaluated the economic impact of treatment alternative programs (TAP) by examining the benefits and costs of diverting offenders from the criminal justice system into substance abuse treatment. The costs of the program included drug testing, overhead costs of running the program, case management services, detoxification, residential care, alcohol and other drug abuse (AODA) education, medical care, and cost of screening and assessment.

The Mauser et al. (1994) study, although containing a 'valid' cost-benefit analysis, did not have a control group, and the number of participants in the evaluation was small. The study concluded that pre-trial diversion to drug treatment was cost-beneficial, using the main outcome measure of savings to the criminal justice system by averting prison costs. This finding is supported by MacKenzie (1997; 2002) who found that drug treatment combined with urine testing was 'promising' in terms of effectiveness, as were drug courts combining both rehabilitation and criminal justice control.

Imprisonment for High-Risk Repeat Offenders.   This study by Piehl and DiIulio (1995) was one of only two 'complete' cost-benefit analyses identified in this systematic review. Piehl and DiIulio (1995) used known costs of incarceration, assessments of re-offending rates from a prisoner self-report survey of 4% of male entrants to state prisons (711,000 adults), and savings in crimes averted by incapacitation, comparing the costs of an additional year in prison to the benefits of reduced crimes. Their conclusion was that 'prison pays for most state prisoners' and comprised either violent or repeat offenders who presented a real danger to the physical safety or property of their community. However, Piehl and DiIulio (1995) did point out that the incapacitation of criminals is subject to the law of diminishing returns and concluded that for 25% of the sample group, essentially made up of offenders committing high-rate auto thefts at a rate of three a year, burglaries at a rate of six a year, and petty thefts at a rate of 24 a year, costs of imprisonment outweighed the social benefits of imprisonment. Piehl and DiIulio concluded that there could be beneficial savings if 10% to 25% of the prison sample were given a non-custodial sentence.

In her review of the research evidence, Mackenzie (1997; 2002) found support for the imprisonment of high-risk repeat offenders in preventing crime. We agree that there are diminishing returns. There also needs to be a greater awareness of the fact that the "impact [of high levels of imprisonment] on ethnic minority communities has been disastrous" (MacKenzie, 2002: 386).

The Piehl and DiIulio (1995) conclusion, that the costs of imprisonment in many cases outweighed the benefits, was considered to be particularly true in the case of drug offenders. They argue that the incapacitation effect of imprisonment on drug-only offenders is zero, and they value drug crimes (sales and possession) as zero social cost. A similar conclusion was reached by Caulkins (1997). Using an economic model, Caulkins found that enhanced sentences were not cost-effective for drug dealers, except high-level dealers.

Intensive Supervision Following Shock Incarceration. Pearson (1988) and Pearson and Harper (1990) evaluated an Intensive Supervision (ISP) program that incorporated a short period of 'shock' incarceration followed by intensive supervision that included face-to-face contacts, curfew checks, and drug tests. The program excluded violent offenders and required participants to be employed (if fit for employment) and provide a minimum of 16 hours per month of community service. They found that the ISP cost less than prison and yielded lower levels of recidivism than the control group that was given prison. The studies did not contain a complete cost-benefit analysis, omitting the intangible benefits of reduced crime. However, even if we incorporated the intangible benefits of reduced crime into the equation, the basic result – that the benefits of the intensive supervision program exceeded its costs – would still hold (even more so).

In addition to the validity of the Pearson (1988) and Pearson and Harper (1990) benefit-cost ratios, the studies were also among the better research designs. The ISP groups had significantly lower reconviction rates at the end of two years. The ISP results are, however, contrary to a substantial amount of other research evidence (see Sherman et al., 1997; 2002). Summarized by MacKenzie (2002), there is no evidence that recidivism is reduced by increasing the surveillance and other restraints over offenders on ISP. In fact, the increased surveillance may be associated with increases in technical violations. However, MacKenzie (2002) acknowledged that insufficient research has been conducted on ISP combined with other interventions (e.g., ISP combining restraints with treatment). There is evidence that increased treatment associated with ISP may be related to reduced rearrests (Petersilia and Turner, 1993).

Family and Juvenile Offender Treatment Programs Vs. Parole. The Roberts and Camasso (1991) study was rated as having a 'valid' cost-benefit analysis. While the authors did not include all benefits from the programs being studied, the additional information would not have changed the direction of the benefit-cost ratio. Two studies were described by Roberts and Camasso (1991). One study was of a family treatment program in which two co-therapists followed a model where the family is viewed as a system with family members behaving in a maladaptive and dysfunctional way to the delinquent. The family is required to change as a unit. The second study was of a youth wilderness program in which juveniles were placed in an outdoor experiential program, given challenging and structured opportunities to exercise self-discipline and overcome challenging physical and psychological obstacles through individual and group effort.

Both programs were found by Roberts and Camasso (1991) to be cost-benefi-cial. The family treatment program was the less rigorous of the two in terms of experimental design, as there was no control group. The youth wilderness program did have a control group, matched by age, IQ, race, religion, current offense, and prior adjudications, whose subjects underwent routine Division of Youth Services processing and parole.

There is research support for the effectiveness of family-based crime prevention programs (see Farrington and Welsh, 2002) but, since most of the programs are multi-dimensional, it has not been possible to identify the active ingredients of successful programs. Without a control group, it is not possible to be certain about the effectiveness of this program, although the authors consider it to be cost-beneficial.

Conversely, MacKenzie (1997; 2002) found no evidence that programs, of the type described in the youth wilderness program, were effective in reducing reconvictions. The Roberts and Camasso (1991) study was however well designed, and was judged to have a 'valid' cost-benefit analysis. Caution should however be taken in accepting results from a single study, which is contrary to most of the other research evidence.

Cost-Beneficial (Unknown)

This part includes studies in which the authors claim intervention is cost-beneficial, but the cost-benefit analysis quality is such that one cannot be certain that the direction of the benefit-cost ratio would not change if missing costs or benefits were included. There are three program types:

- House arrest with electronic monitoring;
- Early release from prison; and
- Burglars sentenced to probation vs. prison.

House Arrest with Electronic Monitoring.   Courtright et al. (1997) described a house arrest program with electronic monitoring that was developed to provide jails with relief from excessive overcrowding. This particular intermediate sentence required offenders to take part in alcohol/drug treatment and pay a daily fee for the electronic monitoring equipment and then a monthly fee for regular supervision. There were minimal technical violations of the conditions of this sentence.

While Courtright et al. reported that the benefits outweighed the costs of crime, they did not include all victim costs for offenses committed during electronic monitoring. When victim costs were included, that might well have resulted in costs outweighing benefits. There can therefore be no confidence in the direction of the benefit-cost ratio in this case.

Other authors (Bonta et al., 2000; Dodgson et al., 2001) have found that electronic monitoring did not deter re-offending, and hence offending should be taken into account when assessing costs of the intervention.

Early Release from Prison.   Similar problems of omission from the cost-benefit analysis applied in the Austin (1986) study. Austin (1986) compared a sample of offenders who were released early to a comparable sample who served their full prison term. While Austin (1986) reported that the benefits of early release programs outweighed their costs, Cohen (1988) argued that once intangible costs of crime (e.g., victim costs) were included in the analysis, costs outweighed benefits and the program failed to pass a benefit-cost test. For this reason there could not be confidence in the direction of the benefit-cost ratio calculated by Austin (1986).

Burglars Sentenced to Probation Vs. Prison. Gray and Olson (1989) conducted a cost-benefit analysis of probation, jail, or prison as alternative sentencing options for burglars. The authors used self-report and official arrest data published in a previous study (Haynes and Larsen, 1984), in which randomly selected sentenced burglars were included, but these had not been randomly sentenced to the probation, jail, or prison options. It was noted by the authors that the less serious offenders were sentenced to probation. Benefits from the three sentences were evaluated in terms of rehabilitation, incapacitation, and deterrence effects, calculating the number of offenses averted by these means.

Gray and Olson (1989) concluded that there were net social benefits to sentencing a burglar to probation, whereas in the case of jail or prison, costs exceeded benefits. In their cost-benefit analysis, Gray and Olson (1989), however, did not include all the possible benefits of crimes averted (e.g., intangible losses to victims). Had these been included in the case of prison and jail, the benefit-cost ratio might have changed direction with benefits exceeding costs. This however is unlikely to have occurred with the probation sentence. If benefits obtained from rehabilitation and hence crimes averted were under-estimated under this sentence, then the benefits might become even greater than the cost estimates, giving an increased benefit-cost ratio. In summary, therefore, one cannot be confident in the direction of the benefit-cost ratio in terms of imprisonment or jail, but can in the case of those sentenced to probation.

CONCLUSIONS AND POLICY IMPLICATIONS

The systematic review found that there are very few studies of sentencing that incorporated cost and benefit information and, of these, the standards of cost-benefit analysis and research design are variable. Therefore, caution must be exercised in drawing conclusions from these to inform policy unless there is other supporting evidence.

Based on the limited number of cost-benefit studies we were only able to generalize about one type of program that passed a cost-benefit test: sex offender treatment in a correctional setting. Four other programs were found to be 'promising' in cost-benefit terms. The results were as follows:

– Sex offender treatment in a secure institution passed a cost-benefit test.
– Family and juvenile offender treatment programs are promising but, without other research evidence, these results should be treated with caution.
– Intensive supervision following a period of incarceration is promising, but there is little supporting evidence for ISP, and the effect of ISP combined with other interventions is unknown.

- Pre-trial diversion programs with drug treatment are promising.
- Incarceration for high-risk repeat offenders is promising, but with diminishing returns for less serious offenders.

The application of research evidence is being seen in the development of government policy internationally, and in the UK it is evident that research has had an influence on proposals for sentencing reform (Halliday, 2001). The Halliday Report (2001) was set up to review the sentencing framework for England and Wales. It concluded that: "Reform and rehabilitation, within the 'punitive' envelope to reduce risks of re-offending, offers the best prospects for improved outcomes" (p. II). As a further objective the Halliday Report recognized "... the need for wider crime reduction strategies outside sentencing aimed at preventing offending ... ." (p. II).

The combination of rehabilitation within a punitive envelope is broadly supported by research evidence that structured risk-focused rehabilitation and cognitive-behavioral interventions are effective, and that punitive interventions alone are not effective (MacKenzie, 1997; 2002). Developmental prevention is also supported by research (Farrington and Welsh, 2002).

Evidence from the small number of studies in this review of the costs and benefits of sentencing would suggest that such approaches may also be cost-beneficial, particularly those incorporating sex offender treatment into custodial penalties (Donato and Shanahan, 1999; Prentky and Burgess, 1990) and pre-trial diversion with drug treatment (Mauser et al., 1994). In this systematic review the evidence linking the research to sentencing policy is sparse. However, the current direction of UK sentencing policy and the research on cost-benefit approaches appear to be congruent with the review findings.

Two other studies (Gray and Olson, 1989; Piehl and DiIulio, 1995) identified in the systematic review may contribute to public discussion about the use of imprisonment for particular offenses (e.g., burglary) and the rising prison population. These studies give an economic rather than a political perspective; however, it is evident that consideration should be given to determining at which point imprisonment ceases (or begins) to be cost-beneficial and a non-custodial alternative may or may not be appropriate. To date there is no specific research guidance on this, nor evidence on the types of offender for which a custodial sentence is or is not cost-beneficial. This is an appropriate question for further research.

Since there is so little research on the costs and benefits of sentencing, there is a clear need for future research. Strategies for implementation of new sentencing policies should incorporate a planned evaluation, rigorously conducted to quality research standards, with 'complete' cost-benefits analyses. Simultaneously, there is a need for routine application of cost-benefit analysis in research studies on sentencing and for development and standardization of cost-benefit analysis techniques, as highlighted by Halliday (2001) and Welsh and Farrington (2000). Only in this way will our store of knowledge on sentences be improved so that we can know 'what works', 'with whom', at 'what cost' and with 'what benefits.'

REFERENCES

Austin, James. 1986. Using Early Release to Relieve Prison Crowding: A Dilemma in Public Policy. *Crime & Delinquency* 32: 404–502.

Barnett, W. Steven, and Colette M. Escobar. 1990. "Economic Costs and Benefits of Early Intervention." In *Handbook of Early Childhood Intervention*, edited by Samuel J. Meisels and Jack P. Shonkoff, 560–582. New York: Cambridge University Press.

Bonta, James, and Suzanne Capretta Wallice, and Jennifer Rooney. 2000. Can Electronic Monitoring Make a Difference? An Evaluation of Three Canadian Programs. *Crime & Delinquency* 46: 61–75.

Caulkins, Jonathon. 1997. Sense and Sensitivity Analysis: Landmark Study Models the Cost Effectiveness of Mandatory Minimum Drug Sentences. *Operations Research/Management Science Today* 24: 24–28.

Centre for Reviews and Dissemination. 1996. *Undertaking Systematic Reviews of Research on Effectiveness*. CRD Report, No. 4. York, UK: University of York.

Cohen, Mark A. 1988. Pain, Suffering, and Jury Awards: A Study of the Cost of Crime to Victims. *Law and Society Review* 22: 537–555.

——, Raymond Swaray, and Cynthia McDougall. 2002. Cost-Benefit Validity Scale. Available at: www.york.ac.uk/criminaljustice/.

Courtright, Kevin E., Bruce L. Berg, and Robert J. Mutchnick. 1997. The Cost-Effectiveness of Using House Arrest with Electronic Monitoring for Drunk Drivers. *Federal Probation* 61: 19–22.

Dodgson, Kath, Phillippa Goodwin, Philip Howard, Sian Llewllyn-Thomas, Ed Mortimer, Neil Russell, and Mark Weiner. 2001. *Electronic Monitoring of Released Prisoners: An Evaluation of the Home Detention Curfew Scheme*. Home Office Research Study, No. 222. London: Home Office Research, Development and Statistics Directorate.

Donato, Ron, and Martin Shanahan. 1999. The Economics of Implementing Intensive In-Prison Sex Offender Treatment Programs. *Trends and Issues in Crime and Criminal Justice* 134. Canberra: Australian Institute of Criminology.

Farrington, David P., and Brandon C. Welsh. 2002. "Family-Based Crime Prevention." In *Evidence-Based Crime Prevention*, edited by Lawrence W. Sherman, David P. Farrington, Brandon C. Welsh, and Doris Layton MacKenzie, 22–55. London: Routledge.

Gray, Tara, and Kent W. Olson. 1989. A Cost-Benefit Analysis of the Sentencing Decision for Burglars. *Social Science Quarterly* 70: 708–722.

Halliday, John. 2001. *Making Punishment Work: Report of a Review of the Sentencing Framework for England and Wales*. London: Home Office.

Haynes, Peter, and Clark R. Larsen. 1984. Financial Consequences of Incarceration and Alternatives: Burglary. *Crime & Delinquency* 30: 529–550.

MacKenzie, Doris Layton. 1997. "Criminal Justice and Crime Prevention." In *Preventing Crime: What Works, What Doesn't, What's Promising*, by Lawrence W. Sherman, Denise C. Gottfredson, Doris Layton MacKenzie, John E. Eck, Peter Reuter, and Shawn D. Bushway, chapter 9. Washington, DC: National Institute of Justice, U.S. Department of Justice.

——. 2002. "Reducing the Criminal Activities of Known Offenders and Delinquents: Crime Prevention in the Courts and Corrections." In *Evidence-Based Crime Prevention*, edited by Lawrence W. Sherman, David P. Farrington, Brandon C. Welsh, and Doris Layton Mackenzie, 330–404. London: Routledge.

Marshall, William L., and Howard E. Barbaree. 1988. "An Out-Patient Treatment Program for Child Molesters." In *Human Sexual Aggression: Current Perspectives*, edited by Robert A. Prentky and Vernon L. Quinsey, 205–214. New York: Annals of the New York Academy of Sciences.

Mauser, Elizabeth, Kit R. Van Stelle, and D. Paul Moberg. 1994. The Economic Impact of Diverting Substance-Abusing Offenders into Treatment. *Crime & Delinquency* 40: 568–588.

McDougall, Cynthia, Mark A. Cohen, Raymond Swaray, and Amanda Perry. 2003. The Costs and Benefits of Sentencing: A Systematic Review. *Annals of the American Academy of Political and Social Science* 587: 160–177.

Pearson, Frank S. 1988. Evaluation of New Jersey's Intensive Supervision Program. *Crime & Delinquency* 34: 437–448.

——, and Alice G. Harper. 1990. Contingent Intermediate Sentences: New Jersey's Intensive Supervision Program. *Crime & Delinquency* 36: 75–86.

Piehl, Anne M., and John J. DiIulio. 1995. Does Prison Pay? Revisited. *Brookings Review* 13: 20–25.

Petersilia, Joan, and Susan Turner. 1993. *Evaluating Intensive Supervision Probation/Parole: Results of a Nationwide Experiment.* Washington, DC: National Institute of Justice, U.S. Department of Justice.

Prentky, Robert A., and Ann W. Burgess. 1990. Rehabilitation of Child Molesters: A Cost-Benefit Analysis. *American Journal of Orthopsychiatry* 60: 108–117.

Roberts, Albert R., and Michael J. Camasso. 1991. Juvenile Offender Treatment Programs and Cost-Benefit Analysis. *Juvenile and Family Court Journal* 42: 37–47.

Sherman, Lawrence W., Denise C. Gottfredson, Doris Layton MacKenzie, John E. Eck, Peter Reuter, and Shawn D. Bushway. 1997. *Preventing Crime: What Works, What Doesn't, What's Promising.* Washington, DC: National Institute of Justice, U.S. Department of Justice.

Sherman, Lawrence W., David P. Farrington, Brandon C. Welsh, and Doris Layton MacKenzie, eds. 2002. *Evidence-Based Crime Prevention.* London: Routledge.

Welsh, Brandon C., and David P. Farrington. 2000. Correctional Intervention Programs and Cost-Benefit Analysis. *Criminal Justice and Behavior* 27: 115–133.

PART III: WHAT WORKS FOR VICTIMS

CHAPTER 9

MANDATED BATTERER INTERVENTION PROGRAMS TO REDUCE DOMESTIC VIOLENCE*

Lynette Feder

Portland State University

David B. Wilson

George Mason University

INTRODUCTION

Domestic violence is defined as assaultive behavior involving adults who are married, cohabitating, or who have an ongoing prior intimate relationship (Goolkasian, 1986). Due to the very private nature of this act, incidences of domestic assaults are less likely to come to the attention of police than are other crimes and therefore to be included in the official crime counts (Berk et al., 1984; Dutton, 1987; Hirschel et al., 1992). However, results from a number of well-regarded national studies (Straus and Gelles, 1986; Tjaden and Thoennes, 2000) indicate just how pervasive this problem continues to be.

After many years of neglect, domestic violence has recently received a tremendous amount of attention from policymakers, researchers, and agency personnel. At first, shelters for abused women and their children appeared followed by programs for male batterers. With the dramatic growth in laws mandating or presuming an arrest response when police responded to domestic assault calls in the late 1980s, increasing numbers of batterers began appearing in courts throughout the nation. Judges saw that mandating these abusers into treatment programs provided an alternative sanction while simultaneously holding out the hope of breaking the cycle of violence and, in that way, truly helping victims of domestic violence.

Obviously, the large numbers of individuals who are affected by domestic violence speaks to the importance of finding meaningful interventions to successfully deal with this problem. However, studies evaluating the effectiveness of batterer intervention programs show very mixed results. This systematic review

* This research was funded by the Smith Richardson Foundation and the Campbell Collaboration Crime and Justice Group. The views expressed are those of the authors. Please address all correspondence to Lynette Feder at Portland State University, Administration of Justice, College of Urban & Public Affairs, 570G Urban Center, Portland, Oregon 97201; email: lfeder@pdx.edu.

Brandon C. Welsh and David P. Farrington, eds.
Preventing Crime: What Works for Children, Offenders, Victims, and Places, 131–145
© 2007 *Springer.*

uses meta-analytic procedures to decipher beneficial, as well as unintended harmful, effects of mandated batterer intervention programs as reported in the research literature.

BACKGROUND

Decades of overlooking domestic violence as a social problem has recently been followed by an intense amount of public, private, and professional interest in this subject. One of the earliest responses to family violence was the development and growth of shelters for battered women and their children (Johnson and Kanzler, 1993). Soon after their establishment, shelter staff noted that they were receiving calls from abusive men seeking services to help them end their violent behavior (Jennings, 1987). Simultaneously, staff noticed that a large percentage of abused women returned to their abusive partners (Hamberger and Hastings, 1993; Snyder and Scheer, 1981). It occurred to these dedicated professionals that the only way to stop the cycle of violence was to change the behavior of the abuser (Feazell et al., 1984).

That counseling abusive men was born directly out of the women's shelter movement largely explains the early focus of these programs. Typically, they were unstructured groups working with abusive men through a combination of consciousness-raising and peer self-help provided within a context of feminist theory that spoke of men's need to control women (Adams and McCormick, 1982; Johnson and Kanzler, 1993). Over the next few years, batterer programs developed independently at various sites across the country. As their numbers grew (Pirog-Good and Stets-Kealey, 1985), the earlier unstructured consciousness-raising groups were replaced by more structured groups using psychoeducational and/or cognitive behavioral techniques. Still, all of this was done within a feminist context (Gondolf, 1997; Healey et al., 1998; Jennings, 1987). Typically, the various programs encouraged men to confront their sexist beliefs and accept responsibility for their past abuse while teaching them alternative behavioral responses like anger management, assertiveness, relaxation techniques, and communication skills (Davis and Taylor, 1999; Healey et al., 1998; Jennings, 1987).

The Domestic Abuse Intervention Project, out of Duluth, Minnesota (usually just called the Duluth Model), has emerged as one of the most prevalent and widely cited programs for treating battering men. It uses a psychoeducational feminist-oriented approach, whereby men are taught that battering is part of a range of male behaviors used to control women. To stop the battering, men are taught alternative methods like time-outs, empathizing, problem solving, and tension-reducing exercises (Pence, 1983). The structured curriculum is usually offered in groups that run from six to 32 weeks in duration (Tolman and Edelson, 1995).

But by far the greatest growth in all these batterer intervention programs occurred in the late 1980s due to the rise in pro-arrest laws occurring throughout the nation (Hotaling and Sugarman, 1986; Gondolf, 1997; Johnson and Kanzler, 1993). With increasing numbers of jurisdictions presuming or mandating arrest for misdemeanor domestic violence (Dutton and McGregor, 1991; Feder, 1997), pressure was placed on the courts to deal with these offenders (Ford and Regoli, 1993; Pence, 1983). At the same time, this population was proving difficult to work with, evidencing high rates of attrition from these treatment programs (Pirog-Good and Stets-Kealey, 1985; Roberts, 1982). Having the courts mandate their attendance to these batterer intervention programs, therefore, seemed to be one method of ensuring greater compliance with the treatment program while simultaneously serving as an alternative to over-crowded jails (Klein, 1997; Johnson and Kanzler, 1993; Healey et al., 1998).

Soon after these court-mandated programs began appearing, studies evaluating their effectiveness materialized in the research literature. In this first wave of evaluation research, the results indicated suspiciously high rates of success in reducing the frequency and/or severity of subsequent violence amongst this offender population. In response, a number of researchers noted that these findings probably reflected the methodological shortcomings inherent in these studies rather than the programs' actual effectiveness in reducing violence (Ford and Regoli, 1993; Gondolf, 1987). Since then, more rigorous research has been conducted. Unlike the earlier studies, they indicated mixed results in terms of the effectiveness of mandated batterer intervention programs (Dutton, 1986; Gondolf, 1998; Harrell, 1991; Chen et al., 1989).

As more communities are called upon to develop coordinated responses to the problem of domestic violence we will most likely see a continued increase in the number of court-mandated treatment programs. Evaluation of these interventions, therefore, becomes increasingly important. A number of researchers have recently written about the importance of recognizing the possibility that well-intended programs can have unintended harmful effects (Dishion et al., 1999; McCord, 2003; Petrosino et al., 2000). If these counseling programs are ineffective in reducing violence, to continue to mandate them necessarily means that limited resources are being diverted away from alternative programs for battered women and their children (Tolman and Bennett, 1990). Even worse is the possibility that these programs might place victims in greater danger than no treatment at all, as was found in one of the studies conducted on a court-mandated batterer program (Harrell, 1991). All of this speaks to the importance of rigorously evaluating these interventions' effectiveness in reducing the future likelihood of re-assault.

SUMMARY OF RESEARCH METHODS

Criteria for Inclusion of Evaluation Studies

We sought to assess the effects of post-arrest mandated interventions (including pre-trial diversion programs) in reducing domestic violence offenders' future likelihood of re-assaulting. Our goal, stemming from the systematic review perspective, was to identify and include all studies that met explicit criteria for inclusion. These criteria dealt with the type of research design, intervention, participants, and outcome measures that were used in the study.

Specifically, to be included a study had to use an experimental design with random assignment into an experimental (court-mandated program) or a no-treatment control group. The no-treatment control groups could include routine treatment by the criminal justice system, such as probation or short jail stays. We restricted our systematic review to evaluations that used experimental designs, because they provide the most rigorous evaluative tool for assessing an intervention's effectiveness, as well as any unintended consequences (Berk et al., 1985; Farrington, 1983; McCord, 2003). Additionally, we restricted our systematic review to evaluations that included mandated interventions that, in part or exclusively, were aimed at the batterer and had as its goal decreasing the batterers' future likelihood of re-assaulting that victim or others.

Our third criterion was to include only studies that used adult participants of heterosexual intimate domestic violence, whether presently or formerly married, separated, divorced, cohabiting, or dating. The study had to include at least one outcome measure on repeat violence to that victim or others that included something other than offenders' self-reported repeat violence (i.e., victim reports or official measures of recidivism, including arrest, charges, or convictions). Finally, the study also had to follow the offender for at least six months post-treatment. The decision to follow offenders for a period post-treatment was based on Dunford's findings that evaluation studies collecting outcome data at the end of treatment were more likely to find effectiveness than those measuring outcomes for some period post-treatment (Dunford, 2000a). This suggests that evaluations that are based solely on end-of-treatment assessments should be viewed cautiously.

Search Strategy for Identification of Relevant Studies

All published and unpublished works from January 1984 to January 2003, including studies conducted in the United States or elsewhere, were eligible for inclusion in our systematic review. We conducted searches of the following databases: Criminal Justice Abstracts, Criminal Justice Periodical Index, Dissertation Abstracts International, ERIC, GPO Monthly Catalog (MOCAT), MEDLINE, National Criminal Justice Research Service (NCJRS), PsiTri Database of Randomized and Controlled Trials in Mental Health, Social, Psychological, Criminological and Educational Trials Register (SPECTR), Social Science Citation Index, Social Work Abstracts, and Sociological Abstracts.

We used three clusters of keywords to search for all experiments conducted on mandated batterer interventions for domestic violence offenders. Whenever appropriate we used a "wildcard" so as to search for the root of the word allowing for other possible derivations. (For instance, we used the term "eval*" to pick up evaluation, evaluate, evaluating, etc.) Cluster one related to the subject matter and included the terms "anger management," "batterer," "domestic assault," "family violence," "spouse abuse," "physical abuse," "Minneapolis Model," and "Duluth Model." Cluster two sought to find citations using program words, such as "treatment," "intervention," "diversion," and "program." Finally, cluster three related to outcomes and included search terms, such as "research," "evaluation," "experiment," "random," "outcome," "comparison," and "matched." Terms within a cluster were connected with the Boolean "or" (i.e., an abstract with any one of the terms would get selected) and the clusters were then connected with the Boolean "and" (i.e., an abstract with at least one of the terms in each cluster would get selected). To make the resulting list more manageable, the search was restricted to titles and abstracts. If the title or abstract looked promising, the entire study was retrieved and reviewed.

Studies determined eligible for inclusion in the systematic review were coded for all relevant data. To ensure data coding reliability, all studies were double coded by the authors and all differences in coding were resolved through discussion.

Statistical Procedures

This systematic review used standard meta-analytic methods. More specifically, dichotomous indicators of program effects were encoded as odds-ratio type effect sizes and continuous indicators of program effects were encoded as standardized mean difference type effect sizes (d). Each outcome reported by a study was coded as a separate effect size and each outcome type (e.g., official reports of reoffending, victim reports of continued abuse) was analyzed separately. Standard methods of combining effect sizes were used (see Lipsey and Wilson, 2001).

RESULTS

Description of Studies

Four studies were identified as meeting the eligibility criteria. Information for two of the studies (Dunford, 2000b; Palmer et al., 1992) came exclusively from peer-reviewed academic journals. Information on the other two studies (Davis et al., 2000; Feder and Forde, 2000) came from non-published reports to a government agency (National Institute of Justice) and peer-reviewed academic journals. When there was conflicting information between the two sources, data from the non-published report was used in the coding of the meta-analysis, because that typically provided more detailed information.

All but one study (Dunford, 2000b) used a general civilian population of batterers who were facing or had faced court prosecution for domestic violence. This study used men living on a Navy base where an incident of domestic violence had been established and the man had been referred to the program. All but one of the studies (Palmer et al., 1992) had a large sample size.

In two studies the generalizability of the sample to the general domestic violence offender population was questionable, due to conditions used for inclusion into their sample. In one of these studies (Palmer et al., 1992) inclusion criteria was suspected of being highly restrictive because the resulting sample size was small (despite the large jurisdiction from which it was pulled and the long time-frame implemented for the study). A second study (Davis et al., 2000) used highly restrictive criteria for inclusion in their sample. In that study, all in the courtroom workgroup, including the batterer, had to agree to this intervention (versus another non-jail alternative). This, as the researchers noted, led to a pool of more highly motivated offenders than is typically found in the generalized batterer population.

All four studies evaluated a psychoeducational or cognitive behavioral approach, or some mix of the two approaches targeted at the batterer and delivered in all-male group settings. One study (Dunford, 2000b) also tested two additional intervention types: a cognitive behavioral group targeted at the male batterer but conducted in conjoint groups, as well as a no-program but rigorously monitored intervention. In the four selected studies, the intervention was delivered over the course of eight weeks (Davis et al., 2000), ten weeks (Palmer et al., 1992), 26 weeks (Davis et al., 2000; Feder and Forde, 2000), or one year (Dunford, 2000b). In all but one of the studies (Dunford, 2000b) it was noted that the program intervention was accompanied by probation.

The nature of the control group varied from study to study. At one extreme was a study (Dunford, 2000b) where the control group received no intervention whatsoever. In the Davis et al. (2000) study, the control group received 40 hours of community service. In the remaining two studies, the control group received probation only.

Meta-Analytic Findings

Two of these studies had multiple treatment conditions compared to a single control group (Dunford, 2000b; Davis et al., 2000), for a total of seven treatment versus control comparisons. The odds-ratio was used as the effect size for dichotomous outcomes, such as official measures of re-arrest, and the standardized mean difference was used for continuous type measures, such as the Conflict Tactics Scales (CTS). For ease of presentation, the odds ratios were transformed into standardized mean difference type effect sizes. This was done using the methods developed by Hasselblad and Hedges (1995) and involved rescaling the logged odds-ratio by a constant. As such, it had no effect on the statistical analyses other than to rescale the values such that they are comparable to the standardized mean difference type effect sizes.

Findings Using Official Reports.   Table 1 presents the random effects mean effect size, 95% confidence interval, and homogeneity statistic (Q) for two outcomes. The first of these represents official reports of domestic violence. These were either official complaints made to the police that may or may not have resulted in an arrest, or actual arrests for domestic violence. If multiple follow-up points were available, the longest was selected. The mean effect size across these seven comparisons was 0.26. This represents a moderate reduction in re-offending, with a 95% confidence interval of 0.03 to 0.50 ($z = 2.23$, $p = .03$).

The distribution of effects and overall mean effect is also presented in Figure 1. As can be seen in this forest plot, all of the effect sizes favored the spouse abuse

TABLE 1.   Random Effects Mean Effect Size and Related Statistics for Official
and Wife's Reported Measures of Domestic Violence

Outcome	Mean d	95% C.I.		k^a
		Lower d	Upper d	
Official measures of domestic violence[b]	0.26*	0.03	0.50	7
All wife reported measures[c]	0.05	−0.07	0.16	6

*Effect statistically significant at $p < .05$.
[a] Number of effect sizes.
[b] $Q = 8.19$, $df = 6$, $p = .22$.
[c] $Q = 2.01$, $df = 5$, $p = .85$.

FIGURE 1.   Standardized Mean Difference Effect Size (d) and 95% Confidence Interval for Official
Measure of Domestic Violence

abatement program, with effects ranging from moderate in size (Palmer et al., 1992; Davis et al., 2000, for the 26 week intervention) to near zero (Davis et al., 2000, for the 8 week intervention). The confidence interval suggests that the true effect of these programs on official measures is likely to be somewhere between trivially small to a meaningful moderate positive effect. The variation in effects across studies is no greater than would be expected due to subject level random error; that is, the difference in effects across studies may simply reflect chance variations that occur with replication.

The evidence from official reports is that spouse abuse abatement programs have a small to modest effect on domestic violence re-offending. In practical terms, this represents a reduction in re-offending from 15% (roughly the average of the control conditions) to 10%. However, these seemingly encouraging findings must be interpreted with caution due to concerns relating to both the generalizability of the findings to the general convicted batterer population, as well as the potential bias of official reports. We discuss these concerns after looking at effects from victim reports.

Findings Using Victim Reports.   In contrast to the official measures of domestic violence, the victim's report of the offender's continued abusive behavior showed no overall benefit of treatment. Three of the four studies measured the victim's

FIGURE 2. Standardized Mean Difference Effect Size (d) and 95% Confidence Interval for All Wife (Victim) Reported Abuse (CTS/Modified CTS) (subscales averaged).

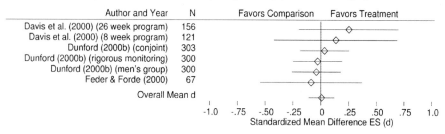

perception of their partner's abusive behavior using either the CTS or modified CTS. For purposes of analysis, we coded all reported subscales and averaged the multiple effect sizes within each treatment-comparison contrast. Thus, the effect size used in Table 1 and Figure 2 represents the mean effect across subscales of the CTS or Modified CTS for each comparison of interest. As shown in Table 1, the mean effect size for victim reports was near zero and was not statistically significant. The 95% confidence interval ranges from a small negative effect to a small positive effect. The distribution of effects is shown in Figure 2. Four of these effects are positive, two are negative, and none are statistically significant. Thus, the outcome measures based on the wife's report do not replicate the finding of a positive benefit of treatment found using the official measures of re-offending. Again, as will be discussed below, there is reason to question each as an indicator of continued abuse.

Moderators of Program Effects.   These four studies differed from one another in many ways. An important issue is whether these differences matter with respect to the effectiveness of the program and its generalizability to the larger convicted batterer population. Unfortunately, with only four studies and seven comparisons, the extent to which we can explore these issues is limited. With this limitation in mind, we conducted a series of analyses examining the relationship between observed effect size and various study characteristics. None of the moderator analyses were statistically significant, although this should not be a surprise given the small number of effect sizes. However, the magnitude of the difference was meaningful for a few of these analyses. This included how the study handled treatment dropouts in their analyses, as well as the restrictiveness of the study's admission criteria.

Turning our attention first to the study characteristics, we coded whether treatment dropouts were included in the analysis of the overall program effect. Failure to do so potentially biases the results and undermines the benefit of randomization. One study (Palmer et al., 1992) both omitted treatment dropouts from the analysis and reported the largest effect size for the batterer intervention's effect on official reports of repeated violence. Removing this study from the analysis only reduces the overall mean effect size slightly (from 0.28 to 0.22), in large part due to the relatively small sample size of this study. The overall distribution remains statistically significant.

Looking next at the representativeness of the sample, we judged two studies (Davis et al., 2000; Palmer et al., 1992) as having samples that were restricted in a manner that reduced the generalizability of their findings. Those studies with more representative samples had a lower overall mean effect size for official reports of domestic violence (0.12) than the studies with a restricted sample (0.39). Importantly, the mean effect for the more representative studies was not statistically significant, raising the possibility that the overall positive findings shown in Figure 1 were, in part, a function of a restricted and presumably easier to treat sample of batterers.

The above analyses of the relationship between study features and effect size need to be interpreted cautiously. Study features tend to be confounded, making it difficult to assign a difference across studies to a specific feature. The small number of studies compounds this problem. The above findings, however, stress the importance of maintaining the integrity of the randomization when analyzing the data and raise concerns regarding the generalizability of the overall positive effect (using official reports) on the larger convicted batterer population.

An additional threat to the validity of a systematic review is the likelihood that statistically non-significant effects have been suppressed, resulting in a "publication bias." We believe that our results are unlikely to be unduly influenced by this well-established phenomenon for a number of reasons. First, only one of the four studies reported a statistically significant effect on the measures presented above. Second, attempts were made to identify unpublished studies and technical reports, rather than rely on published journal articles exclusively, and both sources were used to code two of the four studies. The latter relates to the tendency of some authors to omit effects that are not statistically significant from more formally published works. Finally, Duval and Tweedie's (2000) trim-and-fill method of adjusting for publication bias produced identical results; that is, neither trimmed nor filled effects sizes.

CONCLUSIONS AND POLICY IMPLICATIONS

This systematic review was based on four experimental studies examining the effect of mandating a spouse abuse abatement program relative to a no-treatment or routine-treatment approach for men facing or convicted of misdemeanor domestic violence charges. All of the evaluated programs used a psychoeducational, feminist-oriented and/or cognitive behavioral approach. The results indicated a modest but significant decrease in official reports of continued violent behavior for men mandated to attend these treatment programs in comparison to men not so mandated. Specifically, the meta-analysis indicated that we could expect men in the control group to re-offend 15% of the time in comparison to those mandated into batterer treatment who re-offend 10% of the time.

Interestingly, the studies did not indicate a similar significant benefit for court-mandated batterer treatment when victim reports of continued abuse were used as the outcome measure. The fact that there is disagreement between findings using official reports and those using victim surveys is not new to this field and, therefore, should not be viewed as surprising (see, for instance, Davis et al., 2000).

Given these contradictory findings, what are we to conclude regarding the effectiveness of these programs? We interpret the above findings as equivocal with respect to the effectiveness of court-mandated domestic violence abatement programs. Outcome measures based on official reports suggest that the program may have a moderate impact on reducing future domestic violence. However, as indicated by our further analysis, these beneficial effects may apply only to a select and motivated group of convicted batterers. Additionally, analysis from the victim reports on continued abuse did not confirm these positive findings. Importantly, both outcome measures have weaknesses that are discussed in the next section. This leads to our inability to more definitively answer the question of whether mandating batterer intervention programs reduce the future likelihood of re-assault in a population of convicted batterers.

Due to the private nature of domestic violence, official reports capture only a small fraction of this abuse. The effect of this is to obscure potential benefits of treatment, reducing the size of the observed effect if the program is effective. The lack of sensitivity of official measures affects both groups (treatment and control) and, as such, does not manifest itself as a treatment effect when none exists. Thus, the positive result of the studies reviewed on official reports is encouraging.

There is, however, a concern with using official report measures in domestic violence research. Official measures are highly dependent on the victim's willingness to file a complaint or call the police. As such, it is possible that the abusive partner's assignment to the treatment condition may affect the victim's future willingness to contact the police or other criminal justice officials where the abuse continues. Victims may not report their partner's abuse for a number of reasons. This includes the possibility that she might prefer to see her partner continue in treatment where she believes it will eventually lead to changes in his abusive behavior rather than take the risk of reporting his continued abuse and see him go to jail. Alternately, the victim may resent the criminal justice system's intrusion into her life in the form of mandating a treatment that she is then responsible for paying. (Most programs require the abuser to pay for the treatment. By extension that means that it is the family that pays for the treatment since it is that much less money that is now available to the household (Zorza, 2003).) If treatment is viewed by the victim as ineffective, it may make her critical and suspicious of the system and less likely to cooperate in the case of reporting future incidences of abuse. We have no empirical evidence that this occurs, but the dependence of official reports on the behavior of the victim allows for the plausibility that the different rates noted between batterers in the treatment and comparison conditions may reflect a measurement artifact and not a genuine treatment effect. This possibility is strengthened by the different findings obtained based upon whether we used official reports or victim reports as our outcome measure.

For these and other reasons, the victim is usually viewed as the best source for information on the offender's continued abuse. Victim reports of abuse via standardized measures, such as the Conflict Tactics Scale, are less likely to be affected by the issues raised regarding official reports of continued abuse, provided that the victim is convinced of the confidential nature of her responses. Unfortunately, the percentage of victims responding to follow-up surveys in these studies is low, seriously undermining their utility in establishing the effectiveness (or ineffectiveness) of these programs. The attrition for victim reports for the effect sizes shown in Figure 2 was roughly 30% for the Dunford (2000b) effects, roughly 50% for the Davis et al. (2000) effects, and roughly 80% for the Feder and Forde (2000) effects. High attrition raises the possibility that the victims lost through attrition in the treatment group may differ in meaningful ways from those in the control group. Thus, the absence of an effect for the victim report measures may reflect that the programs are truly ineffective or, alternately, that there is a positive or negative effect that is masked by differential attrition.

The problem of high rates of victim attrition becomes even more critical in light of research indicating that certain victims of domestic violence are more likely to be lost in the research follow-up than are others. Using intensive tracking procedures, Sullivan and her colleagues (1996) were able to retain 97% of the victims of domestic violence for a two-year follow-up period. They found that those victims who were more easily followed "were more likely to be white, were more highly educated, were more likely to have access to cars, were less depressed, and had experienced less psychological and physical abuse compared to the women who were more difficult to find" (Sullivan et al., 1996:273). Findings from the Feder and Forde (2000) experiment provide a good example of this problem. The researchers analyzed differences between women who were followed through the year and those who were lost. They found evidence suggesting that the successfully retained women demonstrated a higher stake in conformity (higher occupational status, partner more likely to be employed).

In all, there is research that strongly suggests that women victims of domestic violence who are more difficult to retain in follow-up research are both more marginal and more likely to be more frequently and severely abused. There is also research that indicates that men who are more marginal are both less likely to obey a court-mandate to treatment and more likely to continue to abuse their partners (Feder and Dugan, 2002). If we can assume that more marginal women are more likely to be partnered with more marginal men, then the need for maintaining contact with a high percentage of victims when assessing the effectiveness of these spouse abuse abatement programs becomes even more apparent. This is especially important in light of analyses of the Spouse Assault Replication Programs, which indicated that an arrest response increased the likelihood of future re-assault for the more marginal batterers, but decreased recidivism for those with higher stakes in conformity (Berk et al., 1992; Sherman, 1992). Any differential loss of these marginal women from the treatment and control groups may therefore produce substantial bias in the findings.

To those ends, additional experiments need to be conducted to more clearly decipher the effectiveness of court-mandated batterer intervention programs. These future experiments must ensure samples of batterers that are representative of the larger convicted batterer population rather than a smaller subset of highly motivated or selected batterers. Additionally, studies must attend to the importance of maintaining high victim retention so as to better ascertain any positive or negative effects from this mandated intervention. In fact, there are established methods that have been used and tested to retain victims of domestic violence in longitudinal follow-up studies (see Rumptz et al., 1991). Finally, additional research is needed to better understand the validity and reliability of official report and victim report measures used in these studies and how they might be affected by treatment assignment (i.e., potential measurement artifacts).

Intervening in the lives of others is a risky business, particularly when the individuals participating in the social intervention are mandated by a court of law to do so. As such, it is incumbent upon us to ensure that we are not inadvertently making things worse for those we are seeking to help. We interpret the existing evidence to suggest that, at a minimum, these programs do not appear to be having negative effects, at least on the outcome measures examined by these studies. However, establishing the absence of harm is methodologically difficult and it remains possible that a harmful effect has gone undetected. What is less convincing, however, is whether they are truly beneficial or whether the evidence of benefit stems from a methodological artifact.

Clearly, what is needed is better research so that policymakers will be able to make more informed decisions. Batterer intervention programs have been in existence since the late 1970s and have been mandated by courts in jurisdictions around the nation since the late 1980s. During these times of limited resources it would seem imperative to have stronger studies upon which to make a more definitive decision on continuing to mandate batterer intervention programs or to search for alternative treatments with batterers and/or their families that may prove more effective in reducing domestic violence.

There is no doubt that, "There is a tremendous sense of urgency and alarm in the treatment of domestic violence – and rightly so. After all, protecting the physical and emotional safety of women and their children is the first priority. Consequently, clinicians feel a primary obligation to 'do something' immediately and decisively to halt and prevent violence" (Jennings, 1987: 204). But as the above review has indicated, doing something may not help. Therefore, we need to be guided by rigorous research in helping us set our course. As Saunders (1988:92) has so elegantly written, "One source of tension seems to arise from the simple fact that social action usually means immediate action, whereas the knowledge gained from science takes a long time to acquire ... Yet action that is not well informed can be less than optimal, ineffective, or worse, counter-productive. Movements for social justice, then, need to use the scientific search for truth as a guide."

REFERENCES

Adams, David, and Anderw McCormick. 1982. "Men unlearning violence: A group approach based on the collective model." In *The Abusive Partner: An Analysis of Domestic Battering*, edited by Maria Roy, 170–197. New York: Van Nostrand Reinhold.

Berk, Richard, Robert Boruch, David Chambers, Peter Rossi, and Ann Witte. 1985. Social policy experimentation: A position paper. *Evaluation Review* 9: 387–429.

Berk, Richard, Sarah Berk, and Phyllis Newton. 1984. Cops on call: Summoning the police to the scene of spousal violence. *Law and Society Review* 18: 479–498.

Berk, Richard, Alec Campbell, Ruth Klap, and Bruce Western. 1992. The deterrent effect of arrest in incidents of domestic violence: A Bayesian analysis of four field experiments. *American Sociological Review* 57: 698–708.

Chen, Huey-tsyh, Carl Bersani, Steven Myers, and Robert Denton. 1989. Evaluating the effectiveness of a court sponsored treatment program. *Journal of Family Violence* 4: 309–322.

Davis, Robert, and Bruce Taylor. 1999. Does batterer treatment reduce violence? *Women & Criminal Justice* 10: 69–93.

——, and Christopher Maxwell. 2000. *Does Batterer Treatment Reduce Violence? A Randomized Experiment in Brooklyn*. Washington, DC: National Institute of Justice, U.S. Department of Justice.

Dishion, Thomas, Joan McCord, and François Poulin. 1999. When Interventions Harm: Peer Groups and Problem Behavior. *American Psychologist* 54: 755–764.

Dunford, Franklyn. 2000a. Determining Program Success: The Importance of Employing Experimental Research Designs. *Crime & Delinquency* 46: 425–434.

——. 2000b. The San Diego Navy Experiment: An assessment of interventions for men who assault their wives. *Journal of Consulting and Clinical Psychology* 68: 468–476.

Dutton, Donald. 1986. The outcome of court-mandated treatment for wife assault: A quasi-experimental evaluation. *Violence and Victims* 1: 163–175.

——. 1987. The criminal justice response to wife assault. *Law and Human Behavior* 11: 189–206.

——, and Barbara McGregor. 1991. "The symbiosis of arrest and treatment for wife assault: The case for combined intervention." In *Woman Battering: Policy Responses*, edited by Michael Steinman, 131–154. Cincinnati, OH: Anderson.

Duval, Sue, and Richard Tweedie. 2000. A nonparametric "trim and fill" method of accounting for publication bias in meta-analysis. *Journal of the American Statistical Association* 95: 89–98.

Farrington, David P. 1983. "Randomized experiments on crime and justice." In *Crime and Justice: An Annual Review of the Research*. Vol. 4, edited by Michael Tonry and Norval Morris, 257–308. Chicago: University of Chicago Press.

Feazell, Carann, Raymond Mayers, and Jeanne Deschner. 1984. Services for men who batter: Implications for programs and policies. *Family Relations* 33: 217–223.

Feder, Lynette. 1997. Domestic violence and police response in a pro-arrest jurisdiction. *Women & Criminal Justice* 8: 79–98.

——, and Laura Dugan. 2002. A Test of the Efficacy of Court-Mandated Counseling for Domestic Violence Offenders: The Broward Experiment. *Justice Quarterly* 19: 343–375.

Feder, Lynette, and David Forde. 2000. *A Test of the Efficacy of Court-Mandated Counseling for Domestic Violence Offenders: The Broward Experiment*. Washington, DC: National Institute of Justice, U.S. Department of Justice.

Ford, David, and Mary Jean Regoli. 1993. "The criminal prosecution of wife assaulters." In *Legal Responses to Wife Assault: Current Trends and Evaluation*, edited by Zoe Hilton, 127–164. Newbury Park, CA: Sage.

Gondolf, Edward. 1987. Seeing through smoke and mirrors: A guide to batterer program evaluations. *Response* 10: 16–19.

——. 1997. Batterer programs: What we know and need to know. *Journal of Interpersonal Violence* 12: 83–98.

——. 1998. Do batterer programs work? A 15 month follow-up of multisite evaluation. *Domestic Violence Report* 3: 65–80.

Goolkasian, Gail. 1986. *Confronting domestic violence: The role of criminal court judges.* Washington, DC: National Institute of Justice, U.S. Department of Justice.

Hamberger, L. Kevin, and James Hastings. 1993. "Court-mandated treatment of men who assault their partner." In *Legal Responses to Wife Assault: Current Trends and Evaluation,* edited by Zoe Hilton, 188–229. Newbury Park, CA: Sage.

Harrell, Adele. 1991. *Evaluation of Court-Ordered Treatment for Domestic Violence Offenders: Final Report.* Washington, DC: Institute for Social Analysis.

Hasselblad, Vic, and Larry V. Hedges. 1995. Meta-analysis of screening and diagnostic tests. *Psychological Bulletin* 117: 167–178.

Healey, Kerry, Christine Smith, and Chris O'Sullivan. 1998. *Batterer Intervention: Program Approaches and Criminal Justice Strategies.* Washington, DC: U.S. Department of Justice.

Hirschel, J. David, Ira Hutchison, and Charles Dean. 1992. The failure of arrest to deter spouse abuse. *Journal of Research in Crime and Delinquency* 29: 7–33.

Hotaling, Gerald, and David Sugarman. 1986. An analysis of risk markers in husband to wife violence: The current state of knowledge. *Violence and Victims* 1: 101–124.

Jennings, Jerry. 1987. History and issues in the treatment of battering men: A case for unstructured group therapy. *Journal of Family Violence* 2: 193–213.

Johnson, John, and Dianne Kanzler. 1993. Treating domestic violence: Evaluating the effectiveness of a domestic violence diversion program. *Studies in Symbolic Interaction* 15: 271–289.

Klein, Andrew. 1997. Batterers' Treatment. *National Bulletin on Domestic Violence Prevention* 3: 1–3.

Lipsey, Mark W., and David B. Wilson. 2001. *Practical Meta-Analysis.* Thousand Oaks: CA: Sage.

McCord, Joan. 2003. Cures That Harm: Unanticipated Outcomes of Crime Prevention Programs. *Annals of the American Academy of Political and Social Science* 587: 16–30.

Palmer, Sally, Ralph Brown, and Maru Barrera. 1992. Group treatment program for abusive husbands: Long-term evaluation. *American Journal of Orthopsychiatry* 62: 276–283.

Pence, Ellen. 1983. The Duluth Domestic Abuse Intervention Project. *Hamline Law Review* 6: 247–275.

Petrosino, Anthony, Carolyn Turpin-Petrosino, and James O. Finckenauer. 2000. Well-Meaning Programs Can Have Harmful Effects! Lessons From Experiments of Programs Such as Scared Straight. *Crime & Delinquency* 4: 354–379.

Pirog-Good, Maureen, and Jan Stets-Kealey. 1985. Male batterers and battering prevention programs: A national survey. *Response* 8: 8–12.

Roberts, Albert. 1982. "A national survey of services for batterers." In *The Abusive Partner: An Analysis of Domestic Battering,* edited by Maria Roy, 230–243. New York: Van Nostrand Reinhold.

Rumptz, Maureen, Cris Sullivan, William Davidson, and Joanna Basta. 1991. An ecological approach to tracking battered women over time. *Violence and Victims* 16: 237–244.

Saunders, Daniel. 1988. "Wife abuse, husband abuse or mutual combat? A feminist perspective on the empirical findings." In *Feminist perspectives on wife abuse,* edited by Kersti Yllo and Michele Bograd, 90–113. Newbury Park, CA: Sage.

Sherman, Lawrence W. 1992. The influence of criminology on criminal law: Evaluating arrests for misdemeanor domestic violence. *Journal of Criminal Law and Criminology* 83: 1–45.

Snyder, Douglas, and Nancy Scheer. 1981. Predicting disposition following brief residence at a shelter for battered women. *American Journal of Community Psychology* 9: 559–566.

Straus, Murray, and Richard Gelles. 1986. Societal change and change in family violence from 1975 to 1985 as revealed by two national surveys. *Journal of Marriage and the Family* 48: 465–479.

Sullivan, Cris, Maureen Rumptz, Rebecca Campbell, Kimberly Eby, and William Davidson. 1996. Retaining participants in longitudinal community research: A comprehensive protocol. *Journal of Applied Behavioral Science* 32: 262–276.

Tjaden, Patricia, and Nancy Thoennes. 2000. Prevalence and consequences of male-to-female and female-to-male intimate partner violence as measured by the National Violence Against Women Survey. *Violence Against Women* 6: 142–161.

Tolman, Richard, and Larry Bennett. 1990. A review of quantitative research on men who batter. *Journal of Interpersonal Violence* 5: 87–118.

Tolman, Richard, and Jeffrey Edelson. 1995. "Intervention for men who batter: A review of research." In *Understanding partner violence: Prevalence, causes, consequences and solutions*, edited by Sandra Stith and Murray Straus, 262–273. Minneapolis, MN: National Council on Family Relations.

Zorza, Joan. 2003. New Research: Broward County Experiment Shows No Benefit From Batterer Intervention Programs. *Domestic Violence Report* 8: 23–25.

CHAPTER 10

RESTORATIVE JUSTICE TO REDUCE VICTIMIZATION

Heather Strang

Australian National University

Lawrence W. Sherman

University of Pennsylvania

INTRODUCTION

What do we know about the effects of restorative justice (RJ) on victimization? The answer to that question depends on *how* we know what we think we know. This chapter answers a traditional question in crime prevention research with a non-traditional method, the systematic review. The aim of this chapter is to describe our conclusions about the effects on victimization of one type of RJ, while simultaneously explaining what is different and important about the new method we have employed for conducting a literature review in crime prevention research.

This chapter focuses on the particular methods we have employed in our review of RJ. It then proceeds to describe all of the randomized controlled trials in RJ that we have identified, and the reasons we have classified them as we have. Based on these classifications, we then show that two out of three valid tests of face-to-face RJ conferences involving offenders, victims, and their friends and families have shown substantial reductions in repeat offending. We conclude by noting that eight more randomized controlled trials are underway, and that the results of that ongoing research could substantially alter the conclusions about the average effects of face-to-face RJ across different populations of offenders, different types of offenses, or different stages in the criminal justice process. But first we discuss the theory that suggests that restorative justice may well be an effective crime prevention mechanism.

BACKGROUND

Restorative justice has the potential to influence future offending at several levels: By reducing the offending of those who experience it (the subject of much of this chapter); by empowering families and friends of offenders to play their role in exercising informal social control over those they care about; and by delivering

Brandon C. Welsh and David P. Farrington, eds.
Preventing Crime: What Works for Children, Offenders, Victims, and Places, 147–160
© 2007 *Springer.*

the motivation and widespread community participation that crime prevention needs to be effective (Braithwaite, 2002).

At the individual level, the dynamics of a RJ encounter provide opportunities for offenders to be confronted with the consequences of their actions far more directly than in a courtroom. Here, as many as possible of the principals involved in the crime meet in the presence of their families, friends, or both. At the conference, any victims (or their representatives) present have the opportunity to describe the full extent of the harm a crime has caused, offenders are required to listen to the victims and to understand the consequences of their own actions, and all participants are invited to deliberate about what actions the offender could take to repair the harm. The pre-condition of such a conference is that the offender does not dispute the fact that he is responsible for the harm caused, and that the conference cannot and will not become a trial to determine what happened.

RJ is usually an emotionally compelling experience, but powerful as it can be, it may not be sufficient to override the effects of long-term drug abuse, unemployment and all the other factors that contribute to offenders' choices to continue their criminal careers. No crime prevention guarantees can flow simply from restorative dialogue, but the advantage that RJ may have is the opportunity presented to put in place concrete measures that focus on crime prevention. These can target the factors underlying offending behavior at a moment when offenders are most likely to acknowledge responsibility for wrongdoing and articulate a willingness to change their future behavior.

It may be critical to the success of RJ to have present family, friends, and others, including professionals, who can play a vital supporting role for offenders. More often than not, the outcomes agreed by participants are targeted principally at reducing the risk of future offending: These kinds of outcomes are usually rated as more important than material or financial restitution for victims by all participants, including the victims themselves (Strang, 2002). These may include drug programs, literacy programs, job training, and so on. But participants in RJ will be aware that failure is the usual life experience of most offenders and that they will need solid support if they are to succeed in their undertakings. RJ provides opportunities for those who care about offenders to specify their own undertakings to help offenders meet their obligations. The willing involvement of families and friends to offer such support is a common feature of RJ: Courts offer no such opportunities, nor would they regard it as their responsibility to provide them. It seems plausible that programs are most likely to be effective when offenders and their supporters willingly undertake to commit to such programs rather than having them imposed.

RJ also provides a deliberative forum for communities to demonstrate their willingness to be involved in crime prevention. Whereas Neighbourhood Watch and similar 'community-based' organizations attract little support in the communities that most need them, the evidence around the world from RJ is that citizens are willing to attend these, often in large numbers. In fact, getting a relatively large and diverse group of people to attend is the best guarantee that the dynamics of the RJ encounter will work well and not be dominated by any one perspective on events. Braithwaite (2002) suggests that discussion of community crime problems in a RJ setting by a group with local knowledge that comes from being affected by the crime in various ways is the best path to a pluralistic and nuanced understanding of the crime. This in turn may be the most effective way of arriving at imaginative solutions to crime in particular settings.

SUMMARY OF RESEARCH METHODS

Objectives

The objective of this review is to derive the most unbiased estimates of the effectiveness of RJ programs in reducing repeat offending and in satisfying victims that justice has been done. Because the randomized controlled trials (RCTs) conducted to date have been heterogeneous with respect to different kinds of offenses and offenders and different stages of the criminal justice process, the review will disaggregate and regroup findings to answer a wide range of questions about RJ structured to create sensitivity to this heterogeneity.

Definition

The varieties of RJ are substantial. The full scope of the concept has been used to describe almost any effort to enable offenders to try to restore or repair some of the damage they have caused to victims or communities by their crimes.

The review attempts to isolate what may be the most theoretically powerful form that these efforts take: Face-to-face RJ. We define this form of RJ as any (a) face-to-face discussion between a RJ facilitator or mediator and (b) anyone affected by a crime (c) with or about offenders who have accepted the responsibility for having caused the crime and (d) addressing the harm they have caused and (e) possible ways the offenders can repair that harm.

The varieties of face-to-face RJ can be distinguished largely on the basis of *who* participates in the RJ process. In mediation, often only the victim and offender meet with the mediator (and they may not always meet face-to-face but rather engage in "shuttle mediation"). In circle sentencing, a form of RJ found mostly in Canadian First Nations communities that combines traditional practices with mainstream judicial process, often those justice officials may take their place in the circle along with victims, offenders, and their supporters. In RJ conferences, led by a facilitator, the victim and offender are usually accompanied by their supporters; professionals, such as probation officers or drug program workers, may also be invited to attend. Sometimes an impersonal victim, such as a representative of a victimized corporation or a victimized community, may participate as well. Sometimes actual practice may be different from the intended program design; for example, program developers may decide that RJ can go ahead even without victim supporters or offender supporters being present, or even in the absence of a personal victim. Sometimes a representative of the victim may be invited to attend if the victim is unwilling to come.

For the purposes of the review, this definition has been narrowed to exclude two forms of face-to-face RJ: victim-offender mediation, where the mediator negotiates between the principals and where supporters of each party are excluded from the negotiation, and sentencing circles. The review focuses on conferencing – the subset of face-to-face RJ that has been studied most carefully and extensively.

Challenges

Several methodological challenges arise in undertaking the review. These include inconsistencies in design in the studies under review, including variability in the measures and analysis of the dependent variable, variability in the time period of analysis of the dependent variable, variability in the characteristics of the offenses and offenders, and variability in the nature of the control treatment. In particular, there was inconsistency in the proportion of cases in the studies in which treatment was delivered as it was supposed to be. We recognize that two solutions are commonly employed to address these problems. First, reviewers compare analysis of effect sizes on all features found in all the studies included in the review (a *lowest common denominator* review); for example, comparing after–only prevalence of repeat offending (percentage of offenders with repeat offenses) because it is the only outcome found in all studies. Second, reviewers disaggregate findings by sample and design characteristics; for example, examining studies that test RJ on violent crimes, as distinct from all types of crimes. We suggest, however, that these two solutions alone may fail to reveal the underlying truth about treatment effects and that a third technique is needed: A methodological test that compares studies using lowest common denominator analysis versus "optimal design analysis," by which we mean a research design that features the strongest logic available for the reduction of bias in the interpretation of treatment effects. If a direct comparison between a subsample of studies allowing optimal design analysis and the same subsample allowing lowest common denominator analysis shows very different results, that test would suggest the dangers of relying on the lowest common denominator analysis in reaching conclusions about treatment effects.

Criteria for Inclusion

As well as the definitional criterion for inclusion we have described – face-to-face RJ conferencing – we have decided to limit studies in the review to those with a randomized design. There have been numerous studies (Braithwaite, 2002) that attempt to evaluate RJ by looking only at its effect on "the treated," that is to say, on the victims and offenders who actually experienced it, rather than its effect on those who were supposed to experience it but did not do so for reasons of implementation failure. Examining the impact of RJ only on those who experienced it is inadequate from a policy perspective if it is the case that promising RJ and failing to deliver it may cause greater harm than never promising it at all, a finding borne out among victims in the Reintegrative Shaming Experiments

(RISE; Strang, 2002). We suggest, therefore, that the problems of selection bias and the difficulties of comparison with alternative treatments are so great that limiting studies for inclusion only to RCTs is justified. Indeed, we were even more rigorous in our methodological criteria. It was not sufficient that a study have a RCT design: The problem of "intention to treat" versus "treatment delivered" is such a serious one in RJ that we have decided to exclude studies where more than 50% of cases failed to receive their assigned treatment.

Search Strategies

Evaluation in RJ is a recent development because these programs are themselves a recent innovation in justice. We use formal search tools, including sociological and criminological databases, but they do not yield as much information as other less formal sources. These include narrative and empirical reviews of literature that examine effects on reoffending, bibliographies of RJ programs, and direct contact with leading researchers.

The present review is designed easily to incorporate both additional studies as they are completed and studies that may have been missed. This is via two mechanisms: First, a registry of RCTs in RJ will be devised that will disaggregate basic features of each study – offense type, offender type, offender age, and so on – that will allow users readily to identify studies relevant for their purpose and allow the ready addition of new studies and, second, forest graphs will show both individual studies and aggregated studies, depending on whether we are commenting on the specific features of any study or wishing to compare effectiveness of the intervention across studies.

Statistical Procedures and Conventions

The review reports the statistical procedures used in each study. There is no attempt to aggregate the statistical findings owing to the heterogeneity in the procedures and designs of the studies, though we note the direction of the results in each study.

RESULTS

Sample Characteristics

Of the seven so-far-completed RCTs in RJ, four were carried out in Canberra, Australia (RISE; see www.aic.gov.au/rjustice/rise/index.html), two in Bethlehem, Pennsylvania (McCold and Wachtel, 1998), and one in Indianapolis (McGarrell et al., 2000).

RISE consisted of separate experiments carried out between 1995 and 2000, involving four separate offenses: Violent crime, shoplifting from large stores, drinking and driving (not involving accidents), and personal property crime. Offenders were randomly assigned either to court in the usual way or diverted to a RJ conference:

a. Violent crime: cases involving offenders under 30 years of age who admitted to middle-level violent offenses, mostly common assault and aggravated assaults.

b. Shoplifting from large stores: cases involving offenders under 18 years of age who admitted to shop theft from large stores where they were apprehended by security staff.

c. Drink driving (drinking and driving): cases involving offenders of all ages who admitted to driving with a blood alcohol level in excess of 0.05.

d. Personal property crime: cases involving offenders under 18 years who admitted to middle-range personal property offenses, including theft, burglary, and car crime.

The Bethlehem (Pennsylvania) Police Family Group Conferencing Project, carried out between 1995 and 1998, consisted of two experiments, one involving property crime and the other violent crime. Offenders under 18 years were randomly assigned either to court in the usual way or diverted to a RJ conference:

a. Property crime: cases involving juvenile offenders who admitted to summary/misdemeanor-level property offenses.

b. Violent crime: cases involving juvenile offenders who admitted to summary/misdemeanor-level violent offenses.

The Indianapolis Juvenile RJ Experiment, carried out between 1997 and 1999, consisted of cases involving first-time offenders under the age of 15 years who admitted to minor property or violent offenses, such as shoplifting, theft, battery, and intimidation. These offenders were randomly assigned either to a RJ conference or to one of 23 diversion programs available to the juvenile court.

These seven experiments were highly variable in a number of ways. The number of cases in each of them ranged from 75 to 900; the offenses were of varying levels of seriousness and related both to direct and indirect victims; and they included both adult and juvenile offenders. Most importantly, they varied in the level of success in achieving random assignment integrity.

We have decided to limit this review to experiments testing the effects of face-to-face RJ for personal victim crimes. As a result, we have excluded two of the four RISE studies: drink driving and large-store shoplifting, neither of which had personal victims. Moreover, we decided to include only those studies in which at least 50% of cases were treated as assigned. This lead to the exclusion of the two Bethlehem studies, one of which (property) achieved a 49.6% delivery rate and the other a 31.6% delivery rate.

Three Valid RCTs of Face-to-Face RJ

Repeat Offending. Three valid RCTs report after–only prevalence of repeat offending (percentage of offenders with repeat offenses). These are the RISE violence and property experiments and the Indianapolis experiment that contained both violent and property offenses. This measure is not the optimal means for drawing causal inferences from these RCTs, individually or collectively, but it is the only measure that allows us to compare all three experiments. In comparing these results the importance and value of "forest analysis" becomes apparent. Even though confidence intervals cross the vertical line indicating zero effect for two of the three experiments (see Figure 1), when the three effect sizes are horizontally displayed as the "trees", the average effect is clearly seen to favor RJ.

FIGURE 1.   *After-Only Offending Prevalence*

Study	Control n/N	RJ n/N	OR (95%CI Fixed)	Weight %	OR (95%CI Fixed)
01 Face-to-Face Restorative Justice Experiments					
Indianapolis (All)	54 / 131	40 / 130		37.2	1.58[0.95,2.63]
RISE (JPP)	38 / 122	41 / 127		43.6	0.95[0.56,1.62]
RISE (JVC)	22 / 59	20 / 62		19.3	1.25[0.59,2.64]
Subtotal(95%CI)	114 / 312	101 / 319		100.0	1.24[0.89,1.72]
Test for heterogeneity chi-square=1.82 df=2 p=0.4					
Test for overall effect z=1.28 p=0.2					
Total(95%CI)	114 / 312	101 / 319		100.0	1.24[0.89,1.72]
Test for heterogeneity chi-square=1.82 df=2 p=0.4					
Test for overall effect z=1.28 p=0.2					

.1   .2   1   5   10
Favors Control   Favors RJ

However, the use of after–only prevalence differences increases the risk of selection bias by baseline differences in offending rates between treatment groups, because of relatively small and heterogeneous sample sizes and because of gaps of varying sizes between treatment as assigned (intention-to-treat) and treatment as actually delivered (effect of treatment-on-treated). It is also a relatively insensitive test, given the fact that a large proportion of all offending is never detected and officially recorded. Only two of the experiments, RISE property and violence, employ an optimal design analysis; that is, the RCT design with the strongest logic available for the reduction of bias in the interpretation of treatment effects, namely before–after frequency differences in offending rates. We would argue, however, on logical grounds that this analysis is superior as a test of treatment effects. The forest analysis in Figure 2 indicates that when effect sizes are combined in these two experiments the one-year before/after frequency of offending also favors RJ.

When we look at changes in offending frequency, comparing one year before with two years after treatment, we find that while the property experiment now favors the control treatment, the violence experiment continues to favor RJ. When the effect sizes are combined for the two experiments, this analysis favours neither treatment (see Figure 3).

Victim Effects.   The views of individual victims on how satisfied they were with their own justice experience may reflect their own levels of confidence about the

FIGURE 2. *Change in 1 Year Before/After Offending Frequency*

Study	Control n	mean(sd)	RJ n	mean(sd)	WMD (95%CI Fixed)	Weight %	WMD (95%CI Fixed)
RISE (JPP)	122	-0.16(2.14)	127	0.13(2.23)		46.1	-0.29[-0.83,0.25]
RISE (JVC)	59	0.17(1.46)	62	-0.26(1.35)		53.9	0.43[-0.07,0.93]
Total(95%CI)	181		189			100.0	0.10[-0.27,0.47]

Test for heterogeneity chi-square=3.65 df=1 p=0.056
Test for overall effect z=0.52 p=0.6

-10 -5 0 5 10
Favors Control   Favors RJ

FIGURE 3. *Change in 1 Year Before/2 Years After Offending Frequency*

Study	Control n	mean(sd)	RJ n	mean(sd)	WMD (95%CI Fixed)	Weight %	WMD (95%CI Fixed)
RISE (JPP)	122	-0.42(2.80)	127	-0.02(1.87)		57.8	-0.40[-0.99,0.19]
RISE (JVC)	59	0.17(1.76)	62	-0.26(2.13)		42.2	0.43[-0.26,1.12]
Total(95%CI)	181		189			100.0	-0.05[-0.50,0.40]

Test for heterogeneity chi-square=3.17 df=1 p=0.075
Test for overall effect z=0.22 p=0.8

-10 -5 0 5 10
Favors Control   Favors RJ

likelihood of revictimization following a RJ conference, compared with the control treatment. Across all available studies, victim satisfaction levels strongly favoured RJ[1] (see Figure 4).

More specific information about victims' fears of revictimization is available

FIGURE 4. *Victim Satisfaction With Their Treatment*

Study	Treatment n/N	Control n/N	OR (95%CI Fixed)	Weight %	OR (95%CI Fixed)
01 All Victims					
Indianapolis (All)	39 / 42	34 / 50		9.6	6.12[1.64,22.81]
RISE (JPP)	43 / 71	37 / 80		59.5	1.78[0.93,3.41]
RISE (JVC)	27 / 45	16 / 36		30.9	1.88[0.77,4.56]
Subtotal(95%CI)	109 / 158	87 / 166		100.0	2.23[1.38,3.59]

Test for heterogeneity chi-square=2.86 df=2 p=0.24
Test for overall effect z=3.30 p=0.0010

| Total(95%CI) | 109 / 158 | 87 / 166 | | 100.0 | 2.23[1.38,3.59] |

Test for heterogeneity chi-square=2.86 df=2 p=0.24
Test for overall effect z=3.30 p=0.0010

.1 .2 1 5 10
Favors Control   Favors RJ

1   Response rates for the RISE property and violence experiments were 87% and 90%, respectively, but lower for the other three experiments: 54% for Bethlehem property, 61% for Bethlehem violence, and 29% for Indianapolis.

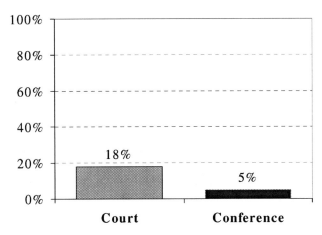

FIGURE 5A.   *Anticipate the Offender will Repeat the Offense on Me – All Victims*

$\chi^2 = 9.727$, df = 1, p ≤ .002; Cohen's d = .777

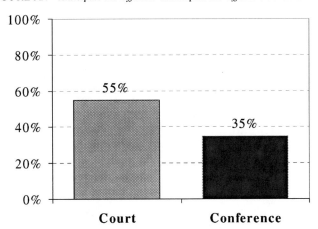

FIGURE 5B.   *Anticipate the Offender will Repeat the Offense on Another – All Victims*

$\chi^2 = 10.038$, df = 1, p ≤ .002; Cohen's d = .468

from RISE data. Victims of middle-level property offenses committed by juveniles and violent offenses committed by offenders up to age 29 were asked whether they expected their offender to revictimize them (see Figure 5A) or to victimize somebody else in the future (see Figure 5B). Those victims who were randomly assigned to attend a RJ conference were significantly less likely to anticipate revictimization than were those whose cases were dealt with in court in the usual way. They also believed it was far less likely that they themselves would be revictimized than their offender would repeat the offense on another victim. When asked about the likelihood of their offender reoffending in general, those randomly assigned to attend a conference were significantly less likely to expect that their offender would repeat their offense than those whose cases were dealt with in court.

Four RCTS on Victim Revenge Crimes

The extent of dissatisfaction that victims of crime, especially violent crime, feel about the way their cases are dealt with by the traditional justice system is little understood and much underestimated. Their feelings of unresolved anger and vengeance were readily apparent in the RISE RCTs on juvenile property crime and young adult violent crime (Strang, 2002). When all these victims were asked whether "the way your case was dealt with made you feel angry," one-third of those whose cases went to court said they felt angry, significantly more than those whose cases were assigned to a conference ($p < .05$). An even stronger indicator of dissatisfaction is when victims are so unhappy that they wish to take the law into their own hands. Twenty percent of all court victims of property or violent crime said they would do some harm to their offender if they had the chance, but only 7% of conference victims said they would do so ($p < .0005$). Moreover, a dramatic difference emerged between victims of violent crimes compared with victims of property crimes in their response here: Fully 45% of violence victims whose cases were dealt with in court wanted revenge compared with only 9% of violence victims whose cases were assigned to a conference ($p < .01$). Given that 40% of violence victims knew their attacker before the offense occurred, the opportunity for acts of retaliation may be plentiful if victims do not resolve their feelings of vengeance via the justice system.

Evidence emerging from two RJ RCTs currently underway in the United Kingdom supports the RISE findings. Here, adult offenders who have pleaded guilty to serious burglary and robbery offenses in London Crown Courts are randomly assigned to take part in a RJ conference prior to court sentencing, or else to proceed to sentence in the usual way. Victims of these crimes have been asked whether they wished they could physically retaliate against their offender (Meyer, forthcoming): Only 9% of those who attended a conference said they wished to retaliate, compared with 23% of those whose cases proceeded to sentence without a conference.[2] Given the exceptional levels of violence that characterize many of these London cases, both in robbery and aggravated burglary, this may indeed be an important means of breaking a cycle of vengeance that could otherwise lead to repeated revictimization.

Eight More RCTs in Progress

These London RJ RCTs are two of eight experiments currently underway in the United Kingdom. All of them are designed to test both possible crime reduction

---

2   Owing to small numbers at this point in the UK project, separate data are not yet available for the burglary and robbery experiments. Given the similarity of these results to the combined property/violence figures in RISE, it seems likely that these figures will be higher for the violent crimes than for the purely property crimes when they are disaggregated.

effects of RJ conferences held in addition to normal criminal justice processes, and also possible benefits to victims of participating in these conferences. The eight experiments are funded by the British Home Office and are located in three sites: London, Northumbria, and the Thames Valley area of central England. They will test RJ under different socio-demographic conditions (poor but well-bonded predominantly white populations in Northumbria compared with ethnically, racially, and economically diverse populations in London), at different points in the criminal justice system (pre-sentence and post-conviction both for offenders sentenced to probation and offenders serving terms of imprisonment), for both adult and juvenile offenders, and for both property and violent offenses.

In London the two experiments involve adult offenders who have pleaded guilty in Crown Court to burglary/aggravated burglary or robbery/street crime offenses. Those randomly assigned to a police-run RJ conference reach an outcome agreement at the end of the conference setting out the actions agreed to by participants, which are designed to repair the harm caused by the offense. This agreement is then put before the sentencing judge in mitigation of the offense. In April 2003, the Court of Appeal decided in *R v Collins* that judges should take into account the fact of the offender's participation in a conference and the contents of the outcome agreement in passing sentence. In this case it was decided that an initial sentence of seven years imprisonment should be reduced to five years. Offenders who attend a conference will be compared with those assigned to the control group on levels of repeat offending.

In Northumbria two experiments involve adult offenders who have pleaded guilty to either property or violent crime in the Magistrates Courts. As in London, offenders may be randomly assigned to a police-run conference that results in an outcome agreement reached between all participants and placed before the magistrate in consideration of mitigation. Another two experiments entail juvenile offenders who have admitted responsibility for violent or property crime and who are to be cautioned under the youth "Final Warning" scheme (their final opportunity to avoid being dealt with in court). Those randomly assigned to a conference participate in the conference in addition to receiving their Final Warning. In all four experiments those offenders participating in a conference will be compared on measures of repeat offending with those randomly assigned to a control group that have been processed by the justice system in the usual way.

A third set of experiments is underway in Thames Valley where adult offenders convicted of violent offenses and sentenced either to community supervision orders or to terms of imprisonment may be randomly assigned to a conference in addition to their sentence. These conferences are run by probation officers, prison officers, or mediators, all trained together in conference facilitation along with the police officers in the other sites. In these experiments as well, reoffending by offenders who were randomly assigned to attend a conference in addition to their sentence will be compared with those in the control group who serve their sentence alone.

CONCLUSIONS AND POLICY IMPLICATIONS

Using the Campbell Collaboration's methods for systematic reviews, we can conclude that face-to-face RJ involving victims and offenders is likely to be an effective way to prevent repeat offending by offenders who have committed, and have admitted committing, violent crimes. Whether that conclusion will hold up, or whether it may even be broadened (or refined) to other offense types or types of offenders, are questions that future research should be able to answer. The same may be said for our second conclusion to date: Face-to-face RJ involving victims and offenders is likely to be an effective way to prevent victims from committing crimes of retaliation.

The most basic difference between this review of RJ and previous reviews is not the method it uses, but the very premise of the review itself. Our premise is that what we know so far is only provisional, and is highly likely to change. We accept no duty to argue a case, or to reach finality. While we accept anyone's right to produce a review and then move on to other topics, we also accept the Campbell obligation to continue to update our review as new evidence becomes available. Taken to its logical conclusion, this implies a duty to recruit others to take over the ongoing updating of our review, for as long as the question remains theoretically and practically important. Just as long-term research projects in life-course criminology have been led by succeeding generations of scholars (some of whom never even met each other, such as the Gluecks and Laub and Sampson), Campbell Reviewers can aspire to attracting others to carry the work on for many decades to come.

The most important thing we can learn from this model of the "never-ending review" is that our conclusions are likely to change. This does not mean we should not act. But it does mean that we should expect to act provisionally, rather than permanently. For many, there is an emotional commitment to procedures of justice being fixed in stone, an "eternal system" of fairness that can be relied upon. While criminologists and policymakers must be sensitive to that view, they must also consider the widespread dissatisfaction with current criminal justice systems, and the growing demand for change.

The demand for better justice can be met in at least three ways. One is to invent a new system based on theory or ideology, and implement it without testing. This is the model employed in New Zealand when a radical alteration to the entire juvenile justice system was introduced in 1989. Another, diametrically opposed model, is to invent a new justice paradigm from the bottom up through careful testing and reviews of evidence. This model is unlikely ever to be fully employed, given the necessity for politicians and policy-makers to do "something," usually within a short electoral cycle that is not conducive to comprehensive theory-testing. A third model is to combine a theory-based plan of innovation with some evidence on a limited number of questions, rather than a comprehensive approach to testing all effects of all variations in the application of a new plan of justice to all possible offense types, offenders, and stages of the justice process.

The future of RJ in England is likely to follow the third model, as the British government recently announced in its White Paper, *Restorative Justice: The Government's Strategy* (see www.homeoffice.gov.uk/justice/victims/restorative/index.html). This broad-ranging document reviews what research to date reveals about what works in RJ and discusses practical issues in its delivery in the criminal justice system as a whole. Finally, it discusses the future of RJ where the intention is to build in RJ at all stages of the criminal justice system on the basis of existing knowledge about how it works and to develop understanding of where it works best and how it could be fully integrated with the existing justice system in the longer term. Moreover, it builds into its ongoing strategy an explicit commitment to proceed on the basis of further research findings.

This refreshing attitude of the British government towards the notion of informing policy by research findings may signal a new opportunity for the research community to make a difference in policy development. But making a difference depends to a large extent on the capacity to make readily available to policymakers the best and most up-to-date research findings. Crime is different from medicine when it comes to implementation of best practice. In medicine practitioners in any speciality can consult the Cochrane Collaboration website for, say, the likely best treatment for lower back pain, and look for a review of all RCTs in the subject area. In crime, governments are almost always the agency most likely to be in a position to implement best practice. But where do governments go for the best information? They often commission their own research, not necessarily aware of existing research findings and sometimes reinventing wheels. The Campbell Collaboration Crime and Justice Group aims to prepare, update, and rapidly disseminate systematic reviews of high quality research conducted worldwide on effective means of reducing crime and improving justice.

So, what do we know about the effects of RJ on preventing victimization? The evidence is robust so far that RJ has a significant crime reduction effect for violent offenders but apparently not for property offenders, at least in the short to medium term. However, all the property experiments for which findings are available so far have involved juveniles, so we do not yet know, for example, whether it is the age of the offenders or the nature of the offense that militates against a crime reduction effect. This and much more will be known soon with the completion of more studies currently underway. It is certainly true that much more remains to be learned but we can be confident that we have made a strong start. The Campbell model provides a transparent means of revealing what is known and also what gaps in knowledge exist as a guide to future research. All knowledge is contingent on the most recent findings and the structure of Campbell with its capacity for absorbing continuous updates, ensures that those who need the latest research findings to inform the development of new policies in crime and justice will eventually have a convenient, accessible, and reliable source for the best available research.

REFERENCES

Braithwaite, John. 2002. *Restorative Justice and Responsive Regulation.* Oxford, England: Oxford University Press.

McCold, Peter, and Ted Wachtel. 1998. *Restorative Policing Experiment: The Bethlehem Pennsylvania Police Family Group Conferencing Project*. Pipersville, PA: Community Service Foundation.

McGarrell, Edmund, Kathleen Olivares, Kay Crawford, and Natalie Kroovand. 2000. *Returning Justice to the Community: The Indianapolis Restorative Justice Experiment*. Indianapolis: Hudson Institute Crime Control Policy Center.

Meyer, Caroline. Forthcoming. *Victims of Crime and Post-Traumatic Stress Disorder*. Unpublished Ph.D. Dissertation. Philadelphia: University of Pennsylvania.

Sherman, Lawrence W. 1992. *Policing Domestic Violence: Experiments and Dilemmas*. New York: Free Press.

Strang, Heather. 2002. *Repair or Revenge: Victims and Restorative Justice*. Oxford, England: Oxford University Press, Clarendon Press.

CHAPTER 11

PREVENTING REPEAT RESIDENTIAL BURGLARY VICTIMIZATION*

Graham Farrell and Ken Pease

Midlands Centre for Criminology and Criminal Justice
Loughborough University

INTRODUCTION

This chapter reviews evaluations of the prevention of repeat residential burglary. These evaluations are a subset of the evaluations relating to the prevention of repeat victimization. The review methodology aims to follow that of the systematic review process proposed by the Campbell Collaboration, which has produced a series of recent reviews including, Farrington and Welsh (2002) and the set of reviews edited by Farrington and Welsh (2001). In keeping with that format, the authors acknowledge a possible interest: We have both previously worked on repeat victimization prevention efforts and elsewhere contended that preventing repeat victimization is a potentially attractive crime prevention strategy.

BACKGROUND

A general definition of repeat victimization is that it is the repeated criminal victimization of a person, household, business, other place or target however defined. The prevention of repeat victimization has gained prominence in the crime prevention literature in recent years in the wake of the Kirkholt burglary prevention project (reviewed below). Although repeat victimization had been recognized as an important component of crime, the Kirkholt project sparked recognition of its potential importance for policy and practice, spurring a range of empirical studies of repeat victimization for different crime types (see Farrell, 1992, 1995; Farrell and Pease, 1993, 1997; Pease, 1998). Efforts to prevent repeat residential burglary to date have been undertaken disproportionately in Britain where repeat victimization has permeated crime policy at the national level.

* Thanks go to Brandon Webster for assistance with preliminary literature searches and data extraction. The first author would like to thank Brandon Welsh and David Farrington for their remarkable patience and friendly encouragement during the preparation of this chapter.

Brandon C. Welsh and David P. Farrington, eds.
Preventing Crime: What Works for Children, Offenders, Victims, and Places, 161–176
© 2007 *Springer.*

Repeat victimization was identified as a potential performance indicator for polic-ing (Tilley, 1995) and by 2000, all police forces in England and Wales had a policy for the prevention of repeat residential burglary, with many having policies to prevent the repetition of other types of crime (Farrell et al., 2001). Readers wishing for an overview of the "repeat victimization story" and the development of the research program in the U.K. since the mid-1980s to the present are referred to Laycock (2001, 2002) and Laycock and Farrell (2003).

Evaluations relating to repeat residential burglary form a prominent part of the evaluation literature relating to the prevention of repeat victimization more generally. However, there is some justification for undertaking a preliminary review for a particular crime type rather than all crime types, as this approach may facilitate the identification of crime-specific aspects of repeat victimization prevention strategies that could go unnoticed if all crime types were reviewed together.

SUMMARY OF RESEARCH METHODS

Criteria for Inclusion of Evaluation Studies

Evaluation studies relating to repeat victimization for all crime types were first identified, and those relating to repeat residential burglary were selected. Both published and unpublished reports were included where identified. Many of the evaluations reviewed herein were familiar to the authors due to previous research on repeat victimization and were also due to contacts with other academics and practitioners working on repeat victimization in Australia, the U.K., and the U.S.

Evaluations with comparison-group designs were included in the review where the comparison groups sometimes had varying degrees of comparability – and in keeping with the keystone notion of methodological transparency, the research designs are assessed.

Search Strategies

Ten online academic and other databases were searched: Criminal Justice Abstracts (1968–2002); Psychological Abstracts (1967–2002); Sociological Abstracts (1963–2002); Criminal Justice Periodicals Index (1970–2002); National Criminal Justice Reference Service (NCJRS) (1972–2002); Child Abuse and Neglect Abstracts (National Child Abuse and Neglect or NCCAN Clearinghouse) (1997–2002); Educational Resources Information Clearinghouse (ERIC) (1966–2002); Lexis-Nexis (1969–2002); Dissertation Abstracts (1861–2002); and Government Printing Office, Monthly catalogue (GPO monthly) (1976–2002).

Key search terms and combinations of terms were entered into each database. Truncation and 'wildcards' were used where possible. In particular, victim* (where * is the wildcard symbol) was used since it is inclusive of victim, victims, victimized, victimization, or any other words that began with 'victim'. The trunca-tion and wildcard use of victim* also captures alternative spellings such as victim-isation and victimization, that is, with 's' and with 'z', respectively. The key search terms entered were: repeat victim*; revictim*; re-victim*; multiple victim*; and recidivist victim*. A series of additional search terms combined 'repeat*' with a list of more specific crime-types: property crime; burglary; burglarization; residen-tial burglary; and residential burglarization. Additional searches using key terms were undertaken using popular Internet search engines to try to capture publica-tions that had not reached the electronic databases.

Evaluations relating to the prevention of repeat residential burglary were iden-tified by reading summaries, abstracts or full reports as necessary. Some evalua-tions, including Tilley and Webb (1994) and Webb (1996) were excluded due to absence of comparison groups or a paucity of information. At the time of writing, some newly published promising results from the U.K.'s national Burglary Reduction Initiative are still emerging but were not disaggregated to allow assess-ment of the evaluations of individual projects focused upon repeat burglary prevention (see e.g., Bowers et al., 2003; Kodz and Pease, 2003).

RESULTS

Critical information on evaluation design, implementation and outcome mea-sures is shown in Tables 1 and 2, with evaluations in chronological order. The details on the projects noted below primarily give the big picture in each case and include any new analysis or reinterpretation of data and findings. Readers should refer to original sources for more detailed information, and page numbers are given to facilitate that process where possible.

Kirkholt, U.K.

The Kirkholt burglary prevention project (Forrester et al., 1988, 1990; Farrington, 1992; Pease, 1991) was the first to explicitly utilize repeat victimiza-tion as the focus of a crime prevention strategy. Treatments included security upgrades at burgled homes with special attention to preventing repeat burglary by the same method of entry. Neighbors of victims were offered free security upgrades as an incentive to develop localized watch groups, each called a Cocoon Neighborhood Watch. In burgled households, coin meters (boxes that held coins used to pay for electricity) were replaced since they were easy and frequent targets. In the second phase of the project, analysis of probation data identified debt as a motivator of burglary, and offenders were offered debt-management services.

The comparison group for the Kirkholt project comprised the remainder of the adjoining police subdivision – a larger area with some privately owned properties and a lower burglary rate. Implementation rates for prevention tactics were 68% for security upgrades (402 of 592 burgled households: see Farrington, 1992: 10–11) and close to 100% for Cocoon Watch, since by the end of the project close

TABLE 1. Features of Treatment and Comparison Groups and Intervention Tactics by Evaluation

Title (Authors)	Treatment Area	Comparison Group(s) (Any differences to treatment area)	Intervention Tactics (Who paid for intervention)
Kirkholt Burglary Prevention Project (Forrester et al., 1988, 1990; Farrington, 1992)	Area of 2,280 households	Remainder of police subdivision (larger area; some privately-owned houses; lower burglary rate)	Victim-oriented: Free focused security upgrades; coin-box removal; cocoon neighborhood watch; Offender-oriented: debt counseling; arrests (free – paid by project)
Site ?R1 (Tilley, 1993)	Area of 8,000 households	Remainder of police subdivision (larger area)	Target-hardening security measures (locks, and Cocoon Watch – also at some non-burgled, vulnerable properties (free to households)
Site ?R2 (Tilley, 1993)	Area of 835 households	Remainder of police subdivision (larger area)	Target-hardening security measures, but offered to all households not just victims (free to households)
Site ?R3 (Tilley, 1993)	Area of 3,936 households	Remainder of police subdivision (larger area)	Target-hardening security measures (free to households)
Huddersfield Biting Back (Anderson et al., 1995; Chenery et al., 1997)	Huddersfield police subdivision with 22,000 population	Remainder of West Yorkshire police force area. Contiguous areas used to examine displacement (larger area)	Graded response system: bronze, silver, gold according to risk, each with multiple tactics including letters to offenders, security, patrols, loan of alarms (mixed: some free, some partially-sponsored security measures)
Preventing Residential Burglary in Cambridge (Bennett and Durie, 1999)	Castle – 2,665 households; Arbury – 3,024 households; one hot spot	Similar non-adjacent local areas and hot spots plus some computer generated treatment and comparison groups	Combined package of victim-oriented security, guardianship measures, and offender-based measures (key security measures depended on means-tested eligibility or purchase by victims)

Continued

TABLE 1. Continued

Title (Authors)	Treatment Area	Comparison Group(s) (Any differences to treatment area)	Intervention Tactics (Who paid for intervention)
Baltimore – Hot Dots in Hot Spots (Weisel et al., 1999)	Three patrol sectors	Patrol sectors matched on population, area, environment, housing stock, socio-economic status	Warning cards of security advice to victims; alert cards and warnings for neighbors; security checks; free property registration; police patrols (all free but note no funding for actual security)
Dallas – Hot Dots in Hot Spots (Weisel et al., 1999)	Part of Northeast police district – 12 square miles, 54,652 population	Comparison area matched on burglary rate; larger area (28 square miles) but similar size population of 45,520	Written notification to generate victim awareness; apartment managers notified of increased risks; home security surveys (all free but note no funding for security)
San Diego – Hot Dots in Hot Spots (Weisel et al., 1999)	Western Division: 26 sq. miles, 173,835 population	Mid-City Division with similar number of burglaries and housing stock	Emphasis on better investigations; home security checks; security brochure for victims (free but note no funding for security)
Beenleigh – Lightning Strikes Twice (Budz et al., 2001)	Area of 41,000 population	Non-neighboring area matched on burglary rate and socio-demographic characteristics	3-tiered responses: Stop Break Response to one-time victims (security advice and materials); Hot Dot Response to two-time victims (more extensive prevention materials); Hot Spot Response to hot spot areas (home-security assessments; property marking)
Tee Tree Gully, Adelaide – Repeat Break and Enter (Ball Public Relations and Walters, 2002; Henderson, 2002)	Tee Tree Gully plus 3 police subdivisions: total population 207,000	Similar non-neighboring comparison areas; similar neighboring areas to measure displacement	Security audit; informal support; referral to other agencies; referral for property marking; links to neighbors

TABLE 2. Measures of Implementation and Outcome by Evaluation

Title (Authors)	Implementation – Measures and Issues	Outcome Measure 1 – Reduced Repeat Burglary	Outcome Measure 2 – Reduction in Overall Burglary (source)	Displacement/Other Issues Arising
Kirkholt Burglary Prevention Project (Forrester et al., 1988, 1990; Farrington, 1992)	68% for security upgrading; close to 100% for Cocoon Watch	Yes – Repeat burglary fell to zero within 6 months (recorded crime data). Pattern of burglary reduction linked temporally to security measures	Burglary fell 60% within 6 months and 75% over 3 years (recorded crime data)	Displacement examined – none found
Site ?R1 (Tilley, 1993)	Cocoon Watch achieved 25% coverage	Not measured	24.3% reduction relative to control area but increase in absolute terms (recorded crime data)	Displacement not measured/The project was not located in a very high crime area
Site ?R2 (Tilley, 1993)	80% of all households in area received security which was offered to all	Not measured	Burglary prevalence fell 57.9% from year 1 to year 3. Burglary incidence fell 65.8% in pre-post comparison of 20 months (recorded crime data)	"Some evidence of displacement to an adjoining beat" (p. 8). Comparison area data not given but inferred from fact that adjoining beat was "the only beat in the subdivision experiencing an increase in burglary" (p. 8)
Site ?R3 (Tilley, 1993)	55% of victims (187 households) received target hardening and 424 households overall	Yes – (1) 40.4% reduction in proportion of repeat burglary; (2) increased mean time to repeats from 81 to 137 days; (3) properties secured without prior burglary did not benefit	54% reduction in burglary incidence relative to comparison group (recorded crime data)	Displacement not measured

Continued

TABLE 2.   *Continued*

Title (Authors)	Implementation – Measures and Issues	Outcome Measure 1 – Reduced Repeat Burglary	Outcome Measure 2 – Reduction in Overall Burglary (source)	Displacement/Other Issues Arising
Huddersfield Biting Back (Anderson et al., 1995; Chenery et al., 1997)	Interviews with victims "suggest implementation a factor in any continuing repeats" (1997: 17)	Victims more satisfied; increased arrests from alarms at victimized properties; reduction over time in number of silver and gold responses suggests reduced repeat burglaries	30% reduction in burglary incidence relative to comparison group (recorded crime data)	Displacement – none found
Preventing Residential Burglary in Cambridge (Bennett and Durie, 1999)	Very low for key tactics: 3.5% (6 of 171 victims) received free Keepsafe door locks; "Some" victims acted on security advice; 9% of victims (n = 15) received loan-alarms; 0% of visited victims required alley gates (p. 36)	No – similar or greater reductions in comparison areas. No – similar or greater reductions in comparison areas	Reduction not attributable to intervention: Reductions greater and/or similar in control areas (recorded crime data)	"The right medicine but the wrong dosage" (p. 41). Implementation failure
Baltimore – Hot Dots in Hot Spots (Weisel et al., 1999)	Few process measures given: police distributed cards and alerted neighbors	No	Police data showed 5.2% decrease in treatment and 24% increase in comparison, but probably spurious – no explanation for it (recorded crime data)	Weak treatment (advice) suggests theory failure produced implementation failure (no strong preventive tactics introduced)
Dallas – Hot Dots in Hot Spots (Weisel et al., 1999)	Victim survey showed: 87% implemented some crime prevention strategy; 13% alarms; 27% moved or moving; 9% boarded windows; 18% changed or added locks (p. 107)	No: Victim survey (51% response rate) showed no change relative to comparison group (but – victims more satisfied with police response – p. 108)	Slight burglary increase relative to control (p. 91) (recorded crime data)	Weak treatment (advice) suggests theory failure combined with implementation failure (no strong preventive tactics introduced)

Continued

TABLE 2. Continued

Title (Authors)	Implementation – Measures and Issues	Outcome Measure 1 – Reduced Repeat Burglary	Outcome Measure 2 – Reduction in Overall Burglary (source)	Displacement/Other Issues Arising
San Diego – Hot Dots in Hot Spots (Weisel et al., 1999)	Few process measures available; changes in police personnel "challenge to implementation" (p. 43); Police "skeptical" about repeat burglaries (p. 43)	No	Burglary fell 12% more than in comparison areas (p. 92), but probably spurious (no explanation for it)	Weak treatment (advice) suggests theory failure produced with implementation failure (no strong preventive tactics introduced)
Beenleigh – Lightning Strikes Twice (Budz et al., 2001)	Victims more likely than controls to use warning stickers (45% v 11%), property marking (42% v 12%), inventory lists (34% v 13%), and lock fitting (39% v 27%); more expensive measures (alarms; new doors or screens) more likely to be adopted than controls but still unlikely overall	Yes – Repeat victims fell 16% and repeat incidents 15% in treatment area and increased in comparison areas. 80+ % of victims reported police advice to be helpful – but no difference in satisfaction	No – burglaries increased relative to comparison group. Report suggests repeats may have displaced to other households within treatment group area but provides no evidence (multiple data sources)	Displacement measured – none found. Evaluation difficult because: "It was difficult to distinguish possible project effects from.. random or seasonal fluctuations" and project was in an area with "low incidence of repeat victimization" (p. 14)
Tee Tree Gully, Adelaide – Repeat Break and Enter (Ball Public Relations and Walters, 2002; Henderson, 2002)	Treatment (advice) given at 31.7% of properties. Result was locks and alarms adopted by 8% and 4% of victims, respectively – low implementation rate	Repeats reduced relative to control (but repeats stable in absolute terms)	No – burglary increased relative to comparison area	No evidence of spatial displacement

to the whole housing area was covered. There were three main outcome indicators: Burglary incidence fell 60% and repeat burglary to zero within six months of the start of the program (Forrester et al., 1990: 4); burglary incidence fell 75% over three years (Forrester et al., 1990: 27); and burglaries declined at households where security was introduced but not at other households. The third indicator was developed by Farrington (1992) in an independent analysis that also excluded regression to the mean as a significant influence. There was no evidence of spatial displacement (Forrester et al., 1990: 29). The evaluators concluded that the project's key characteristic was preventing repeat residential burglary by all locally appropriate means; that is, tailoring multiple tactics to the local crime problem via a crime analysis approach.

Three Putative Replications of Kirkholt

Tilley (1993) evaluated three putative replications of the Kirkholt project. The replications were 'putative' because they varied in the nature and method of replication. Tilley referred to the projects as sites ?R1, ?R2, and ?R3, wherein the question mark raises the issue of whether or not they should be considered replications. The comparison group area constituted the beats of the surrounding police subdivisions in each case – though information on the comparison group for ?R2 is largely inferred and therefore weak. The sites differed from the Kirkholt project in approach and method so that Tilley (1993) argued that only ?R3 could be classified as a replication, but all three are reviewed here. The assessments below involve some re-analysis of the original data.

Site ?R1 contained 8,000 households and was "not a very high crime rate area" (Tilley, 1993: 6). In addition to burgled properties, other "vulnerable," publicly owned households were target hardened while some privately owned burgled homes were not (p. 7). Burglaries in treatment Site ?R1 increased from 571 in the year prior to the project to 991 during the second year of implementation. The comparison group experienced a 229.6% increase from 671 to 1,538 burglaries over the same period (p. 7). If the treatment area had experienced the same magnitude of change, 1,309 burglaries would be expected. Therefore, relative to the control group, the burglaries in the treatment area were 24.3% lower than expected. Data on burglary prevalence was not reported.

Site ?R2 contained 835 dwellings with a 9% burglary prevalence rate in the year prior to the treatment (Tilley, 1993: 7). Instead of a focus upon victims, target hardening "was offered to all on the estate. Security work.. was undertaken at 81% of the properties" but had been offered to all properties in the treatment area (Tilley, 1993: 8). Two outcome measures were reported. The first was the annual change in burglary prevalence which fell from 9.1% (76 households or 1 in 11) in the year before the project, to 1.9% (16 households or 1 in 52) during the second year, to 3.8% (32 households or 1 in 26) during the third year. From the first to the third year this is a 57.9% net reduction in burglary prevalence (76 compared to 32 households). The second outcome measure compared two periods of twenty months before and after the four-months of target hardening in which the number of burglaries fell from 111 before to 38 after, indicating a 65.8% reduction in burglary incidence. Comparison to the control groups found that "there was some evidence of displacement to an adjoining beat, the only beat in the subdivision experiencing an increase in burglary" (Tilley, 1993: 8), though the specific levels of control group burglary rates are not reported. Hence, while the report implies that at any change in the control group was insignificant relative to the findings, the exact data are not reported. The general availability of the treatment suggests this project may not have targeted repeat victimization (this is in agreement with Tilley's interpretation), while the dearth of information available to Tilley for the comparison area detracts from the strength of the overall evaluation design.

Site ?R3 contained 3,936 households and had a prior burglary prevalence rate of 5% (Tilley, 1993: 8). Free target hardening was introduced at the homes of victims. Fifty-five percent of victims (187 households) received security upgrades. Other properties that were "informally identified as at risk" – usually neighbors of victims, elderly, disabled or single-parent residents – were also target hardened (p. 9). From the year prior to the project to the year following, the treatment site experienced a 9% increase in domestic burglaries compared to a 139% increase in the control group (p. 9). When a 139% increase is expected, a 9% increase always produces a figure that is 45.6% lower than the expected level. Hence, relative to the control group, the treatment area experienced the equivalent of a 54.4% reduction in burglary incidence (i.e., 100% minus 45.6%). Three outcome indicators are reported for repeat burglary: There was a steady decline in repeat burglaries from 22.8% to 20.1% to 13.6% of total burglaries over the three-year period, for an overall 40.4% reduction in the proportion of repeat burglaries; the time between burglaries and repeats increased from a mean of 80.5 days to 136.6 days; and those residences which were target hardened due to an informal recommendation (rather than upon being burgled) did not experience less burglaries than the properties that were not target hardened. Each outcome indicator is consistent with an interpretation that the intervention reduced repeat burglaries at previously burgled residences that received the intervention.

Tilley's (1993) report argues that only ?R3 can be considered a replication of Kirkholt according to its method. For present purposes, the set of evaluations also raise the important issue (which can be difficult for evaluation to disentangle) that efforts to prevent repeat victimization can be inappropriately located (in low crime areas) and impact can be difficult to disentangle if tactics focused on repeats are combined with general prevention efforts.

Biting Back – Huddersfield, U.K.

The Huddersfield "Biting Back" project (Anderson et al., 1995; Chenery et al., 1997; Anderson and Pease, 1997) aimed to routinize the prevention of repeat burglaries across a large area. Arguably, the key additional innovation of the project was the introduction of graded responses to repeat victimization – more prevention resources were allocated to more frequently burgled households that remained more at risk (Chenery et al., 1997: 5). The three levels of response were: bronze (the least resource-intensive), silver, and gold (the most resource-intensive for the highest-risk households). The comparison group was the remainder of the area covered by West Yorkshire police, an area larger than that receiving treatment. Victims reported greater satisfaction with the police and were more likely to report having received various types of crime prevention advice from the police. There was an increase in arrests based upon the use of temporary alarms, from 4% of installations to 14% of installations when they were allocated to burgled premises. The main crime rate outcome measure was the 30% reduction in burglary incidence relative to the force as a whole. The evaluation examined burglary patterns by known offenders before and after implementation and found no evidence of spatial displacement.

Cambridge, U.K.

Bennett and Durie (1999) evaluated efforts to prevent residential burglary in two areas (Arbury and Castle) and an overlapping burglary hot spot in Cambridge. Measures were aimed at improving victim security (various measures), increasing guardianship (surveillance measures), and offenders (after-school and youth schemes) (p. 19). This study arguably had the strongest evaluation design of the projects reviewed herein. Multiple comparison groups were similar areas, some with similar pre-treatment burglary rates, plus the city as a whole. Outcome measures of burglary incidence and repeat burglaries showed the small reduction in treatment areas were outweighed by larger reductions in the comparison areas. Any reductions could not be attributed to the treatment. Few victims were eligible for security or wanted advice, and of those who received treatment, few measures were implemented. Re-analysis of implementation data suggests that, of 171 burglary victims in treatment areas, 3.5% ($n = 6$ victims) received free Keepsafe door locks, and 9% ($n = 15$ victims) received loan-alarms, and zero secure alley-gates were purchased. These may well have been the tactics with the strongest prevention mechanisms. Overall, victims declined or did not adopt measures even though project staff implemented them at fairly high rates among those eligible and willing. This reanalysis indicates implementation failure, perhaps more than that identified in the original report where the evaluators concluded there was "the right medicine but in the wrong dosage" (p. 41).

Baltimore, Dallas, and San Diego

The three evaluation sites are shown separately in Tables 1 and 2 but grouped here for brevity. Weisel et al. (1999; see also Stedman and Weisel, 1999) evaluated police efforts to prevent repeat burglaries in Baltimore, Dallas, and San Diego. The report notes that, "no monetary resources were provided to the cities for developing or implementing responses" (p. 19). Police officers were given crime prevention training in each site but "police were not provided with any additional revenue for purchasing crime prevention or intervention tools" (p. 19). The main responses focused on improving information gathered by police at burglary scenes rather than on implementing prevention. Advice leaflets and warning cards were given to victims but there was no provision of security or other measures (see p. 130). The evaluation determined there was implementation failure, noting:

> "The problem-solving efforts developed and implemented by police personnel in each city were relatively weak. The provision of target hardening or other crime prevention advice to the victim was a very hit-or-miss proposition – depending on the knowledge, interest, and motivation of the officer taking the report." (Weisel et al., 1999: 113–114)

The result in relation to Dallas was that: "most of the victims in the experimental area received police advice ... [but] victims in the comparison area were about as likely as victims in the experimental area to make any changes in behavior" (Weisel et al., 1999: 97). These results seemed applicable for each site. This is an important lesson regarding implementation.

Beenleigh, Queensland, Australia

Budz et al. (2001) evaluated efforts to prevent repeat burglary in Beenleigh, a town of 41,000 people with a burglary rate above the regional average (p. 2). Three tiers of response were introduced: 'Stopbreak' was a package of crime prevention material provided to once-burgled households (623 provided); 'Hot Dot' was a response of higher-grade security provided to households burgled more than once (67 such responses provided); and 'Hot Spot' was a response of a security survey and crime prevention advice offered to residents in high burglary rate areas (580 such responses provided). The evaluation design compared burglary for the year of the project to the preceding year for the treatment areas, neighboring areas (to capture displacement), and a comparable non-neighboring area with a similar burglary rate, socio-economic and demographic characteristics (p. 12). Repeat burglaries fell 15% in the treatment area but increased in the comparison areas. There was no reduction in burglary incidence (burglaries fell 2% in the treatment area when one prolific offender was excluded but fell 13% in the comparison area), but since the tactics were focused on preventing repeat burglaries, this second outcome measure does not indicate project failure.

Tee Tree Gully, Adelaide, Australia

The South Australian Residential Break and Enter Pilot Project Evaluation Report details the evaluation of efforts to prevent repeat burglary in Tee Tree Gully and three nearby police subdivisions (Ball Public Relations and Walter, 2002). Five measures composed the treatments introduced at burgled households: a security audit; informal support; referral to other agencies; referral for property marking, and links to neighbors. Implementation occurred at 31.7% of eligible properties ($n = 994$ of 3,137 burgled properties) which "may be the result of police reluctance (during the first half of the project) to ask victims to participate or a victims' willingness to 'get involved' even if the offer is put in the best possible light" (p. 9). However, only 61.2% of treatments resulted in victims following any security advice (833 interventions) – equivelant to a 19.6% implementation rate of any security. Smaller proportions of victims adopted specific measures: 7.4% ($n = 233$) installed door locks, 8.4% ($n = 263$) installed window locks, 3.8% ($n = 121$) installed alarms, and 12.4% ($n = 390$) followed 'some advice' (p. 10). This is a reanalysis of the report data that suggests extremely low implementation rates for key prevention tactics. This strongly indicates implementation failure since a reduction in either repeats or overall burglaries would not be expected based on such low rates of improved security.

The Adelaide project evaluation design incorporated both similar neighboring areas to assess displacement effects, and non-neighboring comparable control areas to assess burglary reduction. The evaluation report concludes that the project reduced repeat burglaries relative to the comparison areas (though repeat burglaries remained stable in the treatment area but increased in the control area), while the treatment areas experienced a 31.3% increase in burglaries compared to a 16.7% increase in the comparison areas (Henderson, 2002: 22).

DISCUSSION AND CONCLUSIONS

There remains a paucity of evidence regarding what works to prevent repeat residential burglary. The most successful efforts appear to involve: (1) A strong preventive mechanism. Specific prevention tactics should be tailored to and be crime and context specific. (2) Multiple tactics. The currently available evidence suggests multiple tactics working together can produce a synergistic effect. While there is little conclusive evidence regarding the effectiveness of particular tactics, opportunity-blocking security aimed at preventing repeat residential burglary by the same modus operandi seems the most likely candidate for effectiveness. (3) Strong implementation. Some prevention efforts failed because the preventive mechanism was not introduced. (4) A focus on high-crime and high-burglary rate situations. Those times and places where rates of repeat burglary rates are highest are the most appropriate focus for prevention efforts.

Conclusions regarding what does not work must be as cautious as those regarding what works. This review suggests (and some of these are mirror-images of what works) the following characteristics of prevention efforts do not work to prevent repeat residential burglary: (1) Weak preventive mechanisms do not work. Further, the same prevention tactic in a different context does not necessarily work if the nature of the burglary problem is different. (2) Poor implementation does not work. In particular, victim-education is an indirect route that does not necessarily mean that effective preventive tactics are implemented: some victims may be unable or unwilling to spend money on security. This suggests better sources of funding for security and other equipment or better motivation and incentives for victims may be required in some instances. (3) Replicating tactics without attention to context does not necessarily work, though some strategic application of measures, such as security upgrades to prevent repeat residential burglary by the same modus operandi appear more generally applicable. (4) Overall impact is less where repeat residential burglary rates are low. This is an issue that may hinge on the apparent disproportionate increase in repeat burglaries in the highest burglary rate areas.

Other Evaluation Issues

Evaluations to date have provided only cursory insight into the impact of prevention efforts upon the time-course of repeat residential burglaries. Evaluations that have shown an extension of the time-between-burglaries have used the mean time to a repeat as the outcome measure. Future research might seek additional measures. Similarly, there is relatively little evaluation data relating to the differential impact of graded responses to higher volume repeat residential burglaries. Evaluation can sometimes be difficult since repeat burglaries can be difficult to measure from recorded crime data (see Farrell and Pease, 2003). Few of the evaluations reviewed herein used pre- and post-treatment victim surveys to develop more accurate outcome measures. Similarly, few evaluations measured the use of prevention tactics in comparison areas, except Weisel et al. (1999) who found that a significant proportion of untreated victims took some form of preventive action. The evaluations demonstrating the greatest reductions in residential burglary and repeats tended to be demonstration projects (notably Kirkholt and Huddersfield's "Biting Back") where researchers were involved with tactic-development and implementation as part of an action-research process.

It is also clear that a key issue relating to implementation is: Who pays for prevention equipment? The evidence suggests that victims are often unable or unwilling to invest in additional security even when warned of increased crime risks. Some evaluation outcomes may need closer examination: Strict adherence to experimental analysis suggests success with a finding of a relative reduction in repeat burglaries even if actual repeat levels are stable or declining (success being relative to the control group), or when a reduction in repeats is concurrent with an overall increase in burglary incidence. Such ambiguities may be due to the inability of most area-based evaluations to assess outcomes based on analysis of individual households, suggesting more discerning evaluation is required.

The widespread adoption of policies to tackle repeat residential burglary by police forces in the U.K. does not necessarily mean that quality prevention efforts have been implemented (Farrell et al., 2000). More recent developments in the empirically derived understanding of repeat residential burglary, such as the 'near-repeat' phenomenon (nearby neighbors are more likely to be victimized; see Townsley et al.; 2001; Johnson and Bowers, 2004) have yet to be integrated into evaluated prevention efforts.

A separate issue of relevance to evaluation is that repeat victimization is a strategy rather than a tactic. As such it can, and should, be integrated with other crime prevention and detection strategies, including more general crime prevention strategies, offender detection efforts, tackling hot spots of crime, preventing theft of hot-products, and environmental design to reduce crime. The combinations of strategies may produce synergies. If so, future evaluations will need to be particularly sophisticated to tease out the various mechanisms at work.

This review and its findings should provide a platform from which to undertake further reviews of efforts to prevent repeat victimization of different types of crime. The current review suggests the need for further evaluation of efforts to prevent repeat residential burglaries. There is evidence the repeat burglary can be prevented when a locally appropriate prevention effort is properly introduced, but prevention does not occur in the absence of either a thorough implementation or a strong preventive mechanism. Hence, the evidence regarding preventive effectiveness is quite sobering in light of the significant progress that has been made in the more general empirical investigation of the nature of repeat residential burglary and repeat victimization.

REFERENCES

Anderson, David, and Ken Pease. 1997. "Biting Back: Preventing Repeat Burglary and Car Crime in Huddersfield." In *Situational Crime Prevention: Successful Case Studies*, Second ed., edited by Ronald V. Clarke, 200–208. Guilderland, New York: Harrow and Heston.

Anderson, David, Sylvia Chenery, and Ken Pease. 1995. *Biting Back: Tackling Repeat Burglary and Car Crime*. Crime Detection and Prevention Series Paper, No. 58. London: Home Office.

Ball Public Relations and Christine Walter. 2002. *The South Australian Residential Break and Enter Pilot Project Evaluation Report – Summary Volume*. Canberra. Australia: Commonwealth Attorney-General's Department.

Bennett, Trevor H., and Linda Durie. 1999. *Preventing Residential Burglary in Cambridge: From Crime Audits to Targeted Strategies*. Police Research Series Paper, No. 108. London: Home Office.

Bowers, Kate, Shane Johnson, and Alex Hirschfield. 2003. *Pushing Back the Boundaries: New Techniques for Assessing the Impact of Burglary Schemes*. London: Home Office.

Budz, Dennis, Neil Pegnall, and Michael Townsley. 2001. *Lightning Strikes Twice: Preventing Repeat Home Burglary*. Queensland, Australia: Criminal Justice Commission.

Chenery, Sylvia, John Holt, and Ken Pease. 1997. *Biting Back II: Reducing Repeat Victimization in Huddersfield*. Crime Detection and Prevention Series Paper, No. 82. London: Home Office.

Farrell, Graham. 1992. Multiple Victimisation: Its Extent and Significance. *International Review of Victimology* 2: 85–102.

——. 1995. "Preventing Repeat Victimization." In *Building a Safer Society: Strategic Approaches to Crime Prevention. Crime and Justice: A Review of Research*, vol. 19, edited by Michael Tonry and David P. Farrington, 469–534. Chicago: University of Chicago Press.

——, and Ken Pease. 1993. *Once Bitten, Twice Bitten: Repeat Victimization and its Implications for Crime Prevention*. Crime Prevention Unit Paper, No. 46. London; Home Office.

——. 1997. Repeat Victim Support. *British Journal of Social Work* 27: 101–113.

——. 2003. "Measuring and Interpreting Repeat Victimization Using Police Data: Findings from Repeat Burglary in Charlotte, North Carolina." In *Theory for Practice in Crime Prevention. Crime Prevention Studies*, vol. 16, edited by Marti Smith and Derek Cornish, 265–289. Monsey, NY: Criminal Justice Press.

Farrell, Graham, Louise Hobbs, Alan Edmunds, and Gloria Laycock. 2000. *RV Snapshot: UK Policing and Repeat Victimization*. Policing and Reducing Crime Unit Paper, No. 5. London: Home Office.

Farrington, David P. 1992. Was the Kirkholt Burglary Prevention Project Effective? Unpublished paper. Cambridge, U.K.: Institute of Criminology, Cambridge University.

——, and Brandon. C. Welsh. 2002. Improved Street Lighting and Crime Prevention. *Justice Quarterly* 19: 313–342.

——, eds. 2001. What Works in Preventing Crime? Systematic Reviews of Experimental and Quasi-Experimental Research. [Full issue.] *Annals of the American Academy of Political and Social Science* 578.

Forrester, David, Mike Chatterton, and Ken Pease. 1988. *The Kirkholt Burglary Prevention Project, Rochdale*. Crime Prevention Unit Paper, No. 13. London: Home Office.

Forrester, David, Samantha Frenzz, Martin O'Connell, and Ken Pease. 1990. *The Kirkholt Burglary Prevention Project: Phase II*. Crime Prevention Unit Paper, No. 23. London: Her Majesty's Stationery Office.

Henderson, Monika. 2002. *Preventing Repeat Residential Burglary: A Meta-Evaluation of Two Australian Demonstration Projects*. Barton, Australia: Commonwealth Attorney-General's Office.

Johnson, Shane D., and Kate Bowers. 2004. The Spatio-Temporal Distribution of Repeat Burglaries. *European Journal of Criminology* 1: 237–255.

Kodz, Jenny, and Ken Pease. 2003. Burglary Reduction Initiative: Early Findings on Burglary Reduction. Home Office Research and Statistics Directorate Findings, No. 204. London: Home Office.

Laycock, Gloria. 2001. Hypothesis-Based Research: The Repeat Victimization Story. *Criminal Justice* 1: 59–82.

——. 2002. "Methodological Issues in Working with Policy Advisers and Practitioners." In *Evaluation for Crime Prevention. Crime Prevention Studies*, vol. 13, edited by Nick Tilley, 205–237. Monsey, NY: Criminal Justice Press.

——, and Graham Farrell. 2003. "Repeat Victimization: Lessons for Implementing Problem-Oriented Policing." In *Problem-Oriented Policing: From Innovation to Mainstream. Crime Prevention Studies*, vol. 15, edited by Johannes Knutsson, 150–175. Monsey, NY: Criminal Justice Press.

Pease, Ken. 1991. The Kirkholt Project: Preventing Burglary on a British Public Housing Estate. *Security Journal* 2: 73–77.

——. 1998. *Repeat Victimisation: Taking Stock*. Police Research Group Paper, No. 90. London: Home Office.

Stedman, John, and Deborah Lamm Weisel. 1999. "Finding and Addressing Repeat Burglaries." In *Problem-Oriented Policing: Crime-Specific Problems, Critical Issues and Making POP Work*, edited by Corina S. Brito and Tracy Allan. Washington, DC: Police Executive Research Forum.

Tilley, Nick. 1993. *After Kirkholt – Theory, Method and Results of Replication Evaluations*. Crime Prevention Unit Series Paper, No. 47. London: Home Office.

——. 1995. *Thinking About Crime Prevention Performance Indicators*. Crime Detection and Prevention Series Paper, No. 57. London: Home Office.

——, and Janice Webb. 1994. *Burglary Reduction: Findings from Safer Cities Schemes*. Crime Prevention Unit Paper, No. 51. London: Home Office.

Townsley, Michael, Ross Homel, and Janet Chaseling. 2003. Infectious Repeats: A Test of the Near Repeat Hypothesis. *British Journal of Criminology* 43: 615–633.

Webb, Janice. 1996. *Direct Line Homesafe*. Lincolnshire, U.K.: Janice Webb Research.

Weisel, Deborah L., Ronald V. Clarke, and John.R. Stedman. 1999. *Hot Dots in Hot Spots: Examining Repeat Victimization for Residential Burglary in Three Cities*. Final Report Submitted to the National Institute of Justice. Washington D.C.: Police Executive Research Forum.

PART IV: WHAT WORKS FOR PLACES

CHAPTER 12

POLICING CRIME HOT SPOTS*

Anthony A. Braga
Harvard University

INTRODUCTION

In recent years, crime scholars and practitioners have pointed to the potential benefits of focusing crime prevention efforts on crime places. A number of studies suggest that crime is not spread evenly across city landscapes. Rather, there is significant clustering of a crime in small places, or "hot spots," that generate half of all criminal events (Pierce et al., 1988; Sherman et al., 1989a; Weisburd et al., 1992). Even within the most crime-ridden neighborhoods, crime clusters at a few discrete locations and other areas are relatively crime free (Sherman et al., 1989a). A number of researchers have argued that many crime problems can be reduced more efficiently if police officers focused their attention to these deviant places (Sherman and Weisburd, 1995; Weisburd and Green, 1995). The appeal of focusing limited resources on a small number of high-activity crime places is straightforward. If we can prevent crime at these hot spots, then we might be able to reduce total crime.

Hot spots policing has become a very popular way for police departments to prevent crime. A recent Police Foundation report found that 7 in 10 departments with more than 100 sworn officers reported using crime mapping to identify crime hot spots (Weisburd et al., 2001). A growing body of research evidence suggests that focused police interventions, such as directed patrols, proactive arrests, and problem-oriented policing, can produce significant crime prevention gains at high-crime 'hot spots' (see e.g. Eck, 1997; 2002). Given the growing popularity of hot spots policing, a systematic review of the empirical evidence on the effects of focused police interventions on crime hot spots is necessary to assess the value of this approach to crime prevention.

---

* This research was supported through funds from the Smith Richardson Foundation. The author would like to thank Phyllis Schultze of Rutgers University's Criminal Justice Library for her assistance in completing the review. David Weisburd, Anthony Petrosino, Brandon Welsh, and David Farrington also deserve thanks for making helpful comments on earlier iterations of this review. This review is limited to hot spots policing evaluations that used randomized controlled trials. Readers interested in a wider assessment of quasi-experimental designs should refer to an earlier published work (Braga, 2001) or consult the Campbell Crime and Justice Group web page for updated reviews (www.aic.gov.au/campbellcj/).

Brandon C. Welsh and David P. Farrington, eds.
Preventing Crime: What Works for Children, Offenders, Victims, and Places, 179–192
© 2007 *Springer.*

Background

Unlike most innovations in policing, the emergence of hot spots policing can be traced directly to emerging theoretical perspectives in criminology that suggested the importance of places in understanding crime (Weisburd and Braga, 2003). Beyond studies observing the *clustering* of criminal events, in their review of the research literature, Eck and Weisburd (1995) identified four other theoretical concepts that illuminate the role of place in crime. *Facilities*, such as bars, churches, and apartment buildings have been found to affect crime rates in their immediate environment depending on the type of people attracted, the way the space is managed, or the possible crime controllers present, such as owners, security, or police. *Site features* such as easy access, a lack of guardians, inept or improper management, and the presence of valuable items have been suggested to influence the decisions offenders make about the place they choose to commit their crimes. Studies of *offender mobility* suggest that offenders' target searching behavior is influenced by personal characteristics (such as gender, age, race, experience, and crime types) and the distribution of crime targets. A direct outgrowth of offender mobility patterns, research on *target selection* posits that offenders seek places with cues that indicate acceptable risks and gains, such as homes on the outskirts of affluent neighborhoods; these places are found during intentional target searches and during offenders' daily legitimate routines.

The study of crime events at places is influenced and supported by three complementary theoretical perspectives: rational choice, routine activities, and environmental criminology. The rational choice perspective assumes that "offenders seek to benefit themselves by their criminal behavior; that this involves the making of decisions and choices, however rudimentary on occasion these choices may be; and that these processes, constrained as they are by time, the offender's cognitive abilities, and by the availability of relevant information, exhibited limited rather than normative rationality" (Cornish and Clarke, 1987: 933). This perspective is often combined with routine activity theory to explain criminal behavior during the crime event (Clarke and Felson, 1993). Routine activity theory posits that a criminal act occurs when a likely offender converges in space and time with a suitable target (e.g., victim or property) in the absence of a capable guardian (Cohen and Felson, 1979). Rational offenders come across criminal opportunities as they go about their daily routines and make decisions whether to take action. Environmental criminology explores the distribution and interaction of targets, offenders, and opportunities across time and space; understanding the characteristics of places, such as facilities, is important as these attributes give rise to the opportunities that rational offenders will encounter during their routine activities (Brantingham and Brantingham, 1991). The assumption is that if victims and offenders are prevented from converging in space and time through the effective manipulation of the environment, police can reduce crime.

Indeed, police officers have long recognized the importance of place in crime problems. Police officers know the locations within their beats that tend to be trouble spots and also are often very sensitive to signs of potential crimes across the places that comprise their beats. As Bittner (1970: 90) suggests in his classic study of police work, some officers know "the shops, stores, warehouses, restaurants, hotels, schools, playgrounds, and other public places in such a way that they can recognize at a glance whether what is going on within them is within the range of normalcy." The traditional response to such trouble spots typically included heightened levels of patrol and increased opportunistic arrests and investigations. Until recently, police crime prevention strategies did not focus systematically on crime hot spots and did not seek to address the underlying conditions that give rise to high-activity crime places.

SUMMARY OF RESEARCH METHODS

This review synthesizes the existing published and unpublished empirical evidence on the effects of focused police crime prevention interventions at high-crime places, and provides a systematic assessment of the preventive value of focused police crime prevention efforts at crime hot spots. The sections below describe the types of studies that were eligible for inclusion in this review.

Types of Studies

In this review, only studies that used randomized controlled trial designs were considered. Crime places that received the hot spots policing intervention were compared to places that experienced routine levels and types of traditional police services such as random patrol and reactive investigations.

Types of Areas

The units of analysis were crime hot spots or high-activity crime "places." As Eck (1997: section 7, 1) suggests, "a place is a very small area reserved for a narrow range of functions, often controlled by a single owner, and separated from the surrounding area ... examples of places include stores, homes, apartment buildings, street corners, subway stations, and airports." All studies using units of analysis smaller than a neighborhood or community were considered. Since this research strategy has the potential to yield a diverse set of high-activity crime places across the identified studies, the quality of the methodological approaches used to identify hot spots in the eligible studies was assessed as part of the review.

Types of Interventions

To be eligible for this review, interventions used to control crime hot spots were limited to police enforcement efforts. Suitable police enforcement efforts included traditional tactics such as directed patrol and heightened levels of traffic enforcement as well as alternative strategies such as aggressive disorder enforcement and problem-oriented policing with limited situational responses and limited engage-ment of the public. Eligible problem-oriented policing initiatives must engage primarily traditional policing tactics such as law enforcement actions, informal counseling and cautioning, and referrals to other agencies. Problem-oriented policing programs that involved multiple interventions implemented by other stakeholders such as community members, business owners, or resident manag-ers, were not considered.

Types of Outcome Measures

Eligible studies had to measure the effects of police intervention in officially recorded levels of crime at places. Appropriate measures of crime included crime incident reports, citizen emergency calls for service, or arrest data. Other out-comes measures such as survey, interview, social observations, physical observa-tions, and victimization measures used by eligible studies to measure program effectiveness were also coded and analyzed.

Particular attention was paid to studies that measure crime displacement effects and diffusion of crime control benefit effects. Policing strategies focused on specific locations have been criticized as resulting in displacement (see Reppetto, 1976). More recently, academics have observed that crime prevention programs may result in the complete opposite of displacement – that crime control benefits were greater than expected and "spill over" into places beyond the target areas (Clarke and Weisburd, 1994). The quality of the methodologies used to measure displacement and diffusion effects, as well as the different types of displacement that were examined (spatial, temporal, target, and modus operandi), was assessed.

Search Strategies for Identification of Studies

To identify the studies meeting the criteria of this review, the following four search strategies were used: searches of on-line databases (see below), searches of narra-tive and empirical reviews of literature that examine the effectiveness of police interventions on crime hot spots (e.g. Sherman, 1990; 1997; Eck, 1997; 2002; Braga, 2001), searches of bibliographies of police crime prevention efforts and place-oriented crime prevention programs (e.g. Sherman, 2002; Sherman and Eck, 2002; Braga, 2002), and contacts with leading researchers. The following eleven databases were searched: Criminal Justice Periodical Index, Sociological Abstracts, Social Science Abstracts (SocialSciAbs), Social Science Citation Index, Arts and Humanities Search (AHSearch), Criminal Justice Abstracts, National Criminal Justice Reference Service (NCJRS) Abstracts, Educational Resources Information Clearinghouse (ERIC), Legal Resource Index, Dissertation Abstracts, and the Government Publications Office Monthly Catalog (GPO Monthly). The following terms were used to search these databases: hot spot, crime place, crime clusters, crime displacement, place-oriented interventions, high crime areas, high crime locations, targeted policing, directed patrol, crackdowns, and enforcement swamping. In addition, two existing registers of randomized controlled trials were consulted. These include (1) the "Registry of Experiments in Criminal Sanctions, 1950–1983 (Weisburd et al., 1990) and (2) the "Social, Psychological, Educational, and Criminological Trials Register" or SPECTR being developed by the United Kingdom Cochrane Centre and the University of Pennsylvania (Petrosino et al., 2000).

RESULTS

Selection of Studies

In May 2003, the four search strategies produced 697 abstracts. Fifty-seven abstracts were selected for closer review and the full-text reports, journal articles, and books for these abstracts were acquired and carefully assessed to determine whether the interventions involved focused police enforcement efforts at crime hot spots and whether the studies used randomized controlled trial designs. Five eligible studies were identified and included in this review: the Minneapolis Repeat Call Address Policing (RECAP) Program (Sherman et al., 1989b), the Minneapolis Hot Spots Patrol Program (Sherman and Weisburd, 1995), the Jersey City Drug Markets Analysis Program (DMAP) (Weisburd and Green, 1995), the Jersey City Problem-Oriented Policing at Violent Places Project (Braga et al., 1999), and the Kansas City Crack House Police Raids Program (Sherman and Rogan, 1995). Since there were only five studies selected, this review was conducted as a structured qualitative exercise. No quantitative analyses were conducted.

Characteristics of Selected Studies

The treatments used to prevent crime at hot spots fell into three broad categories: enforcement problem-oriented policing interventions, directed and aggressive patrol programs, and police crackdowns and raids (see Table 1). The effects of problem-oriented policing initiatives – comprised of mostly traditional tactics with limited situational responses – were evaluated in the Minneapolis RECAP Program and Jersey City POP at Violent Places studies. The Minneapolis Hot Spots Patrol program evaluated the effects of increased levels of preventive patrol on crime. The Jersey City DMAP and Kansas City Crack House Raids Programs evaluated the effects of well-planned crackdowns on street-level drug markets and court authorized raids on crack houses, respectively.

All randomized experiments used crime hot spots as the unit of analysis. With the exception of the Minneapolis RECAP experiment, the experimental designs used sophisticated methodologies to identify crime hot spots. The Minneapolis Hot Spots Patrol, Jersey City DMAP, and Jersey City POP at Violent Places experiments used the most sophisticated methods to identify hot spots. In general, the research teams defined hot spot areas by mapping official police call data to identify high volume street address clusters and intersection areas, ensured that these locations had stable numbers of calls over time, and considered qualitative

TABLE 1. Hot Spots Policing Experiments

Study	Treatment	Hot Spot Definition	Research Design*
Minneapolis (MN) RECAP Sherman et al. (1989b)	Problem-oriented policing interventions comprised of mostly traditional enforcement tactics with some situational responses 1 year intervention period Integrity of treatment threatened by large caseloads that outstripped the resources the RECAP unit could bring to bear	Addresses ranked by frequency of citizen calls for service divided into commercial and residential lists; the top 250 commercial and top 250 residential addresses were included in experiment	Randomized experiment; control and treatment groups were each randomly allocated 125 commercial and 125 residential addresses Differences in the number of calls to each address from a baseline year to the experimental year were compared between RECAP and control groups
Minneapolis (MN) Hot Spots Sherman and Weisburd (1995)	Uniformed police patrol; experimental group, on average, experienced twice as much patrol presence 1 year intervention period Breakdown in the treatment noted during the summer months	110 hot spots comprised of address clusters that experienced high volumes of citizen calls for service, had stable numbers of calls for over two years, and were visually proximate	Randomized experiment; control and treatment groups were each randomly allocated 55 hot spots within statistical blocks Differences of differences between citizen calls in baseline and experimental years, comparing control and experimental groups
Jersey City (NJ) DMAP Weisburd and Green (1995)	Well-planned crackdowns followed by preventive patrol to maintain crime control gains 15 month intervention period Slow progress at treatment places caused intervention time period to be extended by 3 months	56 drug hot spot areas identified based on ranking intersection areas with high levels of drug-related calls and narcotics arrests, types of drugs sold, police perceptions of drug areas, and offender movement patterns	Randomized experiment; control and treatment groups were each randomly allocated 28 drug hot spots within statistical blocks Differences of differences between citizen calls during 7 month pretest and posttest periods, comparing control and experimental groups

Continued

TABLE 1. *Continued*

Study	Treatment	Hot Spot Definition	Research Design*
Jersey City (NJ) POP at Violent Places Braga et al. (1999)	Problem-oriented policing interventions comprised of mostly aggressive disorder enforcement tactics with some situational responses 16 month intervention period Initial slow progress at places caused by resistance of officers to implement intervention	24 violent crime places identified based on ranking intersection areas with high levels of assault and robbery calls and incidents, and police and researcher perceptions of violent areas	Randomized experiment; 24 places were matched into like pairs based on simple quantitative and qualitative analyses; control and treatment groups were each randomly allocated 12 places within matched pairs Differences of differences between a number of indicators during 6 month pretest and posttest periods, comparing control and experimental groups
Kansas City (MO) Crack House Raids Sherman and Rogan (1995)	Court authorized raids on crack houses conducted by uniformed police officers Intervention period was the day of the raid All but 7 cases received randomly assigned treatment as assigned No threats to the integrity of the treatment reported	207 blocks with at least 5 calls for service in the 30 days preceding an undercover drug buy; sample was restricted to raids on the inside of residences where a drug buy was made that was eligible for a search warrant	Randomized experiment; Raids were randomly allocated to 104 blocks and were conducted at 98 of those sites; the other 109 blocks did not receive raids Differences of differences analytic design; pre-post time periods were 30 days before and after raid for experimental blocks, and 30 days before and after controlled buy at treatment block or control blocks

*The control group in each study received routine levels of traditional police enforcement tactics.

indicators, such as police and researcher observations to define hot spot boundaries. The Kansas City Crack House Raid experiment focused on blocks that had at least five calls for service in the month preceding an undercover drug buy made on the inside of a residence. Simple ranking procedures to identify high-volume addresses based on numbers of citizen calls for service were used to define specific locations for focused police interventions in the Minneapolis RECAP experiment.

Effects of Hot Spots Policing Programs on Crime and Disorder

Noteworthy crime reductions were reported in four of the five selected studies (see Table 2). The strongest crime control gains were reported in the Jersey City

TABLE 2. *Results of Hot Spots Policing Experiments*

Study	Crime Outcomes	Other Outcomes	Displacement/Diffusion
Minneapolis (MN) RECAP Sherman et al. (1989b)	No statistically significant differences in the prevalence of citizen calls for service	None	Not measured
Minneapolis (MN) Hot Spots Sherman and Weisburd (1995)	Modest, but statistically significant reductions in total crime calls for service ranging from 6% to 13%	Systematic observations of crime and disorder were half as prevalent in experimental as in control hot spots	Not measured
Jersey City (NJ) DMAP Weisburd and Green (1995)	Statistically significant reductions in disorder calls for service in treatment drug markets relative to control drug markets	None	Examined displacement and diffusion effects in two-block catchment areas surrounding the treatment and control drug places and replicated the drug market identification process Little evidence of displacement; analyses suggest modest diffusion of benefits
Jersey City (NJ) POP at Violent Places Braga et al. (1999)	Statistically significant reductions in total calls for service and total crime incidents All crime categories experienced varying reductions; statistically significant reductions in street fight calls, property calls, narcotics calls, robbery incidents, and property crime incidents	Observation data revealed that social disorder was alleviated at 10 of 11 treatment places relative to control places Non-experimental observation data revealed that physical disorder was alleviated at 10 of 11 treatment places Non-experimental interviews with key community members in target locations suggest no noteworthy improvements in citizen perceptions of places	Examined displacement and diffusion effects in two-block catchment areas surrounding the treatment and control drug places Little evidence of immediate spatial displacement or diffusion
Kansas City (MO) Crack House Raids Sherman and Rogan (1995)	Modest decreases in citizen calls and offense reports that decayed in two weeks	None	Not measured

POP at Violent Places experiment (Braga et al., 1999). In the Jersey City POP experiment, the enforcement problem-oriented policing strategy resulted in statistically significant reductions in total calls for service and total crime incidents, as well as varying reductions in all subcategories of crime types, in the treatment violent crime hot spots relative to the controls. Analyses of systematic observation data collected during the pretest and posttest periods revealed that social disorder was alleviated at 10 of 11 treatment places relative to controls.[1] Non-experimental systematic observation data collected pretest and posttest at treatment places suggested that physical disorder was alleviated at 10 of 11 treatment places.[2] Pretest and posttest interviews with key community members suggested that community perceptions of places improved at 7 of 12 treatment places (Braga, 1997).

The Minneapolis Hot Spots Patrol experiment revealed that roughly doubling the level of patrol in crime hot spots resulted in modest, but significant, reductions in total calls for service, ranging from 6% to 13%, in treatment places relative to control places (Sherman and Weisburd, 1995). Moreover, systematic observations of the hot spots suggested that disorder was only half as prevalent in treatment hot spots as compared to control hot spots. The Jersey City DMAP experiment suggested that well-planned crackdowns followed by patrol maintenance resulted in significant reductions in disorder calls for service at the treatment drug hot spots relative to controls (Weisburd and Green, 1995). The Kansas City Crack House Raid experiment reported modest decreases in citizen calls for service and crime offenses at treatment blocks relative to controls that decayed within two weeks of the raids (Sherman and Rogan, 1995).

The Minneapolis RECAP experiment showed no statistically significant differences in the prevalence of citizen calls for service at addresses that received the problem-oriented policing treatment as compared to control addresses (Sherman et al., 1989b). These results were probably due to the assignment of too many cases to the RECAP unit, thus outstripping the amount of resources and attention the police officers provided to each address (Buerger, 1993). Moreover, the simple randomization procedure led to the placing of some of the highest event addresses into the treatment group; this led to high variability between the treatment and control groups and low statistical power. Although the overall findings suggest that the RECAP program was not effective in preventing crime, a case study analysis revealed that several addresses experienced dramatic reductions in total calls for service (Buerger, 1992).

In addition to the RECAP Experiment, three other studies reported potential threats to the internal validity of the research designs. The Jersey City DMAP experiment and Jersey City POP at Violent Places experiment reported instances where the treatments were threatened by subversion by the participants. The

---

1   One case was excluded from these analyses because the observational data were inappropriately collected (Braga et al., 1999).

2   One case was excluded from these analyses because it did not have any physical disorder in the pretest and posttest periods (Braga et al., 1999).

officers charged with preventing crime at the treatment hot spots were resistant to participating in the programs and this resulted in low levels of treatment during the early months of both experiments. In the Jersey City DMAP experiment, this situation was remedied by providing a detailed crackdown schedule to the Narcotics Squad commander and extending the experiment from 12 months to 15 months. This problem was remedied in the Jersey City POP experiment by changing the leadership of the POP unit, developing an implementation accountability system, providing additional training in the problem-oriented policing approach, and through other smaller adjustments.

The patrol treatment in the Minneapolis Hot Spots experiment was disrupted during summer months due to a peak in the overall calls for service received by the Minneapolis Police Department and a shortage of officers due to vacations; this situation was further complicated by changes in the computerized calls for service system implemented in the fall. The changes in the calls for service system and the disappearance of differences in patrol dosage between treatment and control hot spots during summer months were addressed by conducting separate outcome analyses using different intervention time periods; there were no substantive differences in the outcomes of the experiment across the different time periods. Of course, these implementation problems are not unique to these experiments; many well-known criminal justice field experiments have experienced and successfully dealt with methodological difficulties.[3]

Displacement and Diffusion Effects

Only two studies, the Jersey City experiments, examined whether focused police efforts were associated with crime displacement or diffusion of crime control benefits (see Table 2). Prior to a discussion of the research findings, it must be noted that it is very difficult to detect displacement effects, because the potential manifestations of displacement are quite diverse. As Barr and Pease (1990: 293) suggest, "if, in truth, displacement is complete, some displaced crime will fall outside the areas and types of crime being studied or be so dispersed as to be masked by background variation ... no research study, however massive, is likely to resolve the issue." Diffusion effects are likely to be as difficult to assess. The Jersey City experiments were limited to examining immediate spatial displacement and diffusion effects; that is, whether focused police efforts in targeted areas resulted in crime "moving around the corner" or whether these proximate areas experienced unintended crime control benefits.

Neither study reported substantial immediate spatial displacement of crime

---

3   The landmark Kansas City Preventive Patrol Experiment had to be stopped and restarted three times before it was implemented properly; the patrol officers did not respect the boundaries of the treatment and control areas (Kelling et al., 1974). Likewise, the design of the Minneapolis Spouse Abuse Experiment was modified to a quasi-experiment when randomization could not be achieved because officers chose to arrest certain offenders on a non-random basis (Berk et al., 1988).

into areas surrounding the targeted locations and both suggested possible diffusion effects associated with the focused police interventions. In the two Jersey City experiments, the research teams examined the differences of differences in citizen calls for service in two block catchment areas surrounding treatment and control hot spot areas. The Jersey City POP at Violent Places experiment found little evidence of displacement in the catchment areas and reported significant decreases in total calls for service and disorder calls for service in the catchment areas.[4] The Jersey City DMAP experiment found significant decreases in public morals calls for service and narcotics calls for service in treatment catchment areas relative to controls. The Jersey City DMAP experiment also replicated the drug market identification process and found six new drug hot spots within two blocks of the treatment locations; this result suggests that some modest displacement may have occurred, but it could not be determined whether these new drug hot spots were the result of experimental squad actions, control squad actions, or would have developed naturally without any enforcement efforts.

CONCLUSIONS AND POLICY IMPLICATIONS

The results of this systematic review support the assertion that focusing police efforts at high activity crime places can be used to good effect in preventing crime. Four of five experimental evaluations reported noteworthy crime and disorder reductions. Methodological problems in the research and evaluation design probably accounted for the lack of crime prevention gains in the Minneapolis RECAP experiment. While only two studies measured potential displacement and diffusion effects, this review also supports the growing body of research evidence that suggests that focused crime prevention efforts do not inevitably lead to the displacement of crime problems (Clarke and Weisburd, 1994; Hesseling, 1994; Eck, 1993); rather, when displacement was measured, it was quite limited and often unintended crime prevention benefits were associated with the hot spots policing programs.

Unfortunately, the results of this review provide criminal justice policy makers and practitioners with little insight on what types of policing strategies are most preferable in controlling crime hot spots. Clearly, the enforcement-oriented strategies reviewed here work in preventing crime. We do not know, however, which enforcement strategies are more effective in preventing crime and under what circumstances are certain strategies more appropriate. This review also offers little insight on the effectiveness of enforcement tactics relative to other broader-based community problem-solving policing programs (see e.g., Skogan and Hartnett, 1997). This small body of evaluation research does not unravel the

---

4   Property crime incidents experienced a significant increase while property crime calls for service did not significantly change in the treatment catchment areas relative to controls. The research team viewed this result as an artifact of the experiment rather than a substantive finding (Braga et al., 1999).

important question of whether enforcement-oriented programs result in long-term crime reductions in hot spot areas. Research suggests that a variety of situational factors cause crime to cluster at particular places (Eck and Weisburd, 1995). Proactive patrols, raids, and crackdowns do not specifically address the site features and facilities that cause specific locations to generate high volumes of crime. With the exception of the problem-oriented policing programs with limited situational interventions, the place-oriented interventions in this review consisted of uniform tactics applied across heterogeneous places. Perhaps a greater focus on changing these criminogenic situational characteristics would result in longer lasting crime reductions at crime places.

Beyond thinking about the relative crime prevention value of these programs, we need to know more about community reaction to increased levels of police enforcement action. Police effectiveness studies have traditionally paid little attention to the effects of policing practices upon citizen perceptions of police legitimacy (Tyler, 2000; 2001). Does the concentration of police enforcement efforts lead citizens to question the fairness of police practices? There is some evidence that residents of areas that are subjected to hot spots policing welcome the concentration of police efforts in problem places (Shaw, 1995). Nonetheless, focused aggressive police enforcement strategies have been criticized as resulting in increased citizen complaints about police misconduct and abuse of force in New York City (Greene, 1999). The potential impacts of hot spots policing on legitimacy may depend in good part on the types of strategies used and the context of the hot spots affected. Whatever the impact, we need to know more about the effects of hot spots policing approaches on the communities that the police serve.

REFERENCES

Barr, Robert, and Ken Pease. 1990. "Crime Placement, Displacement, and Deflection." In *Crime and Justice: A Review of Research*, Vol. 12, edited by Michael Tonry and Norval Morris, 277–318. Chicago: University of Chicago Press.

Berk, Richard, Gordon Smyth, and Lawrence W. Sherman. 1988. When Random Assignment Fails: Some Lessons from the Minneapolis Spouse Abuse Experiment. *Journal of Quantitative Criminology* 4: 209–223.

Bittner, Egon. 1970. *The Functions of the Police in Modern Society*. New York: Aronson.

Braga, Anthony. A. 1997. *Solving Violent Crime Problems: An Evaluation of the Jersey City Police Department's Pilot Program to Control Violent Places*. Unpublished Ph.D. dissertation. Newark, NJ: Rutgers University.

——. 2001. The Effects of Hot Spots Policing on Crime. *Annals of the American Academy of Political and Social Science* 578: 104–125.

——. 2002. *Problem-Oriented Policing and Crime Prevention*. Monsey, NY: Criminal Justice Press.

——, David Weisburd, Elin Waring, Lorraine Green Mazerolle, William Spelman, and Francis Gajewski. 1999. Problem-Oriented Policing in Violent Crime Places: A Randomized Controlled Experiment. *Criminology* 37: 541–580.

Brantingham, Paul, and Patricia Brantingham, eds. 1991. *Environmental Criminology*. Second ed. Prospect Heights, IL: Waveland Press.

Buerger, Michael, ed. 1992. *The Crime Prevention Casebook: Securing High Crime Locations.* Washington, DC: Crime Control Institute.

——. 1993. *Convincing the Recalcitrant: An Examination of the Minneapolis RECAP Experiment.* Unpublished Ph.D. dissertation. Newark, NJ: Rutgers University.

Clarke, Ronald V., and Marcus Felson. 1993. "Introduction: Criminology, Routine Activity, and Rational Choice." In *Routine Activity and Rational Choice, Advances in Criminological Theory,* Vol. 5, edited by Ronald V. Clarke and Marcus Felson, 1–14. New Brunswick, NJ: Transaction Press.

Clarke, Ronald V., and David Weisburd. 1994. "Diffusion of Crime Control Benefits: Observations on the Reverse of Displacement." In *Crime Prevention Studies,* Vol. 2, edited by Ronald V. Clarke, 165–183. Monsey, NY: Criminal Justice Press.

Cohen, Lawrence, and Marcus Felson. 1979. Social Change and Crime Rate Trends: A Routine Activity Approach. *American Sociological Review* 44: 588–605.

Cornish, Derek, and Ronald V. Clarke, eds. 1986. *The Reasoning Criminal: Rational Choice Perspectives on Offending.* New York: Springer-Verlag.

Eck, John E. 1993. The Threat of Crime Displacement. *Criminal Justice Abstracts* 25: 527–546.

——. 1997. "Preventing Crime at Places." In *Preventing Crime: What Works, What Doesn't, What's Promising,* by Lawrence W. Sherman, Denise C. Gottfredson, Doris Layton MacKenzie, John E. Eck, Peter Reuter, and Shawn D. Bushway, chapter 7. Washington, DC: National Institute of Justice, U.S. Department of Justice.

——. 2002. "Preventing Crime at Places." In *Evidence-Based Crime Prevention,* edited by Lawrence W. Sherman, David P. Farrington, Brandon C. Welsh, and Doris Layton MacKenzie, 241–294. New York: Routledge.

——, and David Weisburd. 1995. "Crime Places in Crime Theory." In *Crime and Place. Crime Prevention Studies,* Vol. 4, edited by John E. Eck and David Weisburd, 1–33. Monsey, NY: Criminal Justice Press.

Greene, Judith A. 1999. Zero Tolerance: A Case Study of Police Practices and Policies in New York City. *Crime & Delinquency* 45: 171–181.

Hesseling, Rene. 1994. "Displacement: A Review of the Empirical Literature." In *Crime Prevention Studies,* Vol. 3, edited by Ronald V. Clarke, 197–230. Monsey, NY: Criminal Justice Press.

Kelling, George, Anthony Pate, Duane Dickman, and Charles Brown. 1974. *The Kansas City Preventive Patrol Experiment: A Technical Report.* Washington, DC: Police Foundation.

Petrosino, Anthony, Robert F. Boruch, Catherine Rounding, Steve McDonald, and Iain Chalmers. 2000. The Campbell Collaboration Social, Psychological, Educational and Criminological Trials Register (C2-SPECTR) to Facilitate the Preparation and Maintenance of Systematic Reviews of Social and Educational Interventions. *Evaluation and Research in Education* 14: 206–219.

Pierce, Glenn, Susan Spaar, and LeBaron Briggs. 1988. *The Character of Police Work: Strategic and Tactical Implications.* Boston, MA: Center for Applied Social Research, Northeastern University.

Reppetto, Thomas. 1976. Crime Prevention and the Displacement Phenomenon. *Crime & Delinquency* 22: 166–177.

Shaw, James. 1995. Community Policing Against Guns: Public Opinion of the Kansas City Gun Experiment. *Justice Quarterly* 12: 695–710.

Sherman, Lawrence W. 1990. "Police Crackdowns: Initial and Residual Deterrence." In *Crime and Justice: A Review of Research,* Vol. 12, edited by Michael Tonry and Norval Morris, 1–48. Chicago: University of Chicago Press.

——. 1997. "Policing for Crime Prevention." In *Preventing Crime: What Works, What Doesn't, What's Promising,* by Lawrence W. Sherman, Denise C. Gottfredson, Doris Layton MacKenzie, John E. Eck, Peter Reuter, and Shawn D. Bushway, chapter 8. Washington, DC: National Institute of Justice, U.S. Department of Justice.

——. 2002. "Fair and Effective Policing." In *Crime: Public Policies for Crime Control,* edited by James Q. Wilson and Joan Petersilia, 383–412. Oakland, CA: Institute for Contemporary Studies Press.

——, Michael Buerger, and Patrick Gartin. 1989b. *Repeat Call Address Policing: The Minneapolis RECAP Experiment.* Final report to the National Institute of Justice. Washington, DC: Crime Control Institute.

——, and John E. Eck. 2002. "Policing for Crime Prevention." In *Evidence-Based Crime Prevention*, edited by Lawrence W. Sherman, David P. Farrington, Brandon C. Welsh, and Doris Layton MacKenzie, 295–329. New York: Routledge.

Sherman, Lawrence W., Patrick Gartin, and Michael Buerger. 1989a. Hot Spots of Predatory Crime: Routine Activities and the Criminology of Place. *Criminology* 27: 27–56.

Sherman, Lawrence W., and Dennis Rogan. 1995. Deterrent Effects of Police Raids on Crack Houses: A Randomized Controlled Experiment. *Justice Quarterly* 12: 755–782.

Sherman, Lawrence W., and David Weisburd. 1995. General Deterrent Effects of Police Patrol in Crime Hot Spots: A Randomized Controlled Trial. *Justice Quarterly* 12: 625–648.

Skogan, Wesley G., and Susan Hartnett. 1997. *Community Policing, Chicago Style*. New York: Oxford University Press.

Tyler, Thomas. 2000. Social Justice: Outcomes and Procedures. *International Journal of Psychology* 35: 117–125.

——. 2001. Public Trust and Confidence in Legal Authorities: What Do Majority and Minority Groups Members Want From the Law and Legal Institutions? *Behavioral Sciences and the Law* 19: 215–235.

Weisburd, David, and Anthony A. Braga. 2003. "Hot Spots Policing." In *Crime Prevention: New Approaches*, edited by Helmut Kury and Joachim Obergfell-Fuchs, 337–355. Mainz, Germany: Weisser Ring.

Weisburd, David, and Lorraine Green. 1995. Policing Drug Hot Spots: The Jersey City DMA Experiment. *Justice Quarterly* 12: 711–736.

Weisburd, David, Lisa Maher, and Lawrence W. Sherman. 1992. "Contrasting Crime General and Crime Specific Theory: The Case of Hot Spots of Crime." In *Advances in Criminological Theory*, Vol. 4, edited by Freda Adler and William S. Laufer, 45–69. New Brunswick, NJ: Transaction Press.

Weisburd, David, Stephen Mastrofski, and Rosann Greenspan. 2001. *Compstat and Organizational Change*. Washington, DC: Police Foundation.

Weisburd, David, Lawrence W. Sherman, and Anthony Petrosino. 1990. *Registry of Randomized Experiments in Criminal Sanctions, 1950–1983*. Los Altos, CA: Sociometrics Corporation, Data Holdings of the National Institute of Justice.

CHAPTER 13

CLOSED-CIRCUIT TELEVISION SURVEILLANCE*

Brandon C. Welsh
University of Massachusetts Lowell

David P. Farrington
Cambridge University

INTRODUCTION

Closed-circuit television (CCTV) surveillance cameras serve many functions and are used in both public and private settings. The prevention of personal and property crime is among its primary objectives. As an intervention targeted at crime, CCTV is a type of situational crime prevention (Clarke, 1995). According to Clarke and Homel's (1997) classification of situational crime prevention, CCTV is viewed as a technique of "formal surveillance." In this regard, CCTV cameras are seen to enhance or take the place of security personnel.

The mechanisms by which CCTV may prevent crime are numerous. These have been articulated by Armitage et al. (1999:226–227), and the main ones are as follows:

- Caught in the act – perpetrators will be detected and possibly removed or deterred.
- You've been framed – CCTV deters potential offenders who perceive an elevated risk of apprehension.
- Nosy Parker – CCTV may lead more people to feel able to frequent the surveilled places. This will increase the extent of natural surveillance by newcomers, which may deter potential offenders.
- Effective deployment – CCTV directs security personnel to ambiguous situations, which may head off their translation into crime.
- Publicity – CCTV could symbolize efforts to take crime seriously, and the perception of those efforts may both energize law-abiding citizens and/or deter crime.
- Time for crime – CCTV may be perceived as reducing the time available to commit crime, preventing those crimes that require extended time and effort.
- Memory jogging – the presence of CCTV may induce people to take elementary security precautions, such as locking their car, by jogging their memory.

* This research was commissioned by the U.K. Home Office.

Brandon C. Welsh and David P. Farrington, eds.
Preventing Crime: What Works for Children, Offenders, Victims, and Places, 193–208
© 2007 *Springer.*

- Anticipated shaming – the presence of CCTV may induce people to take elementary security precautions for fear that they will be shamed by being shown on CCTV.
- Appeal to the cautious – cautious people migrate to the areas with CCTV to shop, leave their cars, and so on. Their caution and security mindedness reduce the risk.

On the other hand, CCTV may cause reported and actual crime to increase. For example, CCTV may encourage increased reporting to police and recording by police. The presence of CCTV may give people a false sense of security and cause them to stop taking precautions that they would have taken in the absence of this intervention, such as not wearing jewelry or walking in groups when out at night. It may also cause crime to be displaced to other locations, times, or victims.

This chapter reports on the findings of a systematic review – incorporating meta-analytic techniques – of the highest quality available research evidence on the effects of CCTV on crime.

BACKGROUND

In recent years, there has been a tremendous growth in the use of CCTV to prevent crime in public space, especially in Britain (Norris and Armstrong, 1999) and, to a much lesser extent, in the U.S. (Nieto, 1997). In Britain, CCTV has been and continues to be the single most heavily funded non-criminal justice crime prevention measure. Over the three-year period of 1999 through 2001, the British government made available £170 million (approximately $250 million) for "CCTV schemes in town and city centres, car parks, crime hot-spots and residential areas" (Home Office Policing and Reducing Crime Unit, 2001:8). In previous years (1996 through 1998), CCTV accounted for more than three-quarters of total spending on crime prevention by the British Home Office (Koch, 1998). According to a recent report, the number of surveillance cameras in England and Wales has increased from 100 in 1990, to 400 in 1994, to 5,200 in 1997, to 40,000 in 2002 (Armitage, 2002).

During this time there has been much debate about the effectiveness of CCTV to prevent crime and hence, on the wisdom of spending such large sums of money. A key issue is how far funding for CCTV in Britain has been based on high quality scientific evidence demonstrating its efficacy in preventing crime. There is concern that this funding has been based partly on a handful of apparently successful schemes that were usually evaluated using simple one group (no control group) before-after designs, done with varying degrees of competence (Armitage et al., 1999), and done with varying degrees of professional independence from the Home Office (Ditton and Short, 1999). Recent reviews that have examined the effectiveness of CCTV in preventing crime (Eck, 1997; 2002; Phillips, 1999) have also noted the need for higher quality, independent evaluation research.

SUMMARY OF RESEARCH METHODS

Criteria for Inclusion of Evaluation Studies

In selecting evaluations for inclusion in this review, the following criteria were used:

1. CCTV was the focus of the intervention. For evaluations involving one or more other interventions, only those evaluations in which CCTV was the main intervention were included. The determination of the main intervention was based on the author identifying it as such or, if the author did not do this, the importance of CCTV relative to the other interventions. For a small number of included evaluations with multiple interventions, the main intervention was not identified, but it seemed clear from the report that CCTV was the most important.

2. There was an outcome measure of crime. The most relevant crime outcomes were violent and property crimes (especially vehicle crimes).

3. The evaluation design was of high methodological quality, with the minimum design involving before-and-after measures of crime in experimental and comparable control areas.

4. The total number of crimes in each area before the intervention was at least 20. The main measure of effect size was based on changes in numbers of crimes between the before and after time periods. It was considered that a measure of change based on an N below 20 was potentially misleading. Also, any study with less than 20 crimes before would have insufficient statistical power to detect changes in crime. The criterion of 20 is probably too low, but we were reluctant to exclude studies unless their numbers were clearly inadequate.

Search Strategies

The following four search strategies were carried out to identify CCTV evaluations meeting the criteria for inclusion in this review:

1. Searches of on-line data bases. The following data bases were searched: Criminal Justice Abstracts, National Criminal Justice Reference Service (NCJRS) Abstracts, Sociological Abstracts, Social Science Abstracts (SocialSciAbs), Educational Resources Information Clearinghouse (ERIC), Government Publications Office Monthly Catalog (GPO Monthly), Psychology Information (PsychInfo), and Public Affairs Information Service (PAIS) International. These data bases were selected because they had the most comprehensive coverage of criminological, criminal justice, and social science literatures.

The following terms were used to search these data bases: closed circuit television, CCTV, cameras, social control, surveillance, and formal surveillance. When applicable, "crime" was then added to each of these terms (for example, CCTV and crime) to narrow the search parameters.

2. Searches of literature reviews on the effectiveness of CCTV in preventing crime (Eck 1997; 2002; Nieto, 1997; Phillips, 1999; Poyner, 1993).

3. Searches of bibliographies of CCTV reports.

4. Contacts with leading researchers.

Both published and unpublished reports were included in the searches. Furthermore, the searches were international in scope and were not limited to the English language (one non-English language evaluation report is included in the review). The search strategies resulted in the identification of 49 CCTV evaluations. Of these, 47 were obtained and analyzed. Of these 47 evaluations, 22 met the criteria for inclusion and 25 did not and thus, have been excluded from this review. These 25 evaluations were excluded because they did not use a control area ($N = 18$), they had a noncomparable control area, such as the rest of the city ($N = 4$), or they did not report crime data ($N = 3$). The remaining two evaluations that were identified, which may or may not have met the criteria for inclusion, could not be obtained.[1]

RESULTS

How effective is CCTV in reducing crime? What is the effect of CCTV on crime in different settings? What is the effect of CCTV on different crime types? Is there a difference in the effectiveness of CCTV in preventing crime between the U.K. and North America? These are the main questions that this systematic review set out to address.

To address these questions, results obtained in the included evaluations – on the effects of CCTV on crime – were analyzed using the statistical technique of meta-analysis. In the case of CCTV evaluations, the measure of effect size had to be based on the number of crimes in the experimental and control areas before and after the CCTV intervention. This is because this was the only information that was regularly provided in these evaluations. Here, the odds ratio is used as the measure of effect size. For example, in the Doncaster city center CCTV evaluation (Skinns, 1998; see below), the odds of a crime after given a crime before in the control area were 2,002/1,780 or 1.12. The odds of a crime after given a crime before in the experimental area were 4,591/5,832 or 0.79. The odds ratio, therefore, was 1.12/0.79 or 1.42. This was statistically highly significant ($p < .0001$).[2]

---

1   For information on the unobtainable and excluded evaluations, see Welsh and Farrington (2002).
2   The odds ratio (OR) has a very simple and meaningful interpretation. It indicates the proportional change in crime in the control area compared with the experimental area. In this example, the OR of 1.42 indicates that crime increased by 42% in the control area compared with the experimental area. An OR of 1.42 could also indicate that crime decreased by 30% in the experimental area compared with the control area, since the change in the experimental area compared with the control area is the inverse of the OR, or 1/1.42 here. The OR is calculated from the following table:

	Before	After
Experimental	a	b
Control	c	d

Where a, b, c, d are numbers of crimes

    OR = ad/bc

The variance of OR is usually calculated from the variance of LOR (the natural logarithm of OR):

Each of the included evaluations, as well as those that could not be included in the meta-analysis (see below), were rated on their effectiveness in reducing crime. Each evaluation was assigned to one of the following four categories: desirable effect (marked decrease in crime), undesirable effect (marked increase in crime), null effect (evidence of no effect on crime), or uncertain effect (unclear evidence of an effect on crime).

Also important to this review were the issues of displacement of crime and diffusion of crime prevention benefits. Displacement is often defined as the unintended increase in crimes in other locations following from the introduction of a crime reduction scheme. Diffusion of benefits is often defined as the unintended decrease in crimes in adjacent areas following from a crime reduction scheme, or the "complete reverse" of displacement (Clarke and Weisburd, 1994).

In order to investigate these topics, the minimum design should involve one experimental area, one adjacent area, and one non-adjacent control area. If crime decreased in the experimental area, increased in the adjacent area, and stayed constant in the control area, this might be evidence of displacement. If crime decreased in the experimental and adjacent areas and stayed constant or increased in the control area, this might be evidence of diffusion of benefits. Very few of the included evaluations had both adjacent and non-adjacent but comparable control areas. More had an adjacent control area and the remainder of the city as another (non-comparable) control area, for example.

$$V(LOR) = 1/a + 1/b + 1/c + 1/d$$

In order to produce a summary effect size in a meta-analysis, each effect size (here, LOR) is weighted by the inverse of its variance ($1/V$). This estimate of the variance is based on the assumption that total numbers of crimes (a, b, c, d) have a Poisson distribution. Thirty years of mathematical models of criminal careers have been dominated by the assumption that crimes can be accurately modeled by a Poisson process (Piquero et al., 2003). If the number of crimes has a Poisson distribution, its variance should be the same as its mean. However, the large number of changing extraneous factors may cause overdispersion; that is, where the variance of the number of crimes VAR exceeds the number of crimes N.

$$D = VAR/N$$

specifies the overdispersion factor. Where there is overdispersion, V(LOR) should be multiplied by D. Farrington et al. (2005a) estimated VAR from monthly numbers of crimes and found the following equation:

$$D = .0005\,N + 2.2$$

D increased linearly with N and was correlated .81 with N. The median number of crimes in a CCTV study was 755, suggesting that the median value of D was about 2.5. However, this is an overestimate because the monthly variance is inflated by seasonal variations, which do not apply to N and VAR. Our best estimate was that the true value of D was about 2. Hence, V(LOR) calculated from the usual formula above was doubled in all cases.

Pooled Results

From the 19 evaluations that could be used in the meta-analysis,[3] it was concluded that CCTV had a significant but small desirable effect on crime, with a weighted mean odds ratio of 1.09 (95% confidence interval 1.06–1.13, $p < .0001$).[4] This means that crimes increased by 9% after CCTV in control areas compared to experimental areas or, conversely, crimes deceased by 8% in experimental areas compared to control areas. Table 1 summarizes the results of the 19 studies. This shows the odds ratio for total crime measured in each study plus its 95% confidence interval. It can be seen that just over half of the studies (10 out of 19) showed evidence of a desirable effect of CCTV on crime, with odds ratios of 1.27 or greater. Conversely, the other nine studies showed no evidence of any desirable effect of CCTV on crime, with odds ratios of 1.02 or less.

Setting

The 22 CCTV evaluations were carried out in three main settings: city center and public housing, public transport, and car parks.

City Center and Public Housing. Thirteen evaluations met the criteria for inclusion and were carried out in city centers ($N = 11$) or public housing ($N = 2$). Seven of the 13 evaluations were carried out in England, five in the United States, and one in Scotland (see Table 2). On average, the follow-up period in the evaluations was 10.9 months, ranging from a low of three months to a high of 24 months. Only the Doncaster program included other interventions in addition to the main intervention of CCTV. Many of the evaluations used multiple experimental areas (e.g., police beats, apartment buildings), meaning that the coverage of the CCTV intervention was quite extensive in the city or town center. Multiple control areas (e.g., adjacent police beats, remainder of city) were also used by some of the evaluations. We only included comparable control areas in our meta-analysis.

As shown in Table 2, the city center and public housing CCTV evaluations showed mixed results in their effectiveness in reducing crime. Five of the 13 evaluations were considered to have a desirable effect on crime, while three were

---

3   The odds ratio could not be calculated for three evaluations, because numbers of crimes were not reported in the Ilford (Squires, 1998), Brooklyn (Williamson and McLafferty, 2000), or (for the control area) the Sutton city center (Sarno, 1996) evaluations.

4   The weighted mean effect size in a fixed effects model was 1.09. The 19 effect sizes were significantly heterogeneous ($Q = 226.7$, $df = 18$, $p < .0001$). The weighted mean effect size in a random effects model was 1.25 (confidence interval 1.09–1.43, $p < .002$). However, this effect size was misleading. First, in the random effects model, smaller studies had almost the same weight as larger studies, and the smaller studies (especially in car parks) had the largest effect sizes. More weight, however, should be given to effect sizes derived from larger studies. Second, Jones (2005) used four other statistical methods to calculate a weighted mean effect size and found that they all produced results close to the fixed effects value of 1.09. We therefore conclude that the fixed effects value is correct and that the random effects value is not. Fixed effects models are used throughout Table 1.

TABLE 1. *Meta-Analysis of CCTV Evaluations*

	Odds Ratio	Confidence Interval	P Value
American City Center			
New York	0.89	0.30–2.62	n.s.
Cincinnati-N	0.98	0.89–1.09	n.s.
Cincinnati-H	0.91	0.78–1.07	n.s.
Cincinnati-F	1.00	0.93–1.08	n.s
British City Center			
Newcastle	0.90	0.84–0.96	.001
Birmingham	1.91	1.11–3.30	.02
Doncaster	1.42	1.28–1.58	.0001
Burnley	1.27	1.14–1.42	.0001
Airdrie	1.79	1.61–1.99	.0001
Cambridge	0.85	0.74–0.98	.023
Public Transport			
Underground-S	2.58	1.71–3.88	.0001
Underground-N	1.32	0.78–2.23	n.s.
Underground-C	0.89	0.74–1.08	n.s.
Montreal	1.02	0.85–1.22	n.s.
Car Parks			
Guildford	0.23	0.01–4.66	n.s.
Hartlepool	1.78	1.16–2.73	.008
Bradford	2.67	1.21–5.90	.015
Coventry	1.95	1.31–2.91	.001
Sutton	1.49	1.12–1.98	.007
Summary Results			
4 American City Center	0.98	0.93–1.04	n.s.
6 British City Center	1.14	1.09–1.19	.0001
10 City Center	1.08	1.04–1.11	.0001
4 Public Transport	1.06	0.94–1.20	n.s.
5 Car Parks	1.70	1.40–2.07	.0001
14 British	1.16	1.11–1.20	.0001
5 American	0.99	0.94–1.04	n.s.
6 Violent Crime	1.03	0.86–1.24	n.s.
8 Vehicle Crime	1.38	1.23–1.56	.0001
All 19 Studies	1.09	1.06–1.13	.0001

Notes: Cincinnati-N = Northside; Cincinnati-H = Hopkins Park; Cincinnati-F = Findlay Market; Underground-S = southern line; Underground-N = northern line; Underground-C = Oxford Circus.

considered to have an undesirable effect. Of the six British evaluations, four had a significant desirable effect, whereas two had a significant undesirable effect (see Table 1). The remaining five evaluations were considered to have a null ($N = 4$) or uncertain ($N = 1$) effect on crime. An equal number of schemes showed evidence of diffusion of benefits and displacement.

In pooling the data from the ten studies for which effect sizes could be calculated, there was evidence that CCTV led to a small but significant reduction in crime in city centers or public housing. The weighted mean effect size was an

TABLE 2.   *CCTV Evaluations in City Centers and Public Housing*

Author, Publication Date, Location	Other Interventions	Outcome Measure	Follow-up Period	Results and Displacement/Diffusion
Musheno et al. (1978), New York City	None	Crime (multiple offenses)	3 months	Uncertain effect; displacement/diffusion not measured
Brown (1995), Newcastle, England	None	Crime (multiple offenses)	15 months	Undesirable effect; some displacement and diffusion occurred
Brown (1995), Birmingham, England	None	Crime (total, most serious offenses)	12 months	Desirable effect; displacement occurred
Sarno (1996), Sutton, England	None	Crime (total, selected offenses)	12 months	Undesirable effect; diffusion/displacement not measured
Skinns (1998), Doncaster, England	Help points	Crime (total, selected offenses)	24 months	Desirable effect; no displacement occurred
Squires (1998), Ilford, England	None	Crime (total, violent, selected offenses)	7 months	Desirable effect; displacement occurred
Armitage et al. (1999), Burnley, England	None	Crime (total, multiple offenses)	12 months	Desirable effect; diffusion occurred
Ditton and Short (1999), Airdrie, Scotland	None	Crime (total, multiple categories)	24 months	Desirable effect; diffusion occurred
Williamson and McLafferty (2000), Brooklyn, NY	None	Crime (total, multiple categories)	18 months	Null effect; displacement and diffusion did not occur
Mazerolle et al. (2002), Cincinnati (Northside)	None	Calls for police service	6 months	Null effect; little or no displacement occurred
Mazerolle et al. (2002), Cincinnati (Hopkins Park)	None	Calls for police service	4 months	Null effect; displacement/diffusion not measured
Mazerolle et al. (2002), Cincinnati (Findlay Market)	None	Calls for police service	3.5 months	Null effect; some displacement occurred
Farrington et al. (2005b), Cambridge, England	None	Crime (total, multiple categories)	11 months	Undesirable effect; diffusion/displacement not measured

TABLE 3.   *CCTV Evaluations in Public Transport*

Author, Publication Date, Location	Other Interventions	Outcome Measure	Follow-up Period	Results and Displacement/ Diffusion
Burrows (1980), Underground (southern line), London, England	Notices of CCTV, special police patrols	Personal theft, robbery	12 months	Desirable effect; some displacement occurred
Webb and Laycock (1992), Underground (northern line), London, England	Passenger alarms, improved lighting	Robbery	26 months	Desirable effect; diffusion occurred
Webb and Laycock (1992), Underground (Oxford Circus), London, England	Passenger alarms, British Transport Police patrols	Personal theft, robbery, assault	32 months	Undesirable effect; diffusion/ displacement not measured
Grandmaison and Tremblay (1997), Metro, Montreal, Canada	None	Crime (total, multiple offenses)	18 months	Null effect; diffusion/ displacement not measured

odds ratio of 1.08 (95% confidence interval 1.04–1.11, $p < .0001$), which corresponds to a 7% reduction in crimes in experimental areas compared with control areas. However, when these ten studies were disaggregated by country, the six U.K. studies showed quite a large effect on crime (OR = 1.14, $p < .0001$), while the four American studies showed no effect on crime (OR = 0.98, n.s.).

Public Transport.   Four evaluations met the criteria for inclusion and were carried out in public transportation systems. All of the evaluations were conducted in underground railway systems: three in the London Underground and one in the Montreal Metro (see Table 3). The follow-up periods ranged from a low of 12 months to a high of 32 months. With the exception of the Canadian program, all of the programs involved interventions in addition to CCTV. In the first Underground scheme, notices were posted to alert people to the presence of CCTV cameras and special police patrols were in operation prior to the installation of CCTV.[5] For the two other Underground schemes, some of the other interventions that were used included: passenger alarms, kiosks to monitor

---

5   In the evaluation of this program, any effect of the police patrols was controlled by using as the before period the 12 months prior to the patrols coming into operation. The police patrols were discontinued at the time CCTV was implemented, so there was no direct influence of the patrols during the after period.

CCTV, and mirrors. For each of these three Underground schemes, CCTV was, however, the main intervention.

Overall, CCTV programs in public transportation systems present conflicting evidence of effectiveness: two had a desirable effect, one had no effect, and one had an undesirable effect on crime. However, for the two effective programs in the London Underground, the use of other interventions makes it difficult to say with certainty that it was CCTV that produced the observed crime reductions, although in the first of these programs CCTV was more than likely the cause. Only two of the studies measured diffusion of benefits or displacement, with one showing evidence of diffusion and the other displacement.

In pooling the data from the four studies, there was no significant evidence that CCTV led to a reduction in crime in public transport. The average effect size (weighted according to the standard error of each study) was an odds ratio of 1.06 (95% confidence interval 0.94–1.20, n.s.), which corresponds with a 6% reduction in crimes in experimental areas compared with control areas.

Car Parks. Five CCTV evaluations met the criteria for inclusion and were conducted in car parks. All of the programs were implemented in England between the early 1980s and the mid-1990s (see Table 4). The follow-up periods ranged from a low of ten months to a high of 24 months. All of the programs supplemented CCTV with other interventions, such as improved lighting, painting, fencing, payment schemes, notices about CCTV, and security personnel. In each program, however, CCTV was the main intervention.

TABLE 4. CCTV Evaluations in Car Parks

Author, Publication Date, Location	Other Interventions	Outcome Measure	Follow-up Period	Results and Displacement/ Diffusion
Poyner (1991), Guildford, England	Improved lighting, foliage cutback	Theft from vehicles	10 months	Undesirable effect; diffusion occurred
Tilley (1993), Hartlepool, England	Security officers, notices of CCTV, payment scheme	Theft of and from vehicles	30 months	Desirable effect; displacement occurred
Tilley (1993), Bradford, England	Notices of CCTV, improved lighting, painting	Theft of and from vehicles	12 months	Desirable effect; displacement/ diffusion not measured
Tilley (1993), Coventry, England	Lighting, painting, fencing	Theft of and from vehicles	8 and 16 months	Desirable effect; displacement/ diffusion not measured
Sarno (1996), Sutton, England	Locking overnight, lighting	Vehicle crimes (total)	12 months	Desirable effect; displacement/ diffusion not measured

As shown in Table 4, four of the programs had a desirable effect and one had an undesirable effect on vehicle crimes, which was the exclusive focus of each of the evaluations. Most studies did not measure either diffusion of benefits or displacement. The odds ratios showed a significant and desirable effect of CCTV for four of the schemes. In the other scheme (Guildford), the effect was undesirable, but the small number of crimes measured in the before and after periods meant that the odds ratio was not significant. When all five odds ratios were combined, the overall odds ratio was 1.70 (95% confidence interval 1.40–2.07, $p < .0001$). Thus, crime increased by 70% in control areas compared with experimental areas, or conversely crime decreased by 41% in experimental areas compared with control areas.

Crime Type

It was also possible to carry out a meta-analysis of the effect of CCTV on the most frequently measured crime types, which were violent crimes and vehicle crimes.

Violent Crimes. All four of the public transport evaluations provided information about the effects of CCTV on violent crimes (i.e., robbery, assault), but the numbers of violent crimes afterwards were very small in the Underground-S evaluation. The Cambridge, Burnley, and Airdrie city center evaluations also provided information on violent crimes in general. Combining these six evaluations (excluding the Underground-S evaluation), the overall odds ratio for the effect of CCTV on violent crimes was 1.03 (95% confidence interval 0.86–1.24, n.s.), which corresponds to a negligible 3% reduction in violent crimes in experimental areas compared with control areas.

Vehicle Crimes. All five car park evaluations provided information about the effects of CCTV on vehicle crimes (i.e., theft from, theft of, and criminal damage to vehicles), as did the Cambridge, Newcastle, and Burnley city center evaluations. Combining these eight evaluations, the overall odds ratio for the effect of CCTV on vehicle crimes was 1.38 (95% confidence interval 1.23–1.56, $p < .0001$). Thus, CCTV increased vehicle crimes by about 38% in control areas compared with experimental areas, or conversely decreased vehicle crimes by about 28% in experimental areas compared with control areas.

Country Comparison

Out of the 19 evaluations, 14 were from the U.K. and the other five were from North America (four from the U.S. and one from Canada). When the pooled meta-analysis results were disaggregated by country, there was evidence that the use of CCTV to prevent crime was more effective in the U.K. than it was in North America. From the U.K. studies, CCTV had a significant desirable effect on crime, with an overall 14% reduction in crime (OR = 1.16, 95% confidence interval 1.11–1.20, $p < .0001$), while in the North American studies, CCTV showed no desirable effect on crime (OR = 0.99, 95% confidence interval 0.94–1.04, n.s.).

CONCLUSIONS AND POLICY IMPLICATIONS

The studies included in this systematic review and meta-analysis showed that CCTV had a small but significant desirable effect on crime, has been most effective in reducing crime in car parks, has been most effective when targeted at vehicle crimes (largely a function of the successful car park schemes), and has been more effective in reducing crime in the U.K. than in North America.

Exactly what the optimal circumstances are for effective use of CCTV schemes is not entirely clear at present, and this needs to be established by future evaluation research. But it is interesting to note that the success of the CCTV schemes in car parks was limited to a reduction in vehicle crimes (the only crime type measured) and all five schemes included other interventions, such as improved lighting and security officers. Conversely, the evaluations of CCTV schemes in city centers and public housing measured a much larger range of crime types and, with one exception, the schemes did not involve other interventions. These CCTV schemes, and those focused on public transport, had only a small effect on crime. Could it be that a package of interventions focused on a specific crime type is what made the CCTV-led schemes in car parks effective?

Part of the difficulty in attempting to explain why CCTV schemes were more effective in reducing crime in car parks compared to the other settings was that important information on implementation (e.g., How many cameras were installed and where? What was their coverage area? Were the cameras monitored? If so, for how long and by whom?) was not always reported in the evaluation studies. Of course, this issue appears in other evaluations as well.

Another interesting finding to emerge from this review is that CCTV schemes in the U.K. showed a significant desirable effect on crime, while those in North America showed no desirable effect on crime. (Even the Brooklyn public housing scheme that could not be included in the meta-analysis showed evidence of having a null effect on crime; see Table 2.) What might account for this? Or, more importantly, what lessons can be drawn from the U.K. studies to help improve the crime prevention effectiveness of CCTV use in North America? There were some differences in key characteristics between the U.K. and North American CCTV schemes, which may help to address these questions.

First, the average follow-up period of the five North American CCTV schemes was substantially lower than for the 14 U.K. schemes: 6.9 months versus 18.4 to 19.0 months. (Four of the North American studies had the shortest follow-up periods of all 22 CCTV evaluations, ranging from a low of three months to a high of six months.) Because of the short follow-up periods in the North American studies, it is possible that the CCTV schemes were not given enough time to produce a clear effect on crime, either desirable or undesirable (all five of the North American studies showed evidence of either a null or uncertain effect on crime). Longer follow-up periods, as in the majority of the U.K. studies, seem to be warranted for future North American CCTV experiments.

Second, and perhaps most importantly, not one of the five North American schemes used other interventions alongside CCTV, while nine of the 14 U.K. schemes used one or more other types of intervention, such as improved lighting or police patrols. If the five car park schemes are removed, because all of them were carried out in the U.K. and involved other interventions, this leaves four (three with a desirable and one with an undesirable effect on crime) out of nine U.K. studies that used other interventions. It is possible that the absence of policing or other situational crime prevention measures in the North American CCTV schemes may be a contributing factor to their overall poor effect in reducing crime; for example, CCTV on its own may not represent a sufficient deterrent threat to influence an offender's decision making process to commit a crime or not.

Another important issue that may be a contributing factor to the difference in effectiveness between the U.K. and North American CCTV schemes is cultural context. In the U.K., there is a high level of public support for the use of CCTV cameras in public settings to prevent crime (Norris and Armstrong, 1999; Phillips, 1999), while in North America, particularly in the U.S., the public is less accepting of and more apprehensive of "Big Brother" implications arising from this surveillance technology (Murphy, 2002).

It could very well be that the poor showing of the North American CCTV schemes was due in part to a lack of this public support (and maybe even political support) for the schemes, which, in turn, may have resulted in cuts in program funding, the police assigning lower priority to the schemes, or attempts to discourage desirable media coverage, for example. Each of these could potentially undermine the effectiveness of CCTV schemes. In contrast, the U.K. Home Office, who funded many of the U.K. evaluations, wanted to show that CCTV was effective.

Advancing knowledge about the crime prevention benefits of CCTV programs should begin with attention to the methodological rigor of the evaluation designs. The use of a comparable control group by all of the 22 included evaluations went some way towards ruling out some of the major threats to internal validity, such as selection, maturation, history, and instrumentation (see Cook and Campbell, 1979; Shadish et al., 2002). The effect of CCTV on crime can also be investigated after controlling (for example, in a regression equation) not only for prior crime but also for other community-level factors that influence crime, such as neighborhood poverty and poor housing. Another possible research design is to match two areas and then to choose one at random to be the experimental area. Of course, several pairs of areas would be better than only one pair.

Also important in advancing knowledge about the effectiveness of CCTV in preventing crime is attention to methodological problems or changes to programs that take place during and after implementation. Some of these implementation issues include: statistical conclusion validity (adequacy of statistical analyses), construct validity (fidelity), and statistical power (to detect change) (see

Farrington and Painter, 2003). For some of the included evaluations, small numbers of crimes made it difficult to determine whether or not the program had an effect on crime. It is essential to carry out statistical power analyses before embarking on evaluation studies (Cohen, 1988). Few studies attempted to control for regression to the mean, which happens if an intervention is implemented just after an unusually high crime rate period. A long time series of observations is needed to investigate this. The contamination of control areas (that is, by the CCTV intervention) was another, albeit less common, problem that faced the evaluations.

There is also the need for longer follow-up periods to see how far the effects persist. Of the 22 included schemes, four were in operation for six months or less prior to being evaluated. This is a very short time to assess a program's impact on crime or any other outcome measure, and for these programs the question can be asked: Was the intervention in place long enough to provide an accurate estimate of its observed effects on crime? Ideally, time series designs are needed with a long series of crime rates in experimental and control conditions before and after the introduction of CCTV. In the situational crime prevention literature, brief follow-up periods are the norm, but "it is now recognized that more information is needed about the longer-term effects of situational prevention" (Clarke, 2001:29). Ideally, the same time periods should be used in before and after measures of crime.

Research is also needed to help identify the active ingredients of effective CCTV programs and the causal mechanisms linking CCTV to reductions in crime. One-third of the included programs involved interventions in addition to CCTV, and this makes it difficult to isolate the independent effects of the different components, and interactional effects of CCTV in combination with other measures. Future experiments are needed that attempt to disentangle elements of effective programs. Also, future experiments need to measure the intensity of the CCTV dose and the dose-response relationship, and need to include alternative methods of measuring crime (surveys as well as police records).

Research is also needed on the financial costs and benefits of CCTV programs. Only one of the 22 programs presented data on financial costs and benefits or conducted a cost-benefit analysis. Skinns (1998) found that the criminal justice costs saved from fewer prosecutions and sentences (the benefits) were greater than the costs of running the CCTV program by more than three times, for a benefit-cost ratio of 3.5 to 1. Previous work (Welsh and Farrington, 1999; 2000) has shown that situational crime prevention generally is an economically efficient strategy in preventing crime. It is important to measure the cost-effectiveness of CCTV in preventing crime compared with other alternatives such as improved street lighting.

Overall, it might be concluded that CCTV reduces crime. In light of the successful results, future CCTV schemes should be carefully implemented in different settings and should employ high quality evaluation designs with long follow-up periods.

REFERENCES

Armitage, Rachel. 2002. *To CCTV or Not? A Review of Current Research into the Effectiveness of CCTV Systems in Reducing Crime.* London, England: National Association for the Care and Resettlement of Offenders.

——, Graham Smyth, and Ken Pease. 1999. "Burnley CCTV Evaluation." In *Surveillance of Public Space: CCTV, Street Lighting and Crime Prevention. Crime Prevention Studies*, Vol. 10, edited by Kate Painter and Nick Tilley, 225–250. Monsey, NY: Criminal Justice Press.

Brown, Ben. 1995. *CCTV in Town Centres: Three Case Studies.* Crime Detection and Prevention Series Paper, No. 68. London, England: Home Office.

Burrows, John N. 1980. "Closed Circuit Television on the London Underground." In *Designing Out Crime*, edited by Ronald V.G. Clarke and Patricia Mayhew, 75–83. London, England: Her Majesty's Stationery Office.

Clarke, Ronald V. 1995. "Situational Crime Prevention." In *Building a Safer Society: Strategic Approaches to Crime Prevention. Crime and Justice: A Review of Research*, Vol. 19, edited by Michael Tonry and David P. Farrington, 91–150. Chicago: University of Chicago Press.

——. 2001. Effective Crime Prevention: Keeping Pace with New Developments. *Forum on Crime and Society* 1: 17–33.

——, and Ross Homel. 1997. "A Revised Classification of Situational Crime Prevention Techniques." In *Crime Prevention at a Crossroads*, edited by Steven P. Lab, 17–27. Cincinnati: Anderson.

Clarke, Ronald V., and David Weisburd. 1994. "Diffusion of Crime Control Benefits: Observations on the Reverse of Displacement." In *Crime Prevention Studies*, Vol. 2, edited by Ronald V. Clarke, 165–183. Monsey, NY: Criminal Justice Press.

Cohen, Jacob. 1988. *Statistical Power Analysis for the Behavioral Sciences.* Second ed. Hillsdale, NJ: Erlbaum.

Cook, Thomas D., and Donald T. Campbell. 1979. *Quasi-Experimentation: Design and Analysis Issues for Field Settings.* Chicago: Rand McNally.

Ditton, Jason, and Emma Short. 1999. "Yes, It Works, No, It Doesn't: Comparing the Effects of Open-Street CCTV in Two Adjacent Scottish Town Centres." In *Surveillance of Public Space: CCTV, Street Lighting and Crime Prevention. Crime Prevention Studies*, Vol. 10, edited by Kate Painter and Nick Tilley, 201–224. Monsey, NY: Criminal Justice Press.

Eck, John E. 1997. "Preventing Crime at Places." In *Preventing Crime: What Works, What Doesn't, What's Promising*, Lawrence W. Sherman, Denise C. Gottfredson, Doris L. MacKenzie, John E. Eck, Peter Reuter, and Shawn D. Bushway, chapter 7. Washington, DC: National Institute of Justice, U.S. Department of Justice.

——. 2002. "Preventing Crime at Places." In *Evidence-Based Crime Prevention*, edited by Lawrence W. Sherman, David P. Farrington, Brandon C. Welsh, and Doris L. MacKenzie, 241–294. New York: Routledge.

Farrington, David P., Martin Gill, Sam J. Waples, and Javier Argomaniz. 2005a. Studying the Effects of CCTV on Crime: Meta-Analysis of a National Evaluation. Unpublished paper.

Farrington, David P., Trevor H. Bennett, and Brandon C. Welsh. 2005b. The Cambridge Evaluation of the Effects of CCTV on Crime. In *Imagination for Crime Prevention: Essays in Honor of Ken Pease. Crime Prevention Studies*, edited by Graham Farrell. Monsey, NY: Criminal Justice Press, in press.

Farrington, David P., and Kate A. Painter. 2003. How to Evaluate the Impact of CCTV on Crime. *Crime Prevention and Community Safety* 5: 7–16.

Grandmaison, Rachel, and Pierre Tremblay. 1997. Évaluation des Effets de la Télé-Surveillance sur la Criminalité Commise dans 13 Stations du Métro de Montréal. *Criminologie* 30: 93–110.

Home Office Policing and Reducing Crime Unit. 2001. *Invitation to Tender: Evaluation of CCTV Initiatives.* Unpublished document. London, England: Author.

Jones, Hayley E. 2005. *Measuring Effect Size in Area-Based Crime Prevention Research.* Unpublished M.Phil. thesis. Cambridge, England: Statistical Laboratory, Cambridge University.

Koch, Brigitte C.M. 1998. *The Politics of Crime Prevention.* Aldershot, England: Ashgate.

Mazerolle, Lorraine, David C. Hurley, and Mitchell Chamlin. 2002. Social Behavior in Public Space: An Analysis of Behavioral Adaptations to CCTV. *Security Journal* 15: 59–75.

Murphy, Dean E. 2002. "As Security Cameras Sprout, Someone's Always Watching." *New York Times*, 29 September, pp. 1, 22.

Musheno, Michael C., James P. Levine, and Denis J. Palumbo. 1978. Television Surveillance and Crime Prevention: Evaluating an Attempt to Create Defensible Space in Public Housing. *Social Science Quarterly* 58: 647–656.

Nieto, Marcus. 1997. *Public Video Surveillance: Is It an Effective Crime Prevention Tool?* Sacramento, CA: California Research Bureau, California State Library.

Norris, Clive, and Gary Armstrong. 1999. *The Maximum Surveillance Society: The Rise of CCTV.* Oxford, England: Berg.

Phillips, Coretta. 1999. "A Review of CCTV Evaluations: Crime Reduction Effects and Attitudes Towards Its Use." In *Surveillance of Public Space: CCTV, Street Lighting and Crime Prevention. Crime Prevention Studies*, Vol. 10, edited by Kate Painter and Nick Tilley, 123–155. Monsey, NY: Criminal Justice Press.

Piquero, Alex R., David P. Farrington, and Alfred Blumstein. 2003. "The Criminal Career Paradigm." In *Crime and Justice: A Review of Research*, Vol. 30, edited by Michael Tonry, 359–506. Chicago: University of Chicago Press.

Poyner, Barry. 1991. Situational Crime Prevention in Two Parking Facilities. *Security Journal* 2: 96–101.

——. 1993. "What Works in Crime Prevention: An Overview of Evaluations." In *Crime Prevention Studies*, Vol. 1, edited by Ronald V. Clarke, 185–193. Monsey, NY: Criminal Justice Press.

Sarno, Christopher. 1996. "The Impact of Closed Circuit Television on Crime in Sutton Town Centre." In *Towards a Safer Sutton? CCTV One Year On*, edited by Marjorie Bulos and Duncan Grant, 13–49. London, England: London Borough of Sutton.

Shadish, William R., Thomas D. Cook, and Donald T. Campbell. 2002. *Experimental and Quasi-Experimental Designs for Generalized Causal Inference.* Boston: Houghton Mifflin.

Skinns, David. 1998. *Doncaster CCTV Surveillance System: Second Annual Report of the Independent Evaluation.* Doncaster, England: Faculty of Business and Professional Studies, Doncaster College.

Squires, Peter. 1998. *An Evaluation of the Ilford Town Centre CCTV Scheme.* Brighton, England: Health and Social Policy Research Centre, University of Brighton.

Tilley, Nick. 1993. *Understanding Car Parks, Crime and CCTV: Evaluation Lessons from Safer Cities.* Crime Prevention Unit Series Paper, No. 42. London, England: Home Office.

Webb, Barry, and Gloria Laycock. 1992. *Reducing Crime on the London Underground: An Evaluation of Three Pilot Projects.* Crime Prevention Unit Series Paper, No. 30. London, England: Home Office.

Welsh, Brandon C., and David P. Farrington. 1999. Value for Money? A Review of the Costs and Benefits of Situational Crime Prevention. *British Journal of Criminology* 39: 345–368.

——. 2000. "Monetary Costs and Benefits of Crime Prevention Programs." In *Crime and Justice: A Review of Research*, Vol. 27, edited by Michael Tonry, 305–361. Chicago: University of Chicago Press.

——. 2002. *Crime Prevention Effects of Closed Circuit Television: A Systematic Review.* Home Office Research Study, No. 252. London, England: Home Office.

Williamson, Douglas, and Sara McLafferty. 2000. "The Effects of CCTV on Crime in Public Housing: An Application of GIS and Spatial Statistics." Paper presented at the annual meeting of the American Society of Criminology, San Francisco, November.

CHAPTER 14

IMPROVED STREET LIGHTING*

David P. Farrington
Cambridge University

Brandon C. Welsh
University of Massachusetts Lowell

INTRODUCTION

Improved street lighting serves many purposes, one of them being the prevention of crime. While street lighting improvements may not often be implemented with the expressed aim of preventing crime – pedestrian safety and traffic safety may be viewed as more important aims – and the notion of lighting streets to deter lurking criminals may be too simplistic, its relevance to the prevention of crime has not gone unnoticed in urban centers, residential areas, and other places frequented by criminals and potential victims.

Explanations of the way street lighting improvements could prevent crime can be grouped into two main perspectives:

- Situational crime prevention that focuses on reducing opportunity and increasing perceived risk through modification of the physical environment (Clarke, 1995), such as Crime Prevention Through Environmental Design (Jeffery, 1977).
- A group of perspectives that stress the importance of strengthening informal social control and community cohesion through more effective street use (Angel, 1968; Jacobs, 1961) and investment in neighborhood conditions (Taub et al., 1984; Taylor and Gottfredson, 1986).

The situational approach to crime prevention suggests that crime can be prevented by environmental measures, which directly affect offenders' perceptions of increased risks and decreased rewards. This approach is also supported by theories, which emphasize natural, informal surveillance as a key to crime prevention. For example, Jacobs (1961) drew attention to the role of good visibility combined with natural surveillance as a deterrent to crime. She emphasized the association between levels of crime and public street use, suggesting that less crime would be committed in areas with an abundance of potential witnesses.

---

* This research was commissioned by the U.K. Home Office.

Brandon C. Welsh and David P. Farrington, eds.
Preventing Crime: What Works for Children, Offenders, Victims, and Places, 209–224
© 2007 *Springer.*

Other theoretical perspectives have emphasized the importance of investment to improve neighborhood conditions as a means of strengthening community confidence, cohesion, and social control (Kelling and Coles, 1996; Skogan, 1990; Wilson and Kelling, 1982). As a highly visible sign of positive investment, improved street lighting might reduce crime if it physically improved the environment and signaled to residents that efforts were being made to invest in and improve their neighborhood. In turn, this might lead them to have a more positive image of the area and to have increased community pride, optimism, and cohesion. It should be noted that this theoretical perspective predicts a reduction in both daytime and nighttime crime. Consequently, attempts to measure the effects of improved lighting should not concentrate purely on nighttime crime.

The relationship among visibility, social surveillance, and criminal opportunities is a consistently strong theme to emerge from the literature. A core assumption of both opportunity and informal social control models of prevention is that criminal opportunities and risks are influenced by environmental conditions in interaction with resident and offender characteristics. Street lighting is a tangible alteration of the built environment, but it does not constitute a physical barrier to crime. However, it can act as a catalyst to stimulate crime reduction through a change in the perceptions, attitudes, and behavior of residents and potential offenders.

It is also feasible that improved street lighting could, in certain circumstances, increase opportunities for crime. It may bring greater numbers of potential victims and potential offenders into the same physical space. Increased visibility of potential victims may allow better judgments of their vulnerability and attractiveness (e.g., in terms of valuables). Increased social activity outside the home may increase the number of unoccupied homes available for burglary. Increased illumination may make it easier to commit crimes and to escape.

The effects of improved street lighting are likely to vary in different conditions. In particular, they are likely to be greater if the existing lighting is poor and if the improvement in lighting is considerable. They may vary according to characteristics of the area or the residents, the design of the area, the design of the lighting, and the places that are illuminated. For example, improved lighting may increase community confidence only in relatively stable homogeneous communities, not in areas with a heterogeneous population mix and high residential mobility. The effects of improved lighting may also interact with other environmental improvements, such as closed circuit television (CCTV) cameras or security patrols.

This chapter reports on the findings of a systematic review – incorporating meta-analytic techniques – of the highest quality available research evidence on the effects of improved street lighting on crime.

BACKGROUND

Contemporary interest in the effect of improved street lighting on crime began in the U.S. during the dramatic rise in crime in the 1960s. Many towns and cities embarked upon major street lighting programs as a means of reducing crime, and initial results were encouraging (Wright et al., 1974). This proliferation of projects led to a detailed review of the effects of street lighting on crime by Tien et al. (1979), as part of the National Evaluation Program of Law Enforcement Assistance Agency (LEAA) funding. Their report described how the 103 street lighting projects originally identified were eventually reduced to a final sample of only 15 that were considered by the review team to contain sufficiently rigorous evaluative information. With regard to the impact of street lighting on crime, Tien et al. (1979) found that the results were mixed and generally inconclusive. However, each project was considered to be seriously flawed because of such problems as: weak project designs; misuse or complete absence of sound analytic techniques; inadequate measures of street lighting; poor measures of crime (all were based on police records); and insufficient appreciation of the impact of lighting on different types of crime.

The review by Tien et al. (1979) should have led to attempts to evaluate the effects of improved street lighting using more adequate designs and alternative measures of crime, such as victim surveys, self-reports, or systematic observation. It should also have stimulated efforts to determine in what circumstances improved street lighting might lead to reductions in crime. Unfortunately, it was interpreted as showing that street lighting had no effect on crime and effectively ended research on the topic in the U.S.

In the U.K., very little research was carried out on street lighting and crime until the late 1980s (Fleming and Burrows, 1986). There was a resurgence of interest between 1988 and 1990, when three small-scale street lighting projects were implemented and evaluated in different areas of London (Painter, 1994). In each location crime, disorder, and fear of crime declined and pedestrian street use increased dramatically after the lighting improvements.

In contrast to these generally positive results, a major British Home Office-funded evaluation in Wandsworth (Atkins et al., 1991) concluded that improved street lighting had no effect on crime, and a Home Office review, published simultaneously, also asserted that "better lighting by itself has very little effect on crime" (Ramsay and Newton, 1991:24). However, as further evidence has accumulated, there have been more signs that improved street lighting could have an effect in reducing crime. In the most recent review by Pease (1999), he considered that "the capacity of street lighting to influence crime has now been satisfactorily settled" (68). He also recommended that the debate should be moved from the sterile "does it work or doesn't it?" to the more productive "how can I flexibly and imaginatively incorporate lighting in crime reduction strategy and tactics?" (p. 72).

SUMMARY OF RESEARCH METHODS

Criteria for Inclusion of Evaluation Studies

In selecting evaluations for inclusion in this review, the following criteria were used:

1. Improved street lighting (or improved lighting) was the focus of the intervention. For evaluations involving one or more other interventions, only those evaluations in which improved lighting was the main intervention were included. The determination of what was the main intervention was based on the author identifying it as such or, if the author did not do this, the importance the report gave to improved lighting relative to the other interventions.

2. There was an outcome measure of crime. The most relevant crime outcomes were violent and property crimes.

3. The evaluation design was of high methodological quality, with the minimum design involving before-and-after measures of crime in experimental and comparable control areas.

4. The total number of crimes in each area before the intervention was at least 20. The main measure of effect size was based on changes in numbers of crimes between the before and after time periods. It was considered that a measure of change based on an N below 20 was potentially misleading. Also, any study with less than 20 crimes before would have insufficient statistical power to detect changes in crime. The criterion of 20 is probably too low, but we were reluctant to exclude studies unless their numbers were clearly inadequate.

Search Strategies

In order to locate studies meeting the above criteria, four search strategies were employed:

1. Searches of on-line data bases. The following data bases were searched: Criminal Justice Abstracts, National Criminal Justice Reference Service (NCJRS) Abstracts, Sociological Abstracts, Social Science Abstracts (SocialSciAbs), Educational Resources Information Clearinghouse (ERIC), Government Publications Office Monthly Catalog (GPO Monthly), Psychology Information (PsychInfo), and Public Affairs Information Service (PAIS) International.

The following terms were used to search these data bases: street lighting, lighting, illumination, and natural surveillance. When applicable, "crime" was then added to each of these terms (e.g., street lighting and crime) to narrow the search parameters.

2. Searches of literature reviews on the effectiveness of improved street lighting on crime (Eck, 1997; 2002; Fleming and Burrows, 1986; Painter, 1996; Pease, 1999; Poyner, 1993; Ramsay and Newton, 1991; Tien et al., 1979).

3. Searches of bibliographies of street lighting reports.

4. Contacts with leading researchers.

Both published and unpublished reports were considered in the searches. The searches were international in scope and were not limited to the English language. Importantly, the searches were only done for studies that might potentially be included in the review. As already mentioned, the exhaustive review by Tien et al. (1979) identified 103 street lighting projects carried out in the 1970s, but only considered that 15 (listed on their pp. 51–54) met their minimum methodological standards. An attempt was made to obtain 11 of these 15 evaluation reports. For the other four studies (conducted in Baltimore; Chicago; Richmond, Virginia; and Washington, DC), Tien et al. (1979) could not determine from the report that there was any kind of experimental-control comparison.

These search strategies resulted in the identification of 34 improved street lighting evaluations. Of these, 29 were obtained and analyzed. Of these 29 evaluations, 13 met the criteria for inclusion and 16 did not and thus, have been excluded from this review. These 16 evaluations were excluded for various reasons, including not having a comparable control area and having too few crimes. The remaining five evaluations could not be obtained, but it appeared from secondary sources that none met the methodological criteria for inclusion.[1]

RESULTS

To assess the effectiveness of improved street lighting in reducing crime, meta-analytic techniques were used. In the case of street lighting evaluations, the measure of effect size had to be based on the number of crimes in the experimental and control areas before and after the intervention. This is because this was the only information that was regularly provided in these evaluations. Here, the odds ratio is used as the measure of effect size. For example, in the Atlanta improved street lighting evaluation (Atlanta Regional Commission, 1974; see below), the odds of a crime after given a crime before in the control area were 431/234 or 1.842. The odds of a crime after given a crime before in the experimental area were 151/114 or 1.325. The odds ratio, therefore, was 1.842/1.325 or 1.39, which was substantial but not statistically significant.[2]

---

1 For information on the unobtainable and excluded evaluations, see Farrington and Welsh (2002).

2 The odds ratio (OR) has a very simple and meaningful interpretation. It indicates the proportional change in crime in the control area compared with the experimental area. In this example, the OR of 1.39 indicates that crime increased by 39% in the control area compared with the experimental area. An OR of 1.39 could also indicate that crime decreased by 28% in the experimental area compared with the control area, since the change in the experimental area compared with the control area is the inverse of the OR, or 1/1.39 here. The OR is calculated from the following table:

	Before	After
Experimental	a	b
Control	c	d

Where a, b, c, d are numbers of crimes

 OR = ad/bc

The variance of OR is usually calculated from the variance of LOR (the natural logarithm of OR):

 $V(LOR) = 1/a + 1/b + 1/c + 1/d$

This estimate of the variance is based on the assumption that total numbers of crimes (a, b, c, d) have a Poisson distribution. Thirty years of mathematical models of criminal careers (see e.g., Blumstein et al., 1986; Piquero et al., 2003) have been dominated by the assumption that the commission of crimes can be accurately modeled by a Poisson process. If the number of crimes has a Poisson distribution, its variance should be the same as its mean. However, the large number of changing extraneous factors may cause overdispersion; that is, where the variance of the number of crimes VAR exceeds the number of crimes N.

Each of the included evaluations was rated on their effectiveness in reducing crime. Each evaluation was assigned to one of the following four categories: desirable effect (marked decrease in crime), undesirable effect (marked increase in crime), null effect (evidence of no effect on crime), or uncertain effect (unclear evidence of an effect on crime).

Also important to this review were the issues of displacement and diffusion of benefits. Displacement is often defined as the unintended increase in crimes following a crime reduction scheme (see Barr and Pease, 1990). Five different forms of displacement have been identified by Reppetto (1976): temporal (change in time), tactical (change in method), target (change in victim), territorial (change in place), and functional (change in type of crime). Diffusion of benefits is defined as the unintended decrease in crimes following a crime reduction scheme, or the "complete reverse" of displacement (Clarke and Weisburd, 1994).

In order to investigate these topics, the minimum design should involve one experimental area, one adjacent area, and one non-adjacent comparable control area. If crime decreased in the experimental area, increased in the adjacent area, and stayed constant in the control area, this might be evidence of displacement. If crime decreased in the experimental and adjacent areas and stayed constant or increased in the control area, this might be evidence of diffusion of benefits. Only two of the included evaluations (Portland and Stoke-on-Trent) had both adjacent and non-adjacent but comparable control areas. Two others (Harrisburg and Fort Worth) had an adjacent control area and the remainder of the city as another (non-comparable) control area.

Pooled Results

From the 13 evaluations, it was concluded that improved street lighting had a significant desirable effect on crime, with a weighted mean odds ratio of 1.25 (95% confidence interval 1.08–1.44, $p = .002$). This means that crimes increased by 25% in control areas compared with experimental areas, or conversely crimes

---

$$D = VAR/N$$

specifies the overdispersion factor. Where there is overdispersion, V(LOR) should be multiplied by D. Farrington et al. (2005) estimated VAR from monthly numbers of crimes and found the following equation:

$$D = .0005 N + 2.2$$

D increased linearly with N and was correlated .81 with N. The median number of crimes in a lighting study was 205, suggesting that the median value of D was about 2.3. However, this is an overestimate because the monthly variance is inflated by seasonal variations, which do not apply to N and VAR. Our best estimate was that the true value of D was about 2. Hence, V(LOR) calculated from the usual formula above was doubled in all cases. For a more detailed discussion of the variance in this case, see Farrington and Welsh (2004).

TABLE 1.   Meta-Analysis of Street Lighting Evaluations

	Odds Ratio	Confidence Interval	P Value
American N Studies			
Portland	0.94	0.73–1.21	n.s.
Kansas City	1.24	0.84–1.83	n.s.
Harrisburg	1.02	0.66–1.59	n.s.
New Orleans	1.01	0.85–1.21	n.s.
American ND Studies			
Atlanta	1.39	0.92–2.10	n.s.
Milwaukee	1.37	0.95–1.98	n.s.
Fort Worth	1.38	0.84–2.29	n.s.
Indianapolis	0.75	0.39–1.43	n.s.
British ND Studies			
Dover	1.14	0.49–2.67	n.s.
Bristol	1.35	1.19–1.53	.0001
Birmingham	3.82	1.84–7.93	.0003
Dudley	1.44	1.05–1.96	.023
Stoke-on-Trent	1.72	0.99–2.99	.056
Summary Results			
4 American N Studies	1.02	0.89–1.16	n.s.
4 American ND Studies	1.28	1.02–1.61	.031
5 British ND Studies	1.40	1.26–1.57	.0001
8 American Studies	1.08	0.96–1.21	n.s.
9 ND Studies	1.38	1.25–1.52	.0001
All 13 Studies	1.25	1.08–1.44	.002

Notes: N = only night crimes measured; ND = night and day crimes measured.

decreased by 20% in experimental areas compared with control areas.[3] Both nighttime and daytime crimes were measured in all five British studies and four of the eight U.S. studies. The nine night/day studies also showed a significant desirable effect of improved lighting on crime (OR = 1.38, CI = 1.25–1.52, $p < .0001$).

Table 1 summarizes the results of all 13 studies. This shows the odds ratio for total crime in each study plus its 95% confidence interval and statistical significance. It can be seen that only two studies (Portland and Indianapolis) had odds ratios less than 1, meaning that improved street lighting was followed by an increase in crime, and in neither case was this increase significant. Therefore, the hypothesis that more lighting causes more crime can be firmly rejected.

---

3   Because the 13 effect sizes were significantly heterogeneous ($Q = 26.32$, 12 df, $p = .010$), a random effects model was used here. No other sets of effect sizes were significantly heterogeneous, so fixed effects models were used in other cases. The fixed and random effects models, and the other models used by Jones (2005), all produced very similar weighted mean effect sizes.

American Studies

Of the 13 improved street lighting evaluations included in this review, eight were carried out in the U.S. For the most part, residential neighborhoods was the setting for the intervention. Only four of the eight evaluations specified the degree of improvement in the lighting: by seven times in Milwaukee, four times in Atlanta, three times in Fort Worth, and two times in Portland (see Table 2). However, the description of the lighting in other cases (e.g., "high intensity street lighting" in Harrisburg and New Orleans) suggests that there was a marked improvement in the degree of illumination. Only in Indianapolis was the improved street lighting confounded with another concurrent intervention, and it was sometimes possible to disentangle this.

The control area was often adjacent to the experimental area. Hence, similar decreases in crime in experimental and control areas could reflect diffusion of benefits rather than no effects of improved lighting. In most cases, the reports noted that the control area was similar to the experimental area in sociodemographic factors or crime rates. However, none of the evaluations attempted to control for prior noncomparability of experimental and control areas. Only one evaluation (Portland) included an adjacent area and a comparable non-adjacent control area.

The outcome measure of crime was always based on police records before and after the improved street lighting. The Indianapolis evaluation was based on calls for service to the police, many of which did not clearly involve crimes (e.g., calls for "disturbance"). Only the Atlanta and Milwaukee studies provided total, nighttime, and daytime crimes. The Portland, Kansas City, Harrisburg, and New Orleans studies measured only nighttime crimes, and the Fort Worth and Indianapolis studies reported only total crimes.

As shown in Table 2, improved street lighting was considered to have a desirable effect on crime in four evaluations: Atlanta, Milwaukee, Fort Worth, and Kansas City. In all four cases, the odds ratio was 1.24 or greater. In the other four evaluations, the improved street lighting was considered to have a null effect on crime. The results of the meta-analysis of the eight American studies confirm these conclusions. The average effect size was an odds ratio of 1.08, which was not significant. Overall, crime increased by 8% in control areas compared with experimental areas, or conversely crime decreased by 7% in experimental areas compared with control areas.

The key dimension on which the eight effect sizes differed seemed to be whether they were based on data for both night and day (Atlanta, Milwaukee, Fort Worth, and Indianapolis) or for night only (the other four studies). For the four night/day studies, the average effect size was a significant odds ratio of 1.28 (CI = 1.02–1.61, $p = .031$), meaning that crime increased by 28% in control areas compared with experimental areas. For the four night only studies, the odds ratio was 1.02 (n.s.), indicating a negligible reduction in crime. Therefore, the eight American studies could be divided into two blocks of four, one block showing that crime reduced after improved street lighting and the other block showing that it did not.

TABLE 2. American Street Lighting Evaluations

Author, Publication Date, Location	Context of Intervention and Increase in Lighting	Other Interventions	Outcome Measure	Follow-up Period	Results and Diffusion/Displacement
Atlanta Regional Commission (1974), Atlanta, GA	City center; 4x	None	Crime (robbery, assault, and burglary)	12 months	Desirable effect; no displacement
DIFL (1974), Milwaukee, WI	Residential and commercial area; 7x	None	Crime (property and person categories)	12 months	Desirable effect; some displacement
Inskeep and Goff (1974), Portland, OR	Residential neighborhood (high crime); 2x	None	Crime (robbery, assault, and burglary)	6 or 11 months	Null effect; displacement and diffusion did not occur
Wright et al. (1974), Kansas City, MO	Residential and commercial areas; n.a.	None	Crime (violent and property offenses)	12 months	Desirable effect (for violence); some displacement
Harrisburg Police Department (1976), Harrisburg, PA	Residential neighbor-hood; n.a.	None	Crime (violent and property offenses)	12 months	Null effect; no displacement
Sternhell (1977), New Orleans, LA	Residential and commercial areas; n.a.	None	Crime (burglary, vehicle theft, and assault)	29 months	Null effect; no displacement
Lewis and Sullivan (1979), Fort Worth, TX	Residential neighborhood; 3x	None	Crime (total)	12 months	Desirable effect; possible displacement
Quinet and Nunn (1998), Indianapolis, IN	Residential neighborhood; n.a.	Police initiatives	Calls for service (violent and property crime)	6 to 9 months	Null effect; no displacement

Notes: DIFL = Department of Intergovernmental Fiscal Liaison; 4x = 4 times increase in lighting, and so forth; n.a. = not available.

Surprisingly, evidence of a reduction in crime was only obtained when both daytime and nighttime crimes were measured, although this feature may be a proxy for some other aspect of the different evaluation studies.

Unfortunately, all the American evaluations (except the Indianapolis one) are now rather dated, since they were all carried out in the 1970s. More recent American evaluations of the effect of improved street lighting need to be conducted. We now turn to the British evaluations, which were all published in the 1990s.

British Studies

The five British street lighting studies were carried out in a variety of settings, including a parking garage and a market, as well as residential neighborhoods (see Table 3). Three of the evaluations specified the degree of improvement in lighting: by five times in Stoke-on-Trent and by two times in Bristol (approximately) and Dudley. Control areas were usually located close to experimental areas. The outcome measure of crime was based on police records for three studies and on victim surveys in the other two cases (in Dudley and Stoke-on-Trent). Uniquely, the Dudley project also evaluated the impact of improved street lighting using self-reported delinquency surveys of young people. This project also included self-reports of victimization of young people and measures of fear of crime (Painter and Farrington, 2001).

As shown in Table 3, improved street lighting was considered to be effective in reducing crime in four studies (Bristol, Birmingham, Dudley, and Stoke-on-Trent). In the fifth study (Dover), the improved lighting was confounded with other improvements, including fencing to restrict access to the parking garage and the construction of an office near the main entrance. On the basis of police records, Poyner (1991) concluded that the intervention had reduced thefts *of* vehicles but not theft *from* vehicles.

Results of the meta-analysis of the five British studies confirm these conclusions. Total crimes reduced significantly after improved lighting in Bristol, Birmingham, Dudley, and almost significantly ($p = .056$) in Stoke-on-Trent. When the odds ratios from the five studies were combined, crimes increased by 40% after improved street lighting in control areas compared with experimental areas, or conversely crimes decreased by 29% in experimental areas compared with control areas ($OR = 1.40$, $CI = 1.26–1.57$, $p < .0001$).

In conclusion, these more recent British studies agree in showing that improved lighting reduces crime. They did not find that nighttime crimes decreased more than daytime crimes, suggesting that a "community pride" theory may be more applicable than a "deterrence/surveillance" theory.

CONCLUSIONS AND POLICY IMPLICATIONS

Eight American evaluation studies met the criteria for inclusion in the review, and their results were mixed. Four studies found that improved street lighting

TABLE 3. *British Street Lighting Evaluations*

Author, Publication Date, Location	Context of Intervention and Increase in Lighting	Other Interventions	Outcome Measure	Follow-up Period	Results and Diffusion/ Displacement
Poyner (1991), Dover	Parking garage (in town center); n.a.	Fencing, office constructed	Crime (total and theft of and from vehicles)	24 months	Desirable effect (for theft of vehicles); no displacement
Shaftoe (1994), Bristol	Residential neighborhood; 2x	None	Crime (total)	12 months	Desirable effect; not measured
Poyner and Webb (1997), Birmingham	City center market; n.a.	None	Thefts	12 months (6 months in each of 2 years)	Desirable effect; no displacement, some diffusion
Painter and Farrington (1997), Dudley	Local authority housing estate; 2x	None	Crime (total and types of offenses)	12 months	Desirable effect; no displacement
Painter and Farrington (1999), Stoke-on-Trent	Local authority housing estate; 5x	None	Crime (total and types of offenses)	12 months	Desirable effect; diffusion, no displacement

Notes: 4x = 4 times increase in lighting, and so forth; n.a. = not available.

was effective in reducing crime, while the other four found that it was not effective. Why the studies produced different results was not obvious, although there was a tendency for effective studies to measure both daytime and nighttime crimes and for ineffective studies to measure only nighttime crimes. However, all except one of these American evaluations date from the 1970s.

Five more recent British evaluation studies showed that improved lighting led to decreases in crime. Furthermore, in two studies (Dudley and Stoke-on-Trent), the financial savings from reduced crimes greatly exceeded the financial costs of the improved street lighting. Since these studies did not find that nighttime crimes decreased more than daytime crimes, a theory of street lighting focusing on its role in increasing community pride and informal social control may be more plausible than a theory focusing on increased surveillance and increased deterrence. The results did not contradict the hypothesis that improved street lighting was most effective in reducing crime in stable homogeneous communities. (While lack of systematic information on residential mobility made it difficult to draw clear conclusions about whether improved street lighting was more effective in reducing crime in stable homogeneous communities than in unstable heterogeneous communities, not one of the ten studies[4] that could be included in this analysis clearly contradicted this hypothesis, and four studies (Dudley, Stoke-on-Trent, Harrisburg, and Fort Worth) were clearly concordant with it; for more details, see Farrington and Welsh, 2002.)

An alternative hypothesis is that increased community pride comes first, causing improved street lighting on the one hand and reduced crime on the other, with no causal effect of improved lighting on crime. It is difficult to exclude this hypothesis on the basis of most published evaluation reports. However, it can be excluded in the two evaluations (Dudley and Stoke-on-Trent) in which one of us (Farrington) was involved.

In Dudley, there had been no marked changes on the experimental estate for many years. The tenants on this and other local authority housing estates had complained about the poor lighting for some time, and this was why the local authority decided to improve the lighting on the experimental estate. The improvement in lighting was very obvious, and tenants thought that their quality of life had been improved (Painter and Farrington, 1997). This stimulated the Tenants' Association on the experimental estate to obtain £10 million (approximately $15 million) from the Department of the Environment for a program of neighborhood improvements in the next few years. The improvement in lighting on the experimental estate also stimulated the Tenants' Association on the control estate to petition the local authority to improve their lighting.

In Dudley, it was clear that the improved lighting occurred first, led to increased community pride, and acted as a catalyst for further environmental improvements. A similar chain of events happened in Stoke-on-Trent. While we cannot be sure that the same causal ordering occurred in all other street lighting

---

4   The three studies that could not be included in this analysis were: Indianapolis, Dover, and Birmingham.

evaluations, it might be concluded that in at least some studies improved lighting caused increased community pride and decreased crime.

Future research should be designed to test the main theories of the effects of improved street lighting (i.e., community pride versus surveillance/deterrence) more explicitly. Surveys of youth in experimental and control areas could be carried out, to investigate their offending, their opinions of the area, their street use patterns, and factors that might inhibit them from offending (e.g., informal social control by older residents, increased surveillance after dark). Household surveys of adults could also be carried out, focusing on perceptions of improvements in the community, community pride, informal social control of young people, street use, and surveillance after dark.

Ideally, future research should measure crime using police records, victim surveys, and self-reports of offending. It is possible that one effect of improved street lighting may be to facilitate or encourage reporting of crimes to the police; for example, if victims get a better view of offenders. Therefore, police records may be misleading. Surveys of potential victims and potential offenders are necessary for testing key hypotheses about the effects of improved lighting.

Future research should ideally include several experimental areas and several comparable adjacent and control areas. Adjacent areas are needed to test hypotheses about displacement and diffusion of benefits. The comparability of experimental, adjacent, and control areas should be investigated. The use of several areas would make it more possible to establish boundary conditions under which improved lighting had greater or lesser effects. The numbers of crimes recorded in each area in the before period should be sufficient to detect changes reliably. Ideally, large numbers of potential victims and potential offenders should be surveyed.

Crimes should be measured before and after the intervention in experimental, adjacent, and control areas. Ideally, a long time series of crimes should be studied to investigate pre-existing crime trends and also how far any effects of street lighting persist or wear off over time. Different types of crimes should be measured, and also crimes committed during daytime and the hours of darkness. The improvement in lighting in different areas should be carefully measured, including vertical and horizontal levels of illumination. Cost-benefit analyses of the impact of improved street lighting should be carried out (only 2 of the 13 studies conducted a cost-benefit analysis). Our previous work (Welsh and Farrington, 1999; 2000) has shown that situational crime prevention is an economically efficient strategy in preventing crime.

In testing hypotheses, it would be useful to investigate the effects of street lighting in conjunction with other crime prevention interventions. To the extent that community pride is important, this could be enhanced by other environmental improvements. To the extent that surveillance is important, this could be enhanced by other interventions, such as CCTV cameras. For example, one experimental area could have both improved street lighting and CCTV, a second could have only improved street lighting, and a third could have only CCTV.

This kind of planned evaluation of interactions of crime prevention initiatives has rarely been attempted.

The policy implications of research on improved street lighting have been well articulated by Pease (1999). He pointed out that situational crime prevention involved the modification of environments so that crime involved more effort, more risk, and lower rewards. The first step in any crime reduction program required a careful analysis of situations and how they affected potential offenders and potential victims. The second step involved implementing crime reduction interventions. Whether improved street lighting was likely to be effective in reducing crime would depend on characteristics of situations and on other concurrent situational interventions. Efforts to reduce crime should take account of the fact that crime tends to be concentrated among certain people and in certain locations, rather than being evenly distributed throughout a community.

The British studies included in this review show that improved lighting can be effective in reducing crime in some circumstances. Exactly what are the optimal circumstances is not clear at present, and this needs to be established by future evaluation research. However, improved street lighting should be considered as a potential strategy in any crime reduction program in coordination with other intervention strategies. Depending on the analysis of the crime problem, improved street lighting could often be implemented as a feasible, inexpensive, and effective method of reducing crime.

Street lighting has some advantages over other situational measures that have been associated with the creeping privatization of public space, the exclusion of sections of the population, and the move towards a "fortress" society (Bottoms, 1990). Street lighting benefits the whole neighborhood rather than particular individuals or households. It is not a physical barrier to crime, it has no adverse civil liberties implications, and it can increase public safety and effective use of neighborhood streets at night. In short, improved street lighting has few negative effects and clear benefits for law-abiding citizens.

REFERENCES

Angel, S. 1968. *Discouraging Crime Through City Planning*. Working Paper, No. 5. Berkeley, CA: University of California.

Atkins, Stephen, Sohail Husain, and Angele Storey. 1991. *The Influence of Street Lighting on Crime and Fear of Crime*. Crime Prevention Unit Paper, No. 28. London, England: Home Office.

Atlanta Regional Commission. 1974. *Street Light Project: Final Evaluation Report*. Atlanta, GA: Author.

Barr, Robert, and Ken Pease. 1990. "Crime Placement, Displacement, and Deflection." In *Crime and Justice: A Review of Research*, Vol. 12, edited by Michael Tonry and Norval Morris, 277–318. Chicago: University of Chicago Press.

Bottoms, Anthony E. 1990. Crime Prevention Facing the 1990s. *Policing and Society* 1: 3–22.

Blumstein, Alfred, Jacqueline Cohen, Jeffrey A. Roth, and Christy A. Visher, eds. 1986. *Criminal Careers and "Career Criminals,"* Vol. 1. Washington, DC: National Academy Press.

Clarke, Ronald V. 1995. "Situational Crime Prevention." In *Building a Safer Society: Strategic Approaches to Crime Prevention. Crime and Justice: A Review of Research*, Vol. 19, edited by Michael Tonry and David P. Farrington, 91–150. Chicago: University of Chicago Press.

——, and David Weisburd. 1994. "Diffusion of Crime Control Benefits: Observations on the Reverse of Displacement." In *Crime Prevention Studies*, Vol. 2, edited by Ronald V. Clarke, 165–183. Monsey, NY: Criminal Justice Press.

Department of Intergovernmental Fiscal Liaison. 1974. *Final Report – Milwaukee High Intensity Street Lighting Project*. Milwaukee, WI: Author.

Eck, John E. 1997. "Preventing Crime at Places." In *Preventing Crime: What Works, What Doesn't, What's Promising*, by Lawrence W. Sherman, Denise C. Gottfredson, Doris L. MacKenzie, John E. Eck, Peter Reuter, and Shawn D. Bushway, chapter 7. Washington, DC: National Institute of Justice, U.S. Department of Justice.

——. 2002. "Preventing Crime at Places." In *Evidence-Based Crime Prevention*, edited by Lawrence W. Sherman, David P. Farrington, Brandon C. Welsh, and Doris L. MacKenzie, 241–294. New York: Routledge.

Farrington, David P., and Brandon C. Welsh. 2002. *Effects of Improved Street Lighting on Crime: A Systematic Review*. Home Office Research Study, No. 251. London, England: Home Office.

——. 2004. Measuring the Effects of Improved Street Lighting on Crime: A Reply to Dr Marchant. *British Journal of Criminology* 44: 448–467.

Farrington, David P., Martin Gill, Sam J. Waples, and Javier Argomaniz. 2005. Studying the Effects of CCTV on Crime: Meta-Analysis of a National Evaluation. Unpublished paper.

Fleming, Roy, and John N. Burrows. 1986. The Case for Lighting as a Means of Preventing Crime. *Home Office Research Bulletin* 22: 14–17.

Harrisburg Police Department. 1976. *Final Evaluation Report of the "High Intensity Street Lighting Program."* Harrisburg, PA: Planning and Research Section, Staff and Technical Services Division, Harrisburg Police Department.

Inskeep, Norman R., and Clinton Goff. 1974. *A Preliminary Evaluation of the Portland Lighting Project*. Salem, OR: Oregon Law Enforcement Council.

Jacobs, Jane. 1961. *The Death and Life of Great American Cities*. New York: Random House.

Jeffery, C. Ray. 1977. *Crime Prevention Through Environmental Design*. Second ed. Beverly Hills, CA: Sage.

Jones, Hayley E. 2005. *Measuring Effect Size in Area-Based Crime Prevention Research*. Unpublished M.Phil. thesis. Cambridge, England: Statistical Laboratory, Cambridge University.

Kelling, George L., and Catherine M. Coles. 1996. *Fixing Broken Windows: Restoring Order and Reducing Crime in Our Communities*. New York: Simon and Schuster.

Lewis, Edward B., and Tommy T. Sullivan. 1979. Combating Crime and Citizen Attitudes: A Case Study of the Corresponding Reality. *Journal of Criminal Justice* 7: 71–79.

Painter, Kate. 1994. The Impact of Street Lighting on Crime, Fear, and Pedestrian Street Use. *Security Journal* 5: 116–124.

——. 1996. "Street Lighting, Crime and Fear of Crime: A Summary of Research." In *Preventing Crime and Disorder: Targeting Strategies and Responsibilities*, edited by Trevor H. Bennett, 313–351. Cambridge, England: Institute of Criminology, University of Cambridge.

Painter, Kate, and David P. Farrington. 1997. "The Crime Reducing Effect of Improved Street Lighting: The Dudley Project." In *Situational Crime Prevention: Successful Case Studies*, edited by Ronald V. Clarke, 209–226. Second ed. Guilderland, NY: Harrow and Heston.

——. 1999. "Street Lighting and Crime: Diffusion of Benefits in the Stoke-on-Trent Project. In *Surveillance of Public Space: CCTV, Street Lighting and Crime Prevention. Crime Prevention Studies*, Vol. 10, edited by Kate Painter and Nick Tilley, 77–122. Monsey, NY: Criminal Justice Press.

——. 2001. Evaluating Situational Crime Prevention Using a Young People's Survey. *British Journal of Criminology* 41: 266–284.

Pease, Ken. 1999. "A Review of Street Lighting Evaluations: Crime Reduction Effects." In *Surveillance of Public Space: CCTV, Street Lighting and Crime Prevention*, edited by Kate Painter and Nick Tilley, 47–76. Monsey, NY: Criminal Justice Press.

Piquero, Alex R., David P. Farrington, and Alfred Blumstein. 2003. "The Criminal Career Paradigm." In *Crime and Justice: A Review of Research*, Vol. 30, edited by Michael Tonry, 359–506. Chicago: University of Chicago Press.

Poyner, Barry. 1991. Situational Crime Prevention in Two Parking Facilities. *Security Journal* 2: 96–101.

——. 1993. "What Works in Crime Prevention: An Overview of Evaluations." In *Crime Prevention Studies*, Vol. 1, edited by Ronald V. Clarke, 7–34. Monsey, NY: Criminal Justice Press.

——, and Barry Webb. 1997. "Reducing Theft from Shopping Bags in City Center Markets." In *Situational Crime Prevention: Successful Case Studies*, edited by Ronald V. Clarke, 83–89. Second ed. Guilderland, NY: Harrow and Heston.

Quinet, Kenna D., and Samuel Nunn. 1998. Illuminating Crime: The Impact of Street Lighting on Calls for Police Service. *Evaluation Review* 22: 751–779.

Ramsay, Malcolm, and Rosemary Newton. 1991. *The Effect of Better Street Lighting on Crime and Fear: A Review*. Crime Prevention Unit Paper, No. 29. London, England: Home Office.

Reppetto, Thomas A. 1976. Crime Prevention and the Displacement Phenomenon. *Crime & Delinquency* 22: 166–177.

Shaftoe, Henry. 1994. "Easton/Ashley, Bristol: Lighting Improvements." In *Housing Safe Communities: An Evaluation of Recent Initiatives*, edited by Steven Osborn, 72–77. London, England: Safe Neighbourhoods Unit.

Skogan, Wesley G. 1990. *Disorder and Decline: Crime and the Spiral of Decay in American Neighborhoods*. New York: Free Press.

Sternhell, Robert. 1977. *The Limits of Lighting: The New Orleans Experiment in Crime Reduction*. Final Impact Evaluation Report. New Orleans, LA: Mayor's Criminal Justice Coordinating Council.

Taub, Richard P., D. Garth Taylor, and Jan D. Dunham. 1984. *Paths of Neighborhood Change: Race and Crime in Urban America*. Chicago: University of Chicago Press.

Taylor, Ralph B., and Stephen Gottfredson. 1986. "Environmental Design, Crime and Prevention: An Examination of Community Dynamics." In *Communities and Crime. Crime and Justice: A Review of Research*, edited by Albert J. Reiss, Jr. and Michael Tonry, 387–416. Chicago: University of Chicago Press.

Tien, James M., Vincent F. O'Donnell, Arnold Barnett, and Pitu B. Mirchandani. 1979. *Street Lighting Projects: National Evaluation Program*. Phase 1 Report. Washington, DC: National Institute of Law Enforcement and Criminal Justice, U.S. Department of Justice.

Welsh, Brandon C., and David P. Farrington. 1999. Value for Money? A Review of the Costs and Benefits of Situational Crime Prevention. *British Journal of Criminology* 39: 345–368.

——. 2000. "Monetary Costs and Benefits of Crime Prevention Programs." In *Crime and Justice: A Review of Research*, Vol. 27, edited by Michael Tonry, 305–361. Chicago: University of Chicago Press.

Wilson, James Q., and George L. Kelling. 1982. Broken Windows: The Police and Neighborhood Safety. *Atlantic Monthly* March: 29–38.

Wright, Roger, Martin Heilweil, Paula Pelletier, and Karen Dickinson. 1974. *The Impact of Street Lighting on Crime*. Ann Arbor, MI: University of Michigan.

PART V: POLICY CHOICES FOR A SAFER SOCIETY

CHAPTER 15

CONCLUSIONS AND DIRECTIONS FROM EVIDENCE-BASED CRIME PREVENTION

Brandon C. Welsh

University of Massachusetts Lowell

David P. Farrington

Cambridge University

INTRODUCTION

At the heart of the evidence-based paradigm is the notion that "we are all entitled to our own opinions, but not to our own facts" (Sherman, 1998:4). Many people may be of the opinion that hiring more police officers, for example, will yield a reduction in crime rates. However, an examination of the empirical research evidence on the subject reveals that this is not the case (Sherman and Eck, 2002; Weisburd and Eck, 2004). And there are scores of other crime and justice examples where opinion and fact do not agree. Use of opinion instead of fact to guide crime policy is likely to lead to programs that do not work, result in harmful or iatrogenic effects (McCord, 2003), waste scarce public resources (Welsh and Farrington, 2000), or divert policy attention away from the important priorities of the day.

In an evidence-based society, government crime prevention policy and local practice would be based on interventions with demonstrated effectiveness in preventing crime – using what works best. Equally important, governments would put an end to those interventions that do not work or are harmful. One of the key factors here is the advancement of the science of prevention. This is achieved through the support of high-quality research – experimental (and quasi-experimental) evaluations – on the effects of interventions. Another issue that is likely to be even more important than the research process and its product is the political and policy decision about what evidence gets used and what does not. Here, resources, public opinion, other domestic or international priorities, as well as the politicization of crime and justice can come to dominate.

Systematic reviews are the most comprehensive method to assess the effectiveness of crime prevention measures and, in an evidence-based society, they would be the source that governments would turn to for help in the development of policy. This book reports on 13 systematic reviews of different criminological interventions, organized around four important domains: at-risk children,

Brandon C. Welsh and David P. Farrington, eds.
Preventing Crime: What Works for Children, Offenders, Victims, and Places, 227–237

offenders, victims, and places. Each follows as closely as possible the methodology for conducting systematic reviews as advocated by the Campbell Collaboration. Each of the 13 systematic reviews reported here stands as the leading scientific statement on the topic under investigation and, taken together, they represent the leading source of scientific knowledge on what works best to prevent crime. Also important, this collection demonstrates that some criminological interventions – ones that are well known and remain popular with many constituents in the U.S. – do not work or are harmful. Although the results of these reviews are disappointing news from a policy perspective, they are nevertheless important from a scientific perspective. This is because these results direct our attention toward other crime prevention programs that show evidence of proven effectiveness.

In the next few sections we summarize the key findings from the 13 systematic reviews reported in this book. This is followed by a discussion of future directions for research and policy development to advance evidence-based crime prevention and contribute to a safer society.

WHAT WORKS FOR CHILDREN

In the systematic review of early parent training for families with children under age three years, by Odette Bernazzani and Richard Tremblay, seven studies are included, all using randomized controlled experiments. The impact of the intervention is assessed using the outcome measures of child disruptive behavior (e.g., opposition to adults, truancy, aggression) and delinquency (one study). The review finds mixed results on the effectiveness of parent training in preventing child behavior problems under age three: four studies report no evidence of effectiveness, two report beneficial effects, and one reports mainly beneficial effects with some harmful effects. Control subjects typically received non-intensive, basic services. The one study that did measure delinquency showed beneficial effects on this outcome. The authors call for caution in interpreting these results due to, for example, the limited number of high-quality studies and the modest effect sizes of the beneficial studies. Noting the well-established link between child disruptive behavior and delinquency involvement, the authors recommend the testing of different parent training interventions focused on this early problematic behavior.

In the systematic review of the effects of child social skills or social competence training on antisocial behavior (including delinquency), by Friedrich Lösel and Andreas Beelmann, 55 studies with 89 separate experimental-control group comparisons are included. All of the studies are randomized controlled experiments. A meta-analysis finds that almost half of the comparisons reveal positive results, ranging from small to large effect sizes, favoring the children who received the treatment compared to those who did not, while less than one out of ten reveal negative results (i.e., the control group fared better than the treatment group). Control subjects typically received non-intensive, basic services. Mixed results are found for temporal effects of child social skills training on delinquency. At post-intervention (completion of the intervention) the smallest effect size is for delinquency (the mean effect sizes for all outcomes favor the treatment condition), but at later follow-up periods delinquency is the only outcome that is significantly affected. The meta-analysis also finds that the most effective social skills training programs use a cognitive-behavioral approach and are implemented with older children (13 years and over) and higher risk groups who are already exhibiting some behavioral problems. On the basis of their findings, the authors contend that child social skills training represents a "promising approach to crime prevention." Larger samples, longer follow-up periods, and firm outcome criteria are among the authors' recommendations to advance knowledge on this intervention.

WHAT WORKS FOR OFFENDERS

As with the two systematic reviews of interventions for at-risk children, mixed findings are also found across the five systematic reviews of interventions for offenders. In the case of cognitive-behavioral therapy (CBT), Mark Lipsey and Nana Landenberger find that – using meta-analytical techniques – all but one of the 14 included studies (all randomized controlled experiments) show a desirable effect on recidivism (a reduction) and the overall mean effect size is a statistically significant .25. This corresponds approximately to a decrease in recidivism from 45% in the control group (the mean rate across the studies) to 33% in the treatment group, or a 27% decrease in the recidivism rate. Control subjects typically receive the usual correctional services, such as routine probation, prison, or parole services. The authors find that the most important factor related to the effects of CBT on recidivism is whether the intervention was carried out as part of a research or demonstration project ($n = 10$) or routine criminal justice practice ($n = 4$). A comparison of the treatment-control differences for the two types of studies reveal that the research and demonstration projects are four times more effective than the routine practice projects, for a reduction in recidivism rates of 49% versus 11%. Further analyses show that research-based projects targeted at higher risk offenders and administered by well-trained and well-supervised providers of CBT produce the largest effects on recidivism rates, nearly a 60% reduction. While these findings highlight the diminished potential of CBT for offenders in real-life settings, the authors note that the good news for correctional policy and practice is that treatment effectiveness appears to be mainly a function of the quality of the CBT provided. This "suggests that any representative CBT program delivered in typical amounts might have results in practice that approach those produced in R&D projects if they were implemented well by appropriately qualified personnel and closely monitored" (Lipsey and Landenberger, this volume).

In the systematic review of correctional boot camps, by David Wilson and Doris MacKenzie, 32 studies with 43 separate experimental-control group comparisons are included, and effectiveness is assessed by recidivism. The included studies are randomized controlled experiments and quasi-experiments. A meta-analysis found no overall difference in recidivism between boot camp participants and their control group counterparts, with the average (odds ratio) effect size across the studies being close to 1 (1.02). Put another way, the average success rate for boot camp participants is 60.5% (39.5% recidivating), while the average success rate for the controls is 60% (40% recidivating). For the most part, control subjects received probation or prison. With a wide variation in the distribution of effect sizes, from large reductions to large increases in recidivism, the authors carried out further analyses to investigate if there are conditions under which boot camps may be effective. Some evidence is found for larger positive effects produced by boot camp programs that included a counseling component or had as a primary focus therapeutic programming instead of physical training and the like. While the authors note that some evaluations of boot camps have demonstrated positive effects in other areas (e.g., reduced need for prison beds, prosocial attitudes), they conclude that, "Justifying the adoption or continued use of boot camps should not, however, be made on claims of their potential to reduce crime within a community" (Wilson and MacKenzie, this volume).

In the systematic review of Scared Straight and other juvenile awareness programs (or prison tour programs), by Anthony Petrosino and his colleagues, nine studies are included. All are randomized controlled experiments. The review finds that not one of the interventions was effective in preventing offending by the treatment group compared to the no-treatment control group, and that a majority of interventions produced harmful results. A meta-analysis of seven of the studies (two did not provide the needed data) reveal that those juveniles who went through Scared Straight are more likely to engage in criminal activity compared to those juveniles who did not receive the program. Further analyses did not change the findings.

Incarceration-based drug treatment, which covers a broad range of treatment modalities for substance abusing offenders (e.g., methadone maintenance, psychotherapy), is the subject of a systematic review by Ojmarrh Mitchell and his colleagues. This review brings together 26 studies, with a total of 32 separate experimental-control group comparisons. Program impact is assessed according to recidivism and drug use. The included studies are randomized controlled experiments and quasi-experiments. A meta-analysis finds that three-quarters of the effect sizes (24 out of 32) favored the treatment condition over the control condition, and only a few are in the other direction (i.e., controls did better). For the most part, the control condition received the usual services administered in secure correctional facilities. The overall mean odds ratio is 1.25, which corresponds to an 11% reduction in the recidivism rate: 44.5% for the treatment group versus 50% for the control group. Based on a smaller number of comparisons ($n = 11$), slightly stronger results are found for the intervention's effectiveness in reducing post-program drug use. As with the boot camp studies, the incarceration-based drug treatment studies show considerable variability in effects on recidivism. Further analyses reveal that treatment intensity was particularly important: the more intensive programs like therapeutic communities are more effective in reducing recidivism and drug use.

In the final systematic review in this section, Cynthia McDougall and her colleagues examine the monetary costs and benefits of different types of criminal sanctions in order to assess value for money. As part of this review, the authors utilize an innovative cost-benefit validity scale that they previously developed to rank the comprehensiveness of cost-benefit analyses, from lowest (level 1: cost analysis studies in which benefits are not monetized) to highest (level 5: complete cost-benefit analysis). Nine studies met their inclusion criteria, which included scoring a level 3 (a partial cost-benefit analysis) or higher on the scale. After a detailed review of the studies, the authors report that five program types provide some evidence of value for money: sex offender treatment in prison; pretrial diversion with drug treatment; imprisonment for high-risk repeat offenders; intensive supervision following shock incarceration; and family and juvenile offender treatment programs compared to aftercare or parole. But only the effects and cost-benefit findings of sex offender treatment in prison could be generalized to other settings; the other four program types are only considered promising enough to warrant further testing. The authors call for evaluations of correctional programs routinely to include a cost-benefit analysis component and for the standardization of cost-benefit analysis techniques.

WHAT WORKS FOR VICTIMS

The prevention of repeat victimization in different contexts and the degree of victim satisfaction with an intervention in which crime victims play an integral role is the subject of three systematic reviews. Lynette Feder and David Wilson assess the empirical evidence on the effects of court-mandated batterer intervention programs (i.e., some form of counseling or education for abusive men) to reduce domestic violence. The review brings together four studies, with a total of seven separate experimental-control group comparisons. Program impact is assessed according to repeat violence directed at the same victim using official and victim reports. The included studies are randomized controlled experiments. Control subjects received either no intervention, community service, or probation. A meta-analysis finds differential program impacts on domestic violence depending on the source of the outcome measure. In the case of official reports, there is evidence that batterer intervention programs reduced repeat violence by one-third, from 15% (the average of the control groups) to 10%. However, victim reports suggest that the intervention produced no overall reduction in repeat domestic violence. Further analyses lead the authors to caution that the beneficial effects of the intervention on official reports "may apply only to a select and motivated group of convicted batterers" (Feder and Wilson, this volume).

A systematic review of restorative justice, by Heather Strang and Lawrence Sherman, assesses the impact on offender recidivism and victim satisfaction. The review brings together seven studies, all of which are randomized controlled experiments. For comparability purposes, a meta-analysis is restricted to the three studies that tested the effects of face-to-face restorative justice conferences involving victims and offenders (compared with usual court procedures) for crimes with personal victims. Using the measure of repeat offending, the average effect size is found to favor restorative justice. On the measure of how satisfied individual victims were with their own justice experience, the average effect size is found to strongly favor the intervention. Analyses of victims' fears of re-victimization by their offender reveals that those who attended the restorative justice conferences, compared to those victims who did not, were significantly less likely to "anticipate re-victimization." Evidence is also found to support the conclusion that the involvement of victims in face-to-face conferences is likely to be an effective way to prevent victims from committing crimes of retaliation against their offenders.

Lastly, Graham Farrell and Ken Pease review evaluations on the prevention of repeat residential burglary victimization, a sub-set of overall efforts to prevent repeat victimization (see Farrell, 1995). The included studies use comparison-group designs with varying degrees of equivalence. To date, no randomized experiments have been carried out in this area. The authors find that the most effective schemes to prevent repeat residential burglary victimization involve strong preventive mechanisms that are tailored to the local burglary problem in high burglary-rate areas, often combining multiple tactics usually including security upgrades. Furthermore, strong implementation is required, which is not easy to achieve, and reductions in repeat burglaries do not necessarily coincide with an overall reduction in burglary. In contrast, the least effective schemes have weak preventive mechanisms (e.g., advice to victims that does not ensure that preventive measures are taken) and poor implementation (e.g., failing to contact victims, lack of security equipment). The authors observe that there is broad scope for more rigorous evaluation designs to assess the impact of this crime prevention modality.

WHAT WORKS FOR PLACES

Interventions directed at high-crime places or areas at high risk for criminal activity, such as street corners, car parks, or city centers, are the subject of three systematic reviews. In Anthony Braga's review of hot spots policing, which involves the targeting of police enforcement measures in high-crime areas known as hot spots, five studies are included, all of which are randomized controlled experiments. In the experimental hot spots areas, a number of police tactics were used, including problem-oriented policing. Control hot spots areas were subject to routine levels and types of traditional police services (e.g., random patrol). Effectiveness is assessed on the outcome measures of crime and disorder. Findings suggest that targeted police actions can prevent crime and disorder in hot spots. The review also finds some evidence that spatial crime displacement is rare and that crime control benefits associated with the focused police interventions can be diffused to neighboring areas that did not receive the treatment.

In separate systematic reviews – incorporating meta-analytic techniques – we assess the effects of closed-circuit television (CCTV) surveillance and improved street lighting on crime. Altogether, 35 studies are included: 22 for CCTV and 13 for street lighting. The minimum evaluation design of the included studies involved before-and-after measures of crime in experimental and comparable control areas. To date, no randomized experiments have been carried out with these situational crime prevention measures. In the case of CCTV, findings show that it has a significant but small desirable effect on crime, with an overall reduction in crime of 8% in experimental areas compared to comparable control areas. CCTV is most effective in reducing crime in car parks, most effective when combined with improved street lighting and targeted at vehicle crimes, and more effective in reducing crime in the U.K. than in the U.S. Across the CCTV studies, there were mixed results for territorial displacement and diffusion of benefits. While the optimal circumstances for effective use of CCTV schemes are not entirely clear at present, there is some evidence that CCTV may be most effective when combined with other interventions and focused on a specific crime type.

In the case of improved street lighting, findings reveal that it has a significant desirable effect on crime, with an overall reduction in crime of 20% in experimental areas compared to comparable control areas. Findings also show that street lighting is most effective in reducing crime in city centers, most effective when targeted at property crimes, and, similar to CCTV, more effective in reducing crime in the U.K. than in the U.S. In nine of the 13 street lighting studies, both nighttime and daytime crimes were measured, and findings reveal a significant desirable effect on crime. This suggests that a theory of street lighting focusing on its role in increasing community pride and informal social control may be more plausible than a theory focusing on increased surveillance and increased deterrence. On the matter of crime displacement and diffusion of crime prevention benefits, only three of the street lighting studies reported some or possible evidence of territorial displacement and the other nine reported no evidence of displacement, with two of these studies also reporting at least some evidence of diffusion.

CONCLUSIONS AND FUTURE DIRECTIONS

The good news from these systematic reviews is that most of the interventions are effective in preventing crime, and in many cases produce sizeable effects. Acting on the evidence from these reviews could arguably contribute to a safer society, both now and in the long term. Police enforcement of street-level crime and the use of correctional institutions to reduce repeat offending in the community account for a substantial share of criminal justice expenditure. Expanding the use of hot spots policing, cognitive-behavioral treatment for offenders, and incarceration-based drug treatment for substance-abusing offenders as part of overall police and correctional policy could produce impressive reductions in crime. Importantly, there will be a need to ensure a greater level of adherence to the quality and delivery protocols of cognitive-behavioral therapy as part of routine correctional practice. Furthermore, resources could be reallocated from Scared Straight-type programs and correctional boot camps to the two effective correctional interventions. This injection of resources may have the desirable effect of bolstering the scale at which these effective interventions could be delivered. The last point to be made on this subject may be the most important to policymakers and politicians: Some types of criminal sanctions (or correctional interventions) may provide value for money. While there is by no means a substantial body of economic evaluation research on criminal sanctions, some types definitely show promise in returning dividends to society, and at least one type – sex offender treatment in prison – can be considered economically efficient.

There is wide agreement that for a safer, more sustainable society, crime prevention measures must not be limited to criminal justice responses after the fact. There is a need for early developmental crime prevention, which aims to influence the scientifically identified risk factors or root causes of delinquency and later criminal offending. Some of the most important risk factors include: growing up in poverty, living in poor housing, inadequate parental supervision and harsh or inconsistent discipline, parental conflict and separation, low intelligence and poor school performance, and a high level of impulsivity and hyperactivity (Farrington, 1996). The promising results of child social skills or social competence training to reduce antisocial behavior and delinquency offers further support for the need for greater investments in early childhood programs.

In the case of early parent training in which the results were somewhat mixed for the prevention of child behavior problems under age three, other reviews of programs targeting children and adolescents provide evidence of effectiveness in preventing delinquency and later offending (see Farrington and Welsh, 2003). Future demonstration trials that test the effects of parent training during early childhood on disruptive behavior and delinquency should help to build a more extensive knowledge base for this type of intervention. Information on the effects on delinquency from these new trials will of course take some time to become available. However, periodic updates of this systematic review may produce more information on delinquency in the short term. This is because, of the seven studies included in the review, a number are longitudinal trials and are approaching the age of the participants (or the participant's children) when delinquency can be measured.

There is also good news for reducing the recurrence of harms caused to victims of crime in different social contexts. Consideration should be given to expanding face-to-face restorative justice conferences involving victims and offenders as an alternative to the standard criminal justice response of formal criminal court processing for the offender and doing little or next to nothing for the crime victim. Not only does restorative justice serve as an efficacious alternative (by reducing repeat offending and improving victim satisfaction that justice was served), it may also reduce the likelihood of victim retaliation against the offender, an all too common experience in interpersonal street crime (Prothrow-Stith and Spivak, 2004). Furthermore, restorative justice conferences may save substantial financial resources over the costly use of criminal courts. An ongoing multi-site randomized experiment of this intervention in England should shed light on this important question.

Consideration should also be given to expanding efforts to prevent repeat burglary victimization, by targeting a package of situational crime prevention measures at the highest risk places for burglary. Ideally, greater efforts would be taken by homeowners and landlords, as well as local, state, and federal government housing agencies, to prevent the initial occurrence of this crime, which is a high-rate and costly crime in most Western countries. Perhaps the success of efforts to prevent the repeat victimization of break-ins and other property crimes (see Farrell and Pease 2001) will focus greater attention on the need for a more universal program of situational prevention.

With mixed results of court-mandated batterer intervention to reduce domestic violence, which is based on the source of the outcome measure (police or victim reports), further experimentation seems warranted. Future studies should also investigate if this intervention is more suitable for one type of offender over another (e.g., those motivated to change versus those resistant to change). This review draws attention to the importance of using multiple data sources in evaluating program effects, something that is recommended in evaluation research (Ekblom and Pease, 1995) and has become far more common in randomized experiments in criminology today compared to 30 or 40 years ago (Farrington and Welsh, 2005).

Local efforts to prevent crime might benefit from increased use of CCTV surveillance cameras, so long as they are targeted at vehicle crimes, combined with other situational measures such as street lighting, and implemented in car parks. Expanding the use of the situational crime prevention measure of improved street lighting would also be desirable, but as well under certain conditions. The one difference is that street lighting is seemingly an effective measure on its own. Analyses of the potential effects on crime from combining these two interventions, which are reported elsewhere (Welsh and Farrington, 2004), suggest that such a policy may produce a greater yield in reduced crime rates, but this may be limited to vehicle crimes in car parks. To move beyond this narrow application of (especially) CCTV, there may be some merit in future experimentation of these situational measures combined with problem-oriented policing targeted at high-crime activity places. Indeed, the connection of situational prevention and problem-oriented policing is well established in both theory and practice (Braga, 2002).

The Campbell Crime and Justice Group has begun the important task of preparing systematic reviews of the effectiveness of a wide range of criminological interventions for use by policymakers, practitioners, researchers, and the general public. The systematic reviews of the 13 topics reported here represent only a start; reviews of many other topics are underway and planned for the future. We argue that, alongside the Campbell effort, a program of research on new crime prevention and intervention programs needs to be initiated, and in many different Western countries. These new programs need to be evaluated using the most rigorous research designs, including large samples, long follow-up periods, and follow-up interviews. As discussed in Chapter 1, sample size is particularly important for both individual- and area-based studies. Long-term follow-ups are needed to assess how long effects persist after the intervention ends. This information may point to the need for booster sessions. Long follow-ups are a rarity in criminological interventions and should be a top priority of funding agencies.

Research is needed to identify the active ingredients of successful (and promising) crime prevention programs. Many programs are multimodal, making it difficult to isolate the independent effects of different components. Future experiments that attempt to disentangle the effects of different elements of the most successful programs are needed. It is also important that programs include, as part of the original research design, provision for an economic analysis – either a cost-benefit or cost-effectiveness analysis – to allow for an assessment of the economic efficiency of the program (Welsh and Farrington, 2000; Welsh et al., 2001).

It is well known that having convincing research evidence and having it influence policy and practice are two very different matters. How to overcome some of the misconceived political barriers in order to get more knowledge about what works in preventing crime into policy and practice is by no means an easy task, but fortunately it is receiving some attention in various academic disciplines, criminology included (see Crime and Justice Institute, 2004; Cullen, 2002; Latessa, 2004).

In the final analysis, a great deal of work needs to be done – by researchers, policymakers, practitioners, and politicians – to achieve the well-intentioned yet lofty goal of using the highest quality scientific evidence in the development of public policy and practice for the prevention of crime. We view this collection of systematic reviews as an important step forward towards this goal. Of course, should it spur academic interest, encourage more systematic reviews, inspire further innovation among policymakers and practitioners, and ignite the interest of politicians, these too will be important effects.

REFERENCES

Braga, Anthony A. 2002. *Problem-Oriented Policing and Crime Prevention.* Monsey, NY: Criminal Justice Press.

Cullen, Francis T. 2002. "Rehabilitation and Treatment Programs." In *Crime: Public Policies for Crime Control,* edited by James Q. Wilson and Joan Petersilia, 253–289. Oakland, CA: Institute for Contemporary Studies Press.

Crime and Justice Institute. 2004. *Implementing Evidence-Based Principles in Community Corrections: Leading Organizational Change and Development.* Washington, DC: National Institute of Corrections, Community Corrections Division, U.S. Department of Jutice.

Ekblom, Paul, and Ken Pease. 1995. "Evaluating Crime Prevention." In *Building a Safer Society: Strategic Approaches to Crime Prevention. Crime and Justice: A Review of Research,* Vol. 19, edited by Michael Tonry and David P. Farrington, 585–662. Chicago: University of Chicago Press.

Farrell, Graham. 1995. "Preventing Repeat Victimization." In *Building a Safer Society: Strategic Approaches to Crime Prevention. Crime and Justice: A Review of Research,* Vol. 19, edited by Michael Tonry and David P. Farrington, 469–534. Chicago: University of Chicago Press.

——, and Ken Pease, eds. 2001. *Repeat Victimization. Crime Prevention Studies,* Vol. 12. Monsey, NY: Criminal Justice Press.

Farrington, David P. 1996. "The Explanation and Prevention of Youthful Offending." In *Delinquency and Crime: Current Theories,* edited by J. David Hawkins, 68–148. New York: Cambridge University Press.

——, and Brandon C. Welsh. 2003. Family-based prevention of offending: A meta-analysis. *Australian and New Zealand Journal of Criminology* 36: 127–151.

——. 2005. Randomized experiments in criminology: What have we learned in the last two decades? *Journal of Experimental Criminology* 1: 9–38.

Feder, Lynette, and David B. Wilson. In this volume. "Mandated Batterer Intervention Programs to Reduce Domestic Violence."

Latessa, Edward J. 2004. The challenge of change: Correctional programs and evidence-based practices. *Criminology & Public Policy* 3: 547–560.

Lipsey, Mark. W., and Nana A. Landenberger. In this volume. "Cognitive-Behavioral Interventions."

McCord, Joan. 2003. Cures that harm: Unanticipated outcomes of crime prevention programs. *Annals of the American Academy of Political and Social Science* 587: 16–30.

Prothrow-Stith, Deborah, and Howard R. Spivak. 2004. *Murder is No Accident: Understanding and Preventing Youth Violence in America.* San Francisco, CA: Jossey-Bass.

Sherman, Lawrence W. 1998. *Evidence-Based Policing.* Washington, DC: Police Foundation.

——, and John E. Eck. 2002. "Policing for Crime Prevention." In *Evidence-Based Crime Prevention,* edited by Lawrence W. Sherman, David P. Farrington, Brandon C. Welsh, and Doris L. MacKenzie, 295–329. New York: Routledge.

Weisburd, David, and John E. Eck. 2004. What can police do to reduce crime, disorder, and fear? *Annals of the American Academy of Political and Social Science* 593: 42–65.

Welsh, Brandon C., and David P. Farrington. 2000. "Monetary Costs and Benefits of Crime Prevention Programs." In *Crime and Justice: A Review of Research,* Vol. 27, edited by Michael Tonry, 305–361. Chicago: University of Chicago Press.

——. 2004. Surveillance for crime prevention in public space: Results and policy choices in Britain and America. *Criminology & Public Policy* 3: 497–526.

——, and Lawrence W. Sherman, eds. 2001. *Costs and Benefits of Preventing Crime.* Boulder, CO: Westview Press.

Wilson, David B., and Doris L. MacKenzie. In this volume. "Boot Camps."

INDEX

Printed in the United States
111444LV00008BB/147/A